D0742539

Qaddafi's Libya
in World Politics

QADDAFI'S
LIBYA IN
WORLD
POLITICS

Yehudit Ronen

LYNNE
RIENNER
PUBLISHERS

BOULDER
LONDON

Published in the United States of America in 2008 by
Lynne Rienner Publishers, Inc.
1800 30th Street, Boulder, Colorado 80301
www.rienner.com

and in the United Kingdom by
Lynne Rienner Publishers, Inc.
3 Henrietta Street, Covent Garden, London WC2E 8LU

Library of Congress Cataloging-in-Publication Data
Ronen, Yehudit.
  Qaddafi's Libya in world politics / Yehudit Ronen.
    p. cm.
  Includes bibliographical references and index.
  ISBN 978-1-58826-585-2 (hardcover : alk. paper)
  1. Libya—Politics and government—1969– 2. Libya—Foreign
relations—1969– 3. Qaddafi, Muammar. I. Title.
  DT236.Y44 2008
  327.612—dc22

                                                    2008012818

British Cataloguing in Publication Data
A Cataloguing in Publication record for this book
is available from the British Library.

Printed and bound in the United States of America

  Printed on 30% postconsumer recycled paper

  The paper used in this publication meets the requirements
    of the American National Standard for Permanence of
    Paper for Printed Library Materials Z39.48-1992.

  5 4 3 2 1

Contents

Acknowledgments

Seeing *Qaddafi's Libya in World Politics* from conception to publication proved to be an arduous mission. It was accomplished thanks to the support of colleagues, friends, and family, to whom I am greatly indebted. I would like, therefore, to express my gratitude to Asher Susser and Eyal Zisser, respectively the former and current heads of the Moshe Dayan Center for Middle Eastern and African Studies at Tel Aviv University, who provided me with both moral and financial support; Bruce Maddy-Weitzman, a senior research fellow at the Dayan Center, for his illuminating remarks on Chapters 5 and 6; Ilana Greenberg, Roslyn Loon, Elena Lesnick, Itai Dewar, Marion Gliksberg and her staff at the Dayan Center's library, and Haim Gal and his staff at the Dayan Center's archive, who were all devotedly attentive to my many queries and requests; and Shimon Ohayon, the director of the Aharon and Rachel Dahan Institute for Sephardic Heritage at Bar-Ilan University, and Ephraim Hazan, the chair of the institute's Research Fund, who extended their support. I would also like to express my gratitude to Lynne Rienner and her staff, notably Marilyn Grobschmidt and Shena Redmond, and to Ruth Tobias for advancing this volume to press with highly professional efficiency.

Last but definitely not least, special thanks go to my husband, Uzi, and to my children, Ronit, Orit, and Gil, as well as to Asaf and Guy, whose love injected a constant dose of constructive energy into the demanding process of writing and enabled me to give birth to this book.

—*Yehudit Ronen*

Qaddafi's Libya
in World Politics

1

Revolution and
Qaddafi's Expanding Horizons

Like a flash of lightning in the dark of night, a young army officer, Muammar Qaddafi, shot out of the depths of the Libyan Desert and seized power in Tripoli on 1 September 1969. From that moment, Libya began its precarious journey through what was then its largely chaste landscape of foreign affairs, climbing at times to unprecedented heights—but more often faltering at the edge of a precipice.

The availability of huge oil reserves gave the new Libyan head of state unprecedented leverage with which to conduct his country's affairs. The confluence of Libya's abundant economic resources and resultant military power with his own charismatic personality, powerful political leadership, and uncompromising ideological fanaticism allowed Qaddafi to develop a global vision for an ambitious foreign policy marked by a shift from nearly three decades of bellicosity to diplomatic reconciliation at the beginning of the twenty-first century.

Like concentric ripples caused by a stone thrown into a pond, the horizons of Libyan foreign policy steadily expanded beyond the neighboring Arab Muslim countries that initially comprised the sole sphere of significance for Qaddafi's ideological, political, and emotional affiliations. This sphere, however, was to prove a major disappointment in his first decade of rule, undermining the supposedly solid foundation of his worldview and requiring him to expand the geopolitical scope of his interests and aspirations in order to reinforce his personal prestige and advance Libya's interests as he perceived them.

This book, based largely on Libyan and other primary Arab sources, offers insight into Libya's foreign relations throughout Qaddafi's prolonged tenure. Dealing primarily with international relations and drawing on an interdisciplinary methodology, the book is germane to a variety of fields of inquiry, among them security and strategic studies in the Cold War period as well as in its increasingly globalized aftermath, oil-state politics, and the study of terrorism as a threat to the stability of regimes and the international system. While presenting an overview of the intricate puzzle of Tripoli's foreign affairs mainly through the Libyan prism, the book also examines each interlocking piece, underscoring the effects of reciprocal relations among the various areas of Tripoli's foreign policies since 1969 and thus offering a comprehensive survey of Libya's political history. Additionally, it sheds light on Libya's domestic affairs insofar as they are relevant to a full understanding of its foreign policy, revealing crucial junctures in the political life of the Libyan state, society, and leadership.

Chapters 2 and 3 provide a detailed survey of Libya's relations with the United States during the Cold War era and in its aftermath. Ending in Libya's abandonment of weapons of mass destruction (WMD) and related-munitions stockpiles at the close of 2003, when Qaddafi eschewed any further involvement in terrorism, these two chapters analyze the roots of the chronic conflict between Libya and the United States since the administration of Richard Nixon and through that of George W. Bush. These chapters investigate the currents that affected the deeply troubled relations between a superpower and a lightly populated, Middle Eastern country. This section highlights the extraordinary ways in which the conflict was handled and eventually resolved (though a certain bitter residue remains). It also examines the strategic quandary presented by the international community's pressing need to dismantle the WMD of a pariah state, as Washington depicted Libya. The events described here hold possible implications for other countries that insist on developing or acquiring WMD, suggesting ways in which they may be reincorporated into the international community through diplomatic rather than military means.

Since the Cold War was the backdrop for a large part of Qaddafi's rule, Chapter 4 explores the effects of Libyan-Soviet relations on Tripoli's broader foreign affairs and on Qaddafi's domestic power and politics. Libya's foreign policy, especially its frequent belligerence toward the West—particularly the United States, Israel, and the Arab and African states—may have been entirely different had Libya not been buttressed by the Soviet Union. I explore, then, the tremendous influence Moscow exerted both directly and indirectly over Qaddafi's views on foreign policy and his responses to crises and challenges.

The fifth chapter analyzes Libya's interactions and problematic relations with the Arab world and the wider Middle East, placing emphasis on the country's love-hate relations with Egypt—once the crown jewel of Qaddafi's pan-Arab vision. The chapter delineates his courtship of and rupture with various countries of the Mashriq and the Maghrib as it reveals the many competing interests Libya had in these two closely linked regions.

Chapter 6 sheds light on Libya's conduct in the broader Middle East in the era of the "New World Order," as it struggled under sanctions imposed by the United Nations (UN) without the level of support Qaddafi expected from his Arab neighbors. This perceived lack of solidarity amounted to a sense of betrayal at the hands of the so-called Arab nation.

Chapters 7, 8, and 9 describe Libya's policies toward the African continent, focusing on Tripoli's military interventions in Uganda and Chad in the 1970s and 1980s as well as on Libya's broader diplomatic aims and conduct in Africa during the 1990s and the early 2000s. Following the disintegration of the Union of Soviet Socialist Republics (USSR), the subsequent tightening of the US noose on Tripoli, and the Arab world's perceived treachery toward Libya during the 1990s, an isolated and besieged Qaddafi looked increasingly to Africa for diplomatic backing in his country's confrontation with the West. These three chapters refer to Qaddafi's aspirations for ideological and political influence; for territorial, strategic, and economic gains; and, later, for unity and legitimacy on the continent. He harnessed African diplomacy to press for the lifting of the UN-imposed sanctions, to promote his vision of a "United States of Africa," and to carve a niche for himself as the leading statesman on the continent. Surprisingly, Libya's reputation on the global stage was rehabilitated largely by Qaddafi's success in mobilizing the diplomatic support of African states.

* * *

The conflict with the West—in particular the Lockerbie dispute with the United States and Britain throughout the 1990s—stands out as a conspicuous feature of Qaddafi's tenure. This dispute dominated Libya's foreign policy and had an enormous impact on the country's domestic affairs as well, affecting Qaddafi's efforts to maintain his grip on power. More than anything else, the dispute demonstrated the ability of the US-led New World Order to impose limits on a hostile Middle Eastern state. France—which had collided with Libya over contrasting interests in Africa, particularly in Chad, and which still had the Libyan-ordered 1989 downing of a French airplane over Niger fresh in mind—sided with the international community against Libya's involvement in international terrorism by joining the anti-Qaddafi front, led by the United States and Britain. The efforts of these three Western states significantly affected Libya's external affairs in the last decade of the twentieth century, and their impact continued to make itself felt into the third millennium.

Interestingly, the United States, Britain, and France had molded Libya's preindependence history five decades earlier. The Allied forces of World War II liberated Libya from the Axis powers, thus putting an end to Italy's colonial rule (which lasted from 1911 to 1943). Britain and France, who ruled Libya in the aftermath of the war via a Provisional Military Administration, also played significant roles in shaping the country's political future. L. Carl Brown's definition of a "penetrated system" applies not only to Libya but to the Middle East as a whole, which was subjected to prolonged Western involvement. As B. A. Roberson also argues, international influence over and intervention in the region constitute an enduring, recognizable feature of its history.[1]

On 24 December 1951, under formal UN supervision, Libya became an independent state. In its first years, the Kingdom of Libya, ruled by King Muhammad Idris al-Mahdi al-Sanusi, was "too poor, weak, and inexperienced to have much choice of foreign policy." It therefore took "an unassuming stand between the Western powers, on whose support the economy and ultimately the stability of the state depended, and the growing claims of Arab nationalism."[2] Clearly, the new Libyan state was far removed from the pan-Arab, anti-Israel, and anti-West politics and ideologies espoused by Gamal 'Abd al-Nasser and others leading the Egyptian Free Officers Revolution in July 1952. After becoming a member of the Arab League in early 1953—a move that stamped Libya's Arab identity and affiliation with the formal seal of recognition—the Sanusi monarchy turned fully to the West. As both the Cold War and the need for oil continued to intensify, the West became increasingly interested in the Mediterranean region and in Libya, with its oil resources and strategic assets, in particular. These interests converged with those of Sanusi, who signed agreements with Britain and the United States allowing them to maintain a military presence in Libya. An agreement with France granted it a strategic foothold as well. Following these agreements, the West was determined to further reinforce its position in the new Libyan state.

Meanwhile, during the second half of the 1960s, the young army officer Qaddafi fully identified with the pan-Arab approach of Egypt's Nasser, which he perceived as uniquely effective in fending off the Western presence—in his eyes the essence of all that was evil and a decisive factor in the weakening of the Arab states.[3] Qaddafi also adopted Nasser's stance toward Israel, determining to eradicate what he called the "Zionist Entity," which he viewed as closely linked to the United States. Such nationalist sentiments swept the Arab world, especially after the defeat of Nasser in the 1967 war against Israel—Qaddafi, devastated by the defeat, felt that his country had betrayed the Arab cause by not participating. This feeling served as a major catalyst in his decision to overthrow the king, which he considered a necessary first step toward setting a new agenda for his country and for the entire Arab world. From that point to the seizure of power, the road was short.

Qaddafi's black-and-white, self-styled revolutionary outlook and burning zeal rendered him unable to see more subtle nuances in the multihued picture. Throughout the 1970s, his staunch adherence to ideological doctrine meant that he viewed Libya's foreign affairs only through his own pan-Arab, anti-West, and anti-Israel filters. His guardianship of what he believed to be proper Arab principles and values, inflexible even in the post-pan-Arab era, made him the last of the pan-Arab Mohicans.

Facing aggravated confrontation with the United States on the one hand and increasing disappointment with and often militant hostility toward the Arab world—especially Egypt under the leadership of pro-Western Anwar Sadat—on the other, Qaddafi opted for a new strategy to extricate Libya from the two-pronged threat. In spite of his outright rejection of communism, he made Libya an ally of the Soviet Union in the mid-1970s, hoping that the alignment would provide a counterweight to the tensions in its foreign affairs. Instead, Libya's position in the Soviet orbit accelerated the state's descent into the maelstrom of East-West relations, leading the United States to designate the Qaddafi regime a threat to its interests in the Middle East and beyond and thereby increasing Libya's strategic dependence upon the USSR. The alliance also deepened the rift between Libya and pro-Western Arab countries.

But Libya was no mere accidental participant in the conflict between global powers. Though Qaddafi's Libya faced real perils and external constraints, it was Qaddafi's own confrontational approach to foreign relations during the Cold War, including his military interventions in Africa, that frequently brought Libya into direct clashes with the West. Libyan foreign policy was molded to a considerable extent by the ways Qaddafi negotiated the often-conflicting pressures emanating from three conceptually distinct environments: "(1) the domestic level; (2) the regional systemic level; and (3) the global (or international) level."[4]

The collapse of the USSR represented a foreign-policy earthquake for Qaddafi, who needed new tactics to confront what would soon appear to be an ominous post–Cold War period. Still trapped in antiquated paradigms, however, Qaddafi failed to develop such tactics. In contrast, his son Saif al-Islam—well-versed in the ways of the West and free of the burden of traditional anti-Western sentiments—acted with resolve to internalize the recent global changes. This move was critical, since ending the debilitating dispute with the West was urgently necessary to ensure the survival of the Libyan regime and the country's economic prosperity. The arrival of satellite television and the Internet in the late 1990s—much later than they appeared in most Arab countries—has given rise to what Patrick E. Tyler refers to as an "electronic perestroika," an opening to the outside world that has shocked many Libyans into a realization of "the backward conditions" in which they live.[5] This upheaval in communication was introduced, to a large extent, as an integral part of the opening toward the West, initiated by the reformist camp of which Saif al-Islam was a leading figure. Having successfully crossed the divide between the twentieth and twenty-first centuries, Saif al-Islam has emerged as an effective leader in his own right. Nevertheless, it is not yet clear whether Qaddafi will follow in the footsteps of Syria's Hafiz al-Asad and bequeath Libya's leadership to his son.

Whatever may take place, Saif al-Islam and the reformist camp have orchestrated the process of opening Libya to the West. Their efforts to generate internal reforms—and above all to privatize the socialist-oriented market following years of economic stagnation amid tight state control over all facets of its industry—stand out against the backdrop of long-stalled domestic progress. By the early 2000s, Saif al-Islam, Foreign Minister 'Abd al-Rahman Shalqam, and Prime Minister Shukri Ghanem constituted a vanguard striving to transform Libya into a more Western-style nation. Unlike Qaddafi, they negotiated Tripoli's foreign interests pragmatically—purely on the bases of national concerns and international norms rather than on historical, ideological, or emotional bases. This approach marked a turning point in Libya's foreign policy, providing the Qaddafi regime with new opportunities to ensure its political survival and promote the state's economic growth. During this critical period, as Saif al-Islam and the reformist camp began to play an active role in Libyan politics, Qaddafi loosened his iron-fisted grip on the country's foreign-affairs machinery and allowed the winds of change to blow, although still under the state's close orchestration. Referring to Libya's changed policies toward the international system, senior Arab journalist Ghassan Cherbel has commented that "Arab [Libyan] politics are really the mother of all surprises."[6]

In short, as the target of more Western governmental animosity than any other Arab state except Iraq, Libya has gradually relinquished some of its ideological obstinacy in favor of political pragmatism. It took the Qaddafi regime more than thirty years "to realize the extent to which the achievement of its ideological objectives was being undermined by the means used to pursue them," as Tim Niblock has correctly pointed out.[7] Yet when he finally understood it, Qaddafi did his utmost to remove the hurdles he himself had erected, perceiving the preservation of his position at the helm of the state as his supreme interest.

Qaddafi's political input into his country's foreign policymaking was crucial, especially since, throughout his tenure, he fashioned it to conform to his own personal conceptions and aspirations. Qaddafi has professed that the political system he devised and long controlled, formally known as People's Power *(Sultat al-Sha'b),* was the "sole true democracy in the world." This system, part and parcel of his "Third Universal Theory," which he formulated in his three-part *Green Book,* published in 1976, 1977, and 1978 respectively, was a kind of mechanism for direct, popular rule. While he maintained this facade, his so-called revolutionary system allowed him to dominate both the domestic and the foreign affairs of Libya's social and economic spheres, enabling him to dictate every aspect of the state's agenda. Domestic and foreign motives intertwined and mutually shaped the state's international policy. "For over three decades," as Vandewalle notes, "the rhetoric and brinkmanship of the Libyan leadership partly obscured what transpired inside the country. Much of the West's attention, fueled by an inexhaustible media appetite for the Libyan leader's often eccentric behavior," ignored more profound processes within the country.[8] Indeed, domestic affairs were largely eclipsed but, nevertheless, exerted a profound influence on Libya's foreign policies.

* * *

An Arabic adage holds that governing a state is tantamount to dancing on the head of a viper. In Qaddafi's case, it is not only the serpent that has proven wily; Qaddafi himself also possesses highly developed, serpentine survival skills. More than anything else, these skills—in tandem with the character of Libyan society and the country's rich oil revenues—have contributed to the longevity of his regime. In 2007, he celebrated his thirty-eighth year in power—an unprecedented record of political survival among nonmonarchical regimes in the Middle East.

Notes

1. Brown, *International Politics and the Middle East,* pp. 3–5; Roberson, "The Impact of the International System on the Middle East," p. 56.
2. J. Wright, *Libya: A Modern History,* p. 82.
3. For a broader discussion of colonialism's impact and its interest in the creation of weak Arab states, see Telhami and Barnett, *Identity and Foreign Policy in the Middle East,* p. 1.
4. Hinnebusch, "Introduction: The Analytical Framework," p. 2.
5. See Patrick E. Tyler, "Libyan Stagnation: A Big Factor in Qaddafi Surprise," *New York Times,* 8 January 2003.
6. *Al-Hayat,* 26 March 2004.
7. Niblock, "The Foreign Policy of Libya," p. 231.
8. Vandewalle, *A History of Modern Libya,* p. 6.

2

Libya and the United States: Conflict in the Cold War Era

Following independence on 24 December 1951, Libya's King Muhammad Idris al-Mahdi al-Sanusi and the US administration, under the leadership of President Harry S. Truman, fostered a close relationship on a number of levels. The two countries mutually benefited from this cooperation, which plainly indicated the meeting of their vital interests. The extremely poor, pre-oil-boom Libyan state and its politically inexperienced regime received considerable US military and political support as well as economic assistance, which during the 1950s amounted to "more US foreign aid per capita than any other country."[1] In exchange, Libya put various strategic positions and training facilities at the disposal of the United States. Most important among them was the Wheelus Air Force Base near Tripoli, one link in a chain of US bases strategically built around the Soviet bloc in the early years of the Cold War. The reciprocal relations were further entrenched in the long-term Defense Agreement and Memorandum of Understanding signed in September 1954.

This collaboration—which primarily involved the exploration for and, beginning in 1959, the production of oil in Libya by US companies—faced growing challenges throughout the 1960s mainly stemming from the confluence of two processes that had a crucial impact on the Libyan state and society. The first was Libya's transformation into an oil-exporting state, which brought a considerable influx of foreign currency into the economy and dramatically changed significant parts of the local socioeconomic and political fabric. The second was the inculcation of a generation of young Libyan intelligentsia, workers, and junior army officers into the ideology of Egypt's admired president Gamal Abdul Nasser, marked by strong pan-Arab sentiment, militant nationalism, and anti-Western and anti-Israeli ardor.

The convergence of these two processes generated increasing restiveness within Libyan society, giving rise to an almost tangible sense of grievance toward the monarchial regime for its pronounced pro-Western orientation, even to the point of adopting the term *istiqlal muzayyaf* (false independence) when referring to Libya's rule under the monarch. By the mid-1960s, the nationalist and anti-Western atmosphere of protest had become much more focused and militant, as voices emerged explicitly demanding the evacuation of US and British military bases—the most overt symbols of the Western "aggressive imperialist legacy."[2]

The Six Day War in June 1967 and Israel's crushing victory over the Syrian, Egyptian, and Jordanian armies—which were supported by Iraq and other Arab countries—only intensified the anti-US ferment among Libya's nationalist circles. They believed that the United States had helped Israel—the "Zionist enemy" that Libya considered illegitimate and had sought to annihilate—win the war, with US aircraft using the Wheelus airbase to attack Egypt. Moreover, as a growing number of Libyans had begun to perceive the Libyan monarchy as a US collaborator even before the war, King Sanusi was now considered to have indirectly helped Israel defeat the Arabs.

Nasser's radical pan-Arab ideology, with its relentlessly anti-Western and anti-Israeli orientation, captivated a group of young army officers in Libya with Mu'ammar al-Qaddafi at their head. The liquidation of the US military base and the end of US influence on the Arab scene—and particularly on Libya's politics and fledgling oil industry—became top priorities on their agenda.

It was no surprise, therefore, that on 1 September 1969—the night of Qaddafi's military coup—the rebel forces, known as the Free Unionist Officers, deployed artillery units around the Wheelus base in the event that the United States might act to safeguard the king's reign. However, the swift rise to power of Qaddafi's Revolutionary Command Council and the concurrent proclamation of the Libyan Arab Republic (a kingdom no longer) were promptly recognized by Washington, which wished to preserve and further advance vital US interests in Libya and in the broader Middle Eastern and Mediterranean regions.

The Qaddafi Regime's Hostile Posture: Ideological and Political Motives

From the very beginning of his rule, Qaddafi emphasized his ambition to see Libya entirely freed of Western influence (whether US, British, or Italian), which he perceived as the exemplar of neoimperialism. Just a month and a half after seizing power, the new Libyan leader announced his determination to evacuate the Wheelus Air Force Base—even though the US presence there was not only highly beneficial for Libya economically but legally guaranteed, in accordance with the 1954 agreement, until 1971. Qaddafi perceived this goal as "a main condition for Libya's freedom" or *huriyya*—which, along with Islamic socialism *(ishtirakiyya)* and unity *(wahda),* were the three ideological cornerstones of the revolution. He tinged his message with a clear-cut threat: "We resort to wise and just means [that is, negotiations] to enable us to liberate our land, but if fighting becomes inevitable, then let there be fighting." This actively anti-US posture clearly reflected a broader process Qaddafi was setting in motion in order to achieve national self-determination, using a variety of methods such as the "restoration" of Arab-Islamic identity (its language, religion, and culture), the expulsion of British forces, and the closure of their bases on 28 March 1970.[3]

Notwithstanding his belligerent language, Qaddafi was relatively cautious not to engage in any active confrontation during his first year in power, fearing the dangerous implications of such a move on his still vulnerable political position.[4] Yet he continued to develop anti-US rhetoric with revolutionary zeal. While his verbal campaign definitely mirrored his ideological conviction, his systematic presentation of the former regime as submissively pro-US also reaped immediate political gains, legitimizing Qaddafi's problematic overthrow of Sanusi's reign. Since the king had been not only the first independent ruler in Libyan history but also the prestigious head of the religious order Sanusiyya Sufi and a fighter at the forefront of the struggle against Italian colonial rule, he was considered by many Libyans to be a source of national pride and a symbol of postcolonialism. Therefore, the toppling of the monarchial regime, even one characterized by political instability and social unrest, by military means somewhat diminished Qaddafi's standing, at least in the early days of his leadership.

In addition, by turning the issue of eradicating the US presence into a central item on his public revolutionary agenda, Qaddafi provided the politically heterogeneous Libyan society with a new common interest, further fostering the already-growing sense of national ideological unity. This in turn helped him rally the fragmented and largely tribal population around his leadership and soften the divisions that traditionally prevailed among the three geopolitically and socioeconomically distinct regions of Tripolitania, Cyrenaica, and Fezzan.

Thus, when the United States eventually acceded to Qaddafi's pressure and completed its evacuation of the Wheelus base on 11 June 1970—less than a year after his rise to power—the Libyan leader symbolically renamed the day 'Uqba bin Nafi after the Muslim Arab commander who led the Arab conquest of North Africa in the seventh century. The evacuation was cause for celebration, and the day has since become a central event on Libya's calendar. Qaddafi maximized the achievement politically, portraying it as a great moment in the history of modern Libya as well as in his career: "Now Arabs can speak from the position of the victor," he boastfully stated.[5]

Spurred on by this success, Qaddafi became more ardent than before in accusing the United States of exploiting the oil resources of Libya and other Arab states and of supporting Israel in its conflict with the Arab world. His increasing references to the United States as an enemy figure helped him to foster his own image as a fearless head of state determined to fight for the interests of his people and thus to consolidate his political position at home. In his bid to inherit Nasser's mantle of pan-Arab leadership, Qaddafi also demonstrated his commitment to defend sanctified Arab values.[6] Seen in this context, the energy Qaddafi invested in sporadic yet zealous unification efforts with Egypt, Sudan, and Syria in the early 1970s invoked concern in Washington.[7]

Although all of Qaddafi's unification attempts failed—thus eroding his prestige in the region even as the struggle over the revolutionary image of his country continued—tension between Libya and the United States mounted. It culminated in an unprecedented incident on 21 March 1973, when Libyan Mirage fighters fired on a US Air Force C-130 Hercules transport plane over the Mediterranean, some eighty-three miles off the Libyan coast. The United States reported the extraordinary event, admitting that the aircraft had ignored instructions given by the Libyan fighter planes to follow them and land at a Libyan airfield.[8]

Whoever initiated the incident, it plainly indicated the widening dispute between the two countries. Less than a year before the aerial incident, Libya had declared the airspace within a 100-mile radius of Tripoli restricted. This ran contrary to the declaration drafted at the 1954 Chicago Civil Aviation Convention, which limited restrictions on the airspace over a country's territorial waters to the conventional twelve-mile limit. The United States dismissed the Libyan claim as illegal, mainly concerned that the extension of Libyan airspace would hamper the air activities of the Sixth Fleet and disrupt surveillance of the Soviet Union's Mediterranean missions.

In fact, the aerial encounter was only one cause of the momentum Libya and the United States were gaining as they headed on their collision course, fueled heavily by the Cold War. Other disputes involved the downscaling of US diplomatic representation in Tripoli in protest of what Washington perceived as Libya's diplomatic insults in February 1973 and concern over Libya's role in the assassination by Palestinian organization Black September of two US diplomats—including Cleo A. Noel, the new ambassador to Sudan—during a reception at the Saudi embassy in Khartoum on 1 March of that year.[9]

Tripoli's state-controlled media portrayed these encounters between the "small Arab country" (with a population estimated at 2,096,000 in mid-1972) and the "Imperialist American Superpower" as heroic and serving the Arab cause. Moreover, the sharp shift of Egypt and Sudan, Libya's neighbors to the east, from a pro-Soviet to a pro-US orientation provided the United States with the potential to erect new launching pads into Libya, a development that further strengthened Qaddafi's apprehension about hostile US action against his regime. Indeed, when commemorating the third anniversary of the US evacuation of the Wheelus base, the Libyan head of state heightened his militant rhetoric, asserting that the United States, "which believes it dominates the world . . . , needs to be given a big, hard blow by the Arabs on its cold, insolent face. The time has come for the Arab peoples to confront the United States . . . , regardless of the cost."[10]

The Resort to Oil as a Political Weapon

Qaddafi resorted to oil as an effective weapon in his endeavor to fend off the West, still deeply entrenched in Libya. The harbinger of this tactic was the enactment of laws nationalizing the oil industry. Initially limited to the internal distribution networks of Shell and Esso, it expanded in the summer of 1970; by late 1971, Libya had nationalized British Petroleum, and by 1 September 1973—the anniversary of the revolution—it had nationalized 51 percent of all remaining foreign oil companies.

Libya's "oil war" against US companies—which then held most of the concessions in the country—assumed a new dimension in the wake of the outbreak of the Arab-Israeli war on 6 October 1973. Although vexed and humiliated at having been excluded by Egypt and Syria from their war against Israel, Qaddafi adopted the decision of the Organization of Arab Petroleum Exporting Countries (OAPEC) to halt oil exports to the United States, increasing the tax-reference price of crude oil by 94 percent and cutting production by 5 percent on 19 October 1973. However, according to later allegations, Libya clandestinely violated the 1973–1974 Arab oil boycott on the United States in an attempt to minimize the damages to its own economy.[11]

Concurrent with his strong aversion to Washington was Qaddafi's painful awareness of the emergence of the United States as the dominant superpower in Libya's immediate vicinity, where it was becoming the main source of political, economic, and, most significant, military assistance. Already committed militarily in Chad and Uganda, Libya had political and ideological aspirations in the African as well as the Arab arenas and could not afford to ignore the growing US influence, particularly given that Tripoli itself was, in the early 1970s, bereft of any significant connection to, let alone cooperation with, the Soviet Union and thus all the more vulnerable to US threats.

Qaddafi's perception that US mediation of the talks between Egypt and Israel following the 1973 war amounted to an additional insult further inflamed his burning enmity toward Washington. He rejected any political settlement of the Arab-Israeli conflict, unequivocally negating the right of the State of Israel—the "Zionist entity," in his parlance—to exist. Moreover, he vehemently called on Arab countries to join Libya in annihilating the "Zionist enemy" once and for all.

Libya's radical objection to any political solution to the Arab-Israeli conflict collided with Washington's pronounced effort to achieve a settlement in order to avert any further danger to either US vital strategic and oil interests in the region or the international political and economic order. Confounded by conflicting interests and burning with frustration and anger, Qaddafi again used the most effective weapon in his arsenal: the nationalization of foreign oil companies. On 11 February 1974, he nationalized three more US oil companies: California Asiatic, Texaco, and the Libyan-American Oil Company. Beyond benefiting from the domestic popularity of this move, he also hoped to encourage US oil companies to pressure the administration in Washington—now under a new president, Gerald R. Ford—to be more cooperative toward Tripoli. Though this was not to be, the doubling of the price of Libyan crude oil and its prompt translation into growing economic and military empowerment further boosted Qaddafi's political confidence, and he toughened his militancy toward the United States.

Meanwhile, Qaddafi was threatening the political positions of the pro-US regimes in Cairo and Khartoum and, indirectly, of those in the Gulf region, most notably Saudi Arabia. At the same time, he was providing military support to the anti-Western Ugandan regime as well as to anti-Western opposition in Chad. In response, the United States appeared determined to curb Libya's interventionist policies and political ambitions. Although it came to naught and should be viewed mainly in the context of Libya's inter-Arab relations, Qaddafi's temporary establishment of a unity framework with pro-Western Tunisia in 1974 further piqued US concern.

With his enmity toward the United Sates reinforced and his ideological and political wings clipped by the Arab world, Qaddafi found increasing comfort in the bosom of the Soviet Union, notwithstanding the sharp ideological gap between the two countries. The rapprochement between Tripoli and Moscow manifested itself for the first time in a display of Soviet SAM-3 missiles during a military parade in Tripoli celebrating Qaddafi's fifth anniversary in power on 1 September 1974 (for a detailed discussion of Libya's relations with the USSR, see chapter 4). The US response came shortly, in the form of withholding the delivery of eight C-130 Cargo Hercules aircraft that Libya had already paid for. For Libya, engaged in two African wars—including the geographically remote conflict in Uganda in support of Idi Amin Dada—this was a real blow.

The growing ties between Tripoli and Moscow (as well as Havana and other Eastern European capitals) and the consequent fear that Libya was becoming the spearhead of Soviet expansionism in the Middle East and Africa—particularly around the strategically important Horn of Africa—only exacerbated Washington's antagonism toward Tripoli. Moreover, the political and ideological encroachment of the USSR into Ethiopia after the overthrow of pro-US emperor Haile Selassie in 1974 and the installation of Colonel Mengistu Haile Mariam's Marxist-Leninist Dergue in Addis Ababa seriously worried the United States. It traditionally regarded the Horn of Africa and its periphery as its own concern, and, together with its Arab allies, feared the imposition of a *pax Sovietica* on the region. Not only was it strategically important for ensuring the safe passage of shipping vessels through the Red Sea, but it was also crucial for safeguarding oil routes from Saudi Arabia and the Gulf states to the West. What's more, Ethiopia controlled the sources of the Nile and thus the flow of water to US-friendly Sudan and Egypt. Aggravated by and fearful of Soviet penetration into the Horn, the United States and the Red Sea countries acted to prevent Libya's efforts to promote the interests of its new Soviet ally.

Soviet premier Aleksei Kosygin's visit to Libya in May 1975—during which Moscow concluded a new arms deal with Tripoli—and Qaddafi's visit to Moscow from 6 through 9 December 1976 were both unprecedented shows of diplomacy, indicating to the United States that Libya's rapprochement with the USSR was gathering alarming momentum. Moreover, Libya's crucial role in two military coup attempts—made in September 1975 and July 1976, respectively—against the pro-US Sudanese regime (which may have served the USSR's interests well had they been successful) further highlighted the threat Qaddafi posed to US policy in the Middle East, particularly in the Red Sea region and around the Horn of Africa.

Because of these concerns, bilateral relations deteriorated to a new low. In early 1977, the US Defense Department ranked Libya fourth—after the Soviet Union, China, and North Korea—in its annual report of potential enemies, with Cuba ranked fifth. The Ford administration cited Qaddafi's "irresponsible support for international terrorism," his backing of various anti-Western "liberation movements" throughout the world, and his attempts to subvert pro-Western regimes.[12] Washington's decision to place Libya high on the list also stemmed from Egypt's accusation that Libya and the USSR had played a role in instigating subversive activities against Sadat's regime, primarily the food riots of 18 and 19 January 1977—the most serious antigovernment protests since 1952, which saw the removal of the Farouq monarchy (1936–1952). The riots came in response to the Egyptian government's decision to impose austerity measures to meet the demands of international financial bodies and the US administration in order to improve Egypt's economic conditions. Egypt also leveled other serious allegations of subversion against Libya and the Soviet Union, identifying antiregime activists who, Cairo claimed, acted on behalf of Tripoli and Moscow.

The inclusion of Libya on the US list of potential enemies alarmed and infuriated Qaddafi: "the [United States] carries the banners of war against Arab nationalism. . . . He who allies himself with the [United States] now becomes an enemy of the Arab nation . . . a real enemy, even if he carries the *Ka'ba* [the sacred focus of Muslim pilgrimage to Mecca] over his head." This message, which explicitly denounced the pro-US Saudis, also clearly contained anti-Egyptian and anti-Sudanese criticism. The growing political affinity between Egypt under President Anwar Sadat, Sudan under Ja'far Muhammad al-Numayri—president since 1969—and the United States coincided with the deterioration of Libya's relations with Egypt and culminated in an unprecedented military confrontation initiated by Cairo in the summer of 1977. Libya publicly accused the United States of supplying combat intelligence to the Egyptians during this armed confrontation, while Egypt, for its part, accused the USSR of militarily helping the Libyans. Thus, in 1977, the line of conflict between Libya and the United States largely reflected the lines of conflict at the core of Libya's inter-Arab affairs.[13] Since Middle Eastern politics were increasingly dominated after late 1977 by the US-coordinated Egyptian-Israeli peace effort, Libyan-US enmity was infused with renewed vigor, reflecting this track. As a result of this changed emphasis, the military conflagration between Libya and Egypt was, for the most part, shelved.

Clearly, the dispute with the superpower, which grew increasingly prominent on the agenda of Libya's domestic and foreign affairs, helped Qaddafi to enhance his leadership position both within Libya and abroad. Indeed, with newly bolstered self-confidence as a result both of improved ties with the Kremlin and of what was underscored by Libya as its victorious resistance against the disproportionately powerful Egyptian army in the July 1977 war, Qaddafi committed himself to fomenting further revolutionary zeal among the Libyan people in order to strengthen his grip on power. He further promoted his self-styled system of People's Power, proclaiming his country as a *jamahiriyya*—that is, a state of the masses—and moving in 1978 and 1979 to enthusiastically promulgate the socialist principles of his ideology. These were declared in his Third Universal Theory, the main thesis of which was that "power, wealth, and arms"—the basic determinants of freedom—"must be in one's own hands rather than under government control" (*"al-Sulta wal-tharwa wal-silah fi yad al-sha'b"*). In the latter half of the 1970s, the seemingly smooth implementation of such socialist-revolutionary theories, combined with the economic prosperity that resulted from the continuing boom in oil prices on the world market, substantially strengthened Qaddafi's regime.[14]

The prosperous domestic conditions, although not free of difficulties, helped to lessen the trauma caused by 'Umar al-Muhayshi's attempted coup in mid-1975, which remained fresh in Qaddafi's mind throughout the following years—particularly as Muhayshi continued his vituperative anti-Qaddafi campaign from his shelter in pro-US Tunisia and later in pro-US

Egypt.[15] The substantial escalation of tensions with the United States, although sometimes beneficial for boosting Libyan nationalist sentiments in general and Qaddafi's political prestige in particular, definitely worried the regime in Tripoli.

As the Egyptian-Israeli peace process progressed, its encouragement by the United States provoked a particularly venomous spate of anti-US wrath by Qaddafi and motivated Libya to act against the forces propelling Egypt and Israel toward an agreement. Libya thus became actively involved in the formation of the Arab Front of Steadfastness and Resistance. Composed of Libya, the People's Democratic Republic of Yemen (PDRY), Syria, Algeria, and the Palestine Liberation Organization (PLO), the Front unequivocally opposed any political settlement with Israel. It was also determined to remove Sadat from power, counteract US influence in the Middle East, and strengthen a Soviet presence in the region.

Trying to minimize the damage Qaddafi had done to its interests in the Middle East and, particularly, to deter other radical Arab governments from doing likewise or impairing the US-backed peace policy, Jimmy Carter's administration, installed in January 1977, hardened its position toward Tripoli. On 21 February 1978, shortly after Sadat visited the United States to make a plea for arms support, the Carter administration announced the imposition of a ban on the sale to Libya of equipment worth US$400 million, encompassing spare parts for military transport aircraft, two Boeing airliners, and 400 heavy-duty trucks capable of transporting tanks. Washington explained that the ban was the consequence of Tripoli's support for international terrorism and its attempts to undermine the governments of neighboring countries, clearly alluding to US allies Egypt, Sudan, and Chad.[16] In what soon became a steady exchange of charges, Libya protested the "childish policy," based on "capitalist exploitation" and pandering to "Jewish hatred of . . . Islam and Arabs," and accused the United States of being a "state of world terrorism."[17] Only exacerbating the animosity was Libya's deep-rooted opposition to the US-backed peace process as represented by the Camp David accords of September 1978 and the Israeli-Egyptian peace agreement of March 1979.

Solidifying Perception:
The United States as the "Devil on Earth"

At the end of the 1970s, the United States shifted its attention from the eastern Mediterranean—which, because of the Arab-Israeli conflict, had figured prominently in its policymaking for many years—to the Persian Gulf in pursuit of vital US interests, primarily those pertaining to security and oil. This shift was mainly a response to Iran's radical Islamic Revolution, which had dethroned the pro-US shah in February 1979, and to the Soviet military invasion of Afghanistan in December of that year. Both events eroded the United States' political prestige and strategic position in the broader Middle Eastern arena while enhancing, to some degree, the standing of militantly anti-US countries such as Libya among radical circles in the region.

As the attention of the United States was shifting, so Libya was shifting the emphases of its own Middle Eastern policy. This shift was clearly indicated by Qaddafi's attempt to shape good relations with Ruhollah al-Musavi al-Khomeini's Islamist and anti-US regime during its first months in power in Iran, as well as by his calls for the establishment of "a nucleus of greater Islamic unity." Meanwhile, US concerns about Libya were deepened by several significant events: the taking of US hostages in Tehran on 4 November 1979, allegedly carried out by Libyan-trained militants and publicly supported by Libya;[18] the attack by a Saudi Islamist rebel group on the Grand Mosque of Mecca on 20 November 1979, threatening the pro-US Saudi rule that Libya had long detested; and the deepening crisis between the United States and the Soviet Union, resulting from the Soviet invasion of Afghanistan about a month after the Saudi attack—an invasion politically backed by Libya, whose own troops were on the verge of another vigorous invasion of Chad, the neighbor of pro-US Sudan. The cumulative damage to US standing in the broader Middle East was simultaneously turned to advantage by the Soviets and its client states in the region.

In fact, the detrimental developments for the United States in Iran and Afghanistan liquidated the historic buffer zone between the USSR and the Persian Gulf-Indian Ocean states. The strategic worsening of the US position and the intensification of US hostilities with Iran as well as with other areas of the Arab Muslim world increasingly affected Libya's approach toward the superpower. In early December 1979, in a particularly demonstrative act of bellicosity that showed support for Khomeini's Islamic Revolution, Libyan citizens set fire to the US embassy building in Tripoli. Washington accused the Libyan authorities of responsibility and suspended diplomatic activities in Libya three days later. A second attack against the embassy resulted in its closure by the United States in early February 1980. Bilateral ties were henceforth conducted at a level no higher than that of chargés d'affaires.

In Tunisia, an armed attack on the mining town of Gafsa on 26 and 27 January 1980—perceived by the pro-Western Tunisian government as a subversive act carried out with Libya's help in the hope of installing a pro-Libyan and, possibly, pro-Soviet government in Tunis—also adversely affected Libyan-US relations. Tripoli's backing of opponents of Habib Bourguiba's regime, while denied by Qaddafi, annoyed Washington, which perceived Tunisia as a friendly country of strategic and political importance, situated as it was at the crossroads of Africa, the Middle East, and Europe. Together with France, the United States was quick to assist Tunisia militarily.

Meanwhile, to the increasing alarm of the Libyan regime, the scope and effectiveness of anti-Qaddafi activities by domestic-born opponents was reaching a peak in 1980. These were encouraged and in some cases even launched from outside the country, mostly from the West and from Britain in particular. Particularly frustrating for Qaddafi were the virulent propaganda attacks launched by the opposition through its publications in the West, which claimed responsibility for anti-Qaddafi activities within Libya itself—among them violent clashes and a military uprising in Tobruk in mid-1980 and an assassination attempt against Qaddafi by army officers on 4 October 1980. Not surprising against this background, Qaddafi called on Libyan expatriates—to whom he referred as "stray dogs"—to return home immediately or "be liquidated." This call was part of Qaddafi's subsequent "hit campaign" to stop his opponents' activities in the United States as well as in Europe and the Arab world. Growing animosity between Libya and the United States again escalated into a crisis in late spring 1980. The Carter administration expelled Libyan diplomats, whom it charged with urging Libyan students in the United States to assassinate Qaddafi's political opponents. In retaliation, Tripoli expelled twenty-five US citizens and arrested two others, all on charges of "spying and having connections with terrorist organizations." Additionally, Libya threatened to cut off oil supplies to the United States.[19]

Fearing a reduction in backing from Moscow due to the Soviets' draining war in Afghanistan and aware that the US ban on the sale of military equipment had led to an acceleration of socioeconomic and political ferment in his country, Qaddafi made an uncharacteristically conciliatory gesture toward the Carter administration. In an extraordinary step, on 11 December 1979 the Libyan leader granted an interview to the *New York Times* in which he apologized for the attack on the US embassy, expressed opposition to the taking of US hostages in Iran, and even pledged not to let any Soviet naval vessels enter Libyan ports. Qaddafi also hoped that close cooperation with Billy Carter, brother of the US president, would aid reconciliation between the two countries, but in the end these efforts were unsuccessful. Preoccupied with the presidential campaign, faced with the immediate task of freeing the hostages in Iran, and distressed by the growing belligerence toward the United States in the Middle East, the Carter administration ignored Qaddafi's conciliatory gesture. In any case, at that juncture, the United States considered issues pertaining to Iran, Afghanistan, the Red Sea, and the Horn of Africa to be more urgent.

The response disappointed Qaddafi, who viewed any softening of tension with the United States as a blessing in the early 1980s, a difficult and demanding time for his country. Having just extricated itself from a humiliating political and military fiasco in Idi Amin's Uganda, the army—the backbone of Qaddafi's regime—was beginning to criticize the leader internally. Moreover, Libya's relations in the Arab world and in Western Europe were fluctuating between irritation and outright hostility—and even relations with Malta, one of the "success stories" of Libya's foreign policy, cooled over the demarcation of offshore oil-prospecting zones. These tensions coincided with mounting troubles at home. Qaddafi's revolution had lost much of its fervor, while the opposition was gathering momentum. This shift was reflected in recurrent defections by diplomats abroad, in the swelling of the ranks of expatriate opposition groups, and in the aforementioned army uprising in Tobruk in August 1980, in which "more than 400 people were wounded or killed"—an event that Tripoli denied.[20] Viewing the fact that US oil purchases accounted for almost 40 percent of Libya's total annual production,[21] Qaddafi found his failure to defuse enmity between Tripoli and Washington all the more worrying.

Frustrated and anxious, Qaddafi soon reverted to his well-known pattern of confrontation with the "imperialist American superpower," finding it most politically expedient to divert his people's attention away from his own supposedly revolutionary performance toward the foreign arena, where "small, peaceful Libya" faced a threat by the powerful "imperialist enemy" and therefore needed to mobilize all its resources in order to cope with the peril.

The United States had its own motivation to pursue Qaddafi, who was inflicting growing damage to its interests. Not surprisingly, therefore, disputes between the United States and Libya over water and airspace borders in the Mediterranean, which had first surfaced in 1973, reemerged with renewed vigor in late 1980. Following the strengthening of strategic and military links between Tripoli and Moscow and increased Soviet submarine and naval movements in the Mediterranean in the late 1970s and early 1980s, the United States increased its strategic sensitivity toward the region and, accordingly, intensified reconnaissance flights in the area.

In October 1980, about a month after the outbreak of the Iran-Iraq War, Qaddafi—fearing that the United States might take advantage of the unrest to intervene in the Gulf region—addressed a message to incumbent president Jimmy Carter and presidential contender Ronald Reagan, demanding that US naval and air forces keep away "from the Libyan-Arab borders in the Mediterranean" or "the outbreak of armed conflict . . . would regretfully be a real possibility at any moment."[22] He was aware that while the United States was at loggerheads with the regimes in both Baghdad and Tehran, it was committed to securing the flow of oil from the Gulf and protecting its allies in the region, notably Saudi Arabia. Qaddafi was also concerned that the United States might take advantage of the shift in Arab and international attention to the war in the Gulf to militarily attack Libya, whose army had invaded Chad alongside Goukouni Oueddei's anti-Western forces with the aim of deciding the civil war there in the fall of 1980. Libya and its Soviet ally had vital interests in Chad.

The next peak in this bilateral dispute was the US closure of the Libyan embassy ("People's Bureau," in Qaddafi's revolutionary parlance) in Washington on 6 May 1981, thus reducing diplomacy to the lowest level short of a complete severance of relations. The United States explained its decision by referring to "Libya's misconduct," particularly its "support for international terrorism." Qaddafi counterattacked with his usual accusations, describing the punitive act as "childish and infantile" and concluding that the Reagan administration, in power since early 1981, was even "more stupid than that of Carter."[23]

In retrospect, this act heralded the toughening of Reagan's foreign policy in general and of his policy toward Libya in particular, thereby both dispelling the Carter-era perception of the United States as weak (a perception shaped especially by the handling of both the Iranian hostage affair and the Soviet invasion of Afghanistan), and curbing Qaddafi's anti-US drive while threatening to politically eradicate him. The Reagan administration believed in using military solutions to secure its interests in the Middle East and beyond if necessary. At that juncture, the United States clearly perceived Libya not only as an adversary in itself but also as the spearhead of Soviet expansionism in the Middle East and Africa. While neither Qaddafi's unity scheme with pro-Soviet Syria in the fall of 1980 nor his announcement of a merger with Chad in early 1981 achieved any practical results, his visit to Moscow in the spring of 1981 provided Reagan with further ammunition with which to fight what Washington termed Libya's provocations. The Kremlin's pledge to construct an 800 MW nuclear power station in Libya and a subsequent visit by 'Abd al-Salam Jallud, Qaddafi's right-hand man, to Moscow to secure additional weapons in June 1981 only served to reinforce Washington's apprehension.

Thus, when the opportunity arose, the United States acted: in a dogfight over the disputed territorial waters of the Gulf of Sirte on 19 August 1981, two US F-14 fighters shot down two Libyan fighter planes. Libya accused the United States of attacking its fighters while they were on a routine reconnaissance mission in "Libyan airspace." Libya also claimed to have shot down one US fighter plane and called the attack an instance of "international terrorism" that relied "on the law of the jungle and the logic of cowboys" and indicated the Reagan administration's determination "to do everything it feasibly could to arrange to 'tie up' the Libyan dictator" or at least "make life uncomfortable" for him.[24] For its part, the United States denied the loss of aircraft and warned Libya that it would again use military force if any of its ships or aircraft were attacked while participating in Mediterranean exercises. What's more, a US source contended that it was Qaddafi who had ordered Libya's aircraft to attack in the hope that the Soviets would rally to his defense, thereby triggering a superpower confrontation—or at least deterring the United States from taking any military action in the future.[25] Somewhat paradoxically, at this point of escalating tension, Libya remained the third largest supplier of petroleum imports to the United States, and 2,000 US nationals still worked in Libya, mostly in oil-related areas.

Alarmed, yet benefiting at home from having built up his image as the bold Arab adversary of an abhorred "imperialist" superpower, Qaddafi declared that Libya would not stop operating in the Gulf of Sirte "even if it means the death of the last Libyan man and woman . . . [and] even if it means a third world war."[26] Qaddafi's militant rhetoric was nourished at that stage not only by emotional, ideological, and political motivations, but also by a sense of security and strategic prowess resulting from the signing of the Tripartite Friendship and Cooperation Treaty with two other pro-Soviet countries, Ethiopia and the PDRY, in the immediate wake of the August 1981 air fight.

Libya and the USSR perceived the new treaty as an important means of countering "American aggression" in the Arab world, the Persian Gulf, the Mediterranean Sea, and even the Indian Ocean. The treaty was particularly significant in light of the buildup of the US-initiated Rapid Development Force to meet military challenges in the Middle East and other areas. At that juncture, the United States was making an effort to address the advantages the USSR enjoyed based on its greater proximity to the Persian Gulf, including the opportunity to stockpile in Libya and surrounding countries arms and equipment that could be rapidly utilized by airlifted Soviet troops. In addition, the Soviets had access to naval facilities in Ethiopia and the PDRY as well as to intelligence on US naval units in the Indian Ocean.

Aware of the Soviet preoccupation with the taxing war in Afghanistan, Libya was concerned by the United States' increased strategic and military drive against the USSR in the fall of 1981. Qaddafi felt severely threatened by Reagan's militant acts against him (and against Moscow, among them sending weapons to the Afghani rebels). "If the US attacks the Gulf of Sirte again," he warned, "we will intentionally attack the depots of American nuclear weapons" in Sicily, Crete, Greece, and Turkey. This time, the Libyan head of state added a religious note to his anti-US rhetoric, portraying US citizens as "the new crusaders who are fighting a holy war against Islam and the Arabs." He thus implied that the US fight against Libya was also a war between Christianity and Islam and that this struggle was of primary concern to the entire Arab and Islamic world. Emphasizing religious terminology in general and the term "crusade" in particular to justify his uncompromising defiance of the United States and to mobilize domestic political support, Qaddafi revealed not only his ever-growing enmity toward the United States but also his fear that the superpower was determined to eliminate him politically. His rhetoric also reflected the rise of Islamic militancy in the Middle East and beyond, following the Khomeini-led Islamic Revolution in Tehran. Qaddafi, who consistently emphasized the primacy of Islam in Libyan society and posited the Quran as the sole valid authority for Muslims, had not yet been challenged by radical Islamic factions. Qaddafi's fears regarding the intensification of US aggression toward him should be seen against the backdrop of the "growing antipathy [toward] and willingness to think the worst of [the United States]" evidenced in many third-world countries in the early 1980s, an attitude termed "anti-Americanism." This antipathy was a reaction to the United States' growing confidence and determination to reassert its position in the world after overcoming its "Vietnam Syndrome," marked by an aversion to the use of military force as an instrument of foreign policy.[27]

Meanwhile, Libya's relations with the United States were also indirectly affected by the assassination of Egyptian president Anwar Sadat on 6 October 1981. Although Libya was not involved in the affair, it nevertheless caused Qaddafi immediate relief. The United States regarded Egypt as a central pillar of its Middle East strategy and acted to prevent the destabilization of Hosni Mubarak's regime by stepping up its political and military support for the strongly pro-US and anti-Libyan governments in both Egypt and Sudan, each of which considered its security dependent on the other.

Fearing further Soviet expansion along the Middle Eastern–African seamline, the United States also became increasingly involved with Chad—as did France, which still regarded its former colony as an important asset. Together with Soviet advisers, Libya's military leaders appeared determined to exploit the ongoing civil war in Chad and reinforce Tripoli's political and strategic foothold there, thus endangering the interests of the United Sates and its allies in the region. Qaddafi interpreted US intervention in neighboring Chad as a direct threat to Libya's security, stating that "America is preparing to make war against us. . . . America intends to invade Libya."[28]

At that point, Qaddafi believed that the powerful global alliance of the imperialist United States, Zionist Israel, and Arab-reactionary Egypt, Sudan, and Saudi Arabia was poised to take action against Libya. Clearly, Tripoli considered the United States its most dangerous enemy. Interestingly, the radical wing of Islam was not included on Qaddafi's list of enemies, despite the fact that radical Islamists were responsible for Sadat's assassination and the attempt to replace Egypt's entire regime with a Khomeini-type Islamic government.[29] Although Sadat's removal from power pleased Qaddafi, the growing strength of the Islamist radicals as an antiregime force alarmed him. These radicals, who had begun to infiltrate Libya in a low-key manner, would later threaten to liquidate Qaddafi's "infidel" regime.

Increasing tension in Egypt and its environs following Sadat's assassination soon resulted in reinforced economic and political pressure by the United States on Tripoli. On 10 December 1981, the United States called on all its citizens residing in Libya—most of whom were employees of oil companies and their dependents—to leave immediately. Simultaneously, US passports were invalidated for travel to Libya. On 10 March 1982, Reagan imposed an embargo on purchases of Libyan oil and banned the sale of US technology and equipment to Libya's oil-and-gas industry. Explaining these steps, the Reagan administration referred to Libya's support of international terrorism and actions to destabilize US allies. In the summer of 1982, the sympathetic relations between Libya and Iran, a fierce anti-US stronghold that had succeeded in militarily warding off Iraqi troops, further aggravated the United States, fearing a loss of power in the oil-rich Gulf.

At that stage, Libya had abundant reasons for disliking the US administration. Qaddafi's frustration with Washington was reflected in his allegation that the United States supported Israel's military invasion of Lebanon in 1982. Reagan's plan for a settlement of the Arab-Israeli conflict, launched in the fall of 1982, further demonized the United States in Qaddafi's eyes. And the 1982–1983 empowerment of the US-led Rapid Development Force only intensified his alarm. This force comprised 230,000 army, navy, marine, and air force personnel and could be made available in times of emergency to serve as an effective strike force in the Middle East. Symptomatic of the heightened enmity was Tripoli's adoption, in early 1983, of a new name for the United States: "the devil on earth," which echoed Khomeini's label, the "Great Satan."[30]

The Broadening of Western Opposition

Qaddafi's fury was further nourished by what he claimed to be the United States' responsibility for his failure to win the chairmanship of the Organization of African Unity (OAU) for 1983–1984. He earnestly desired the position to counteract the damage done to Libya's image of respectability and political power in Africa by the prolonged fighting in Chad, which had also had considerable political implications at home. These difficulties, together with the development of hostilities with Somalia, Zaire, and Uganda throughout 1982, reinforced Qaddafi's drive to chair the OAU. Tripoli accused the United States of sabotaging Libya's interests in Africa and the OAU in particular.[31]

Another clash between Libyan and US aircraft nearly took place over the Mediterranean off the Libyan Gulf of Sirte on 18 February 1983. Apprehensive of imminent US military action, Qaddafi exploited the escalating tension to rally Libyans around his leadership, threatening to fight back even if it meant the turning of the Gulf of Sirte into "a gulf red with blood in defence of our sea, land, and air." Qaddafi's threat was followed by massive, government-orchestrated demonstrations protesting the US "provocations," during which Reagan's effigy was burned and fierce enmity toward his administration vented.[32]

Frustrated by the increasing irrelevance of the Arab-Israeli peace process, the US administration flexed its own political and military muscles, sending four Airborne Warning and Control System (AWACS) radar planes to Egypt and deploying the nuclear-powered aircraft carrier *Nimitz* to the central and eastern Mediterranean during the first months of 1983. These moves, which coincided with accusations concerning Qaddafi's subversive attempts to topple Numayri's pro-US regime in Khartoum, injected new doses of hostility into the US attitude toward Libya. Shortly thereafter, the bloody blow of a suicide car-bomb attack on the US embassy in Lebanon occurred on 18 April 1983, reinforcing Washington's uneasiness.

Qaddafi perceived the moves made by the "crazy and foolish Reagan administration" as preparation for "open aggression against the Libyan people" aimed at removing him from power. The United States increased its pressure and, later in the summer, ordered the *USS Eisenhower* into the Gulf of Sirte, claimed by Libya as part of its territorial waters. Qaddafi reacted by threatening to sink the nuclear-powered aircraft carrier if it entered the Libyan gulf.[33] At the end of 1983, Washington responded by imposing a ban on all exports to Libya and, for the third consecutive year, renewed the ban on travel by holders of US passports.

A new peak of acrimony between Tripoli and Washington was caused by an air attack on the Sudanese city of Omdurman on 16 March 1984. Sudan accused Libya of the attack, claiming that it aimed to silence Radio Omdurman—which had broadcast strongly worded anti-Qaddafi assaults in the months preceding the attack—and to trigger an uprising against Numayri's regime and install instead a pro-Libyan, and thus pro-Soviet, regime in Khartoum. The Numayri regime—still smarting from the abortive Communist-led coup of 1971, aware of continued pro-Communist sentiment within Sudanese society, and feeling pressure from Soviet-backed Libya and Ethiopia—was seriously aggravated. The swelling of political and industrial unrest in Khartoum in early 1984, which was clearly inspired by the Communist-affiliated trade unions, substantiated Numayri's perception of a Soviet threat to his regime, whether directly or through Libya. Even without these problems, the Numayri regime at that point faced unprecedented turmoil partly as a result of Sudan's return to civil war and partly as a result of the imposition of *Shari'a* or Islamic law in a nation where about a third of the population was Christian or animist. Perceiving the attack on Omdurman as a hostile Libyan operation against US interests in the Middle East (an allegation Qaddafi denied), the United States, in what was becoming routine procedure, sent two AWACS surveillance aircraft to Egypt to guard Sudan's borders. Libya considered the dispatch of the AWACS an act of direct "aggression."[34]

Given the highly charged atmosphere, it was no wonder that Qaddafi accused the United States of involvement in the 8 May 1984 attack on his office and residence in the Bab al-'Aziziyya barracks in Tripoli. Though Libya claimed that the perpetrators of the attack were members of the Libyan Muslim Brotherhood using as a cover name the National Front for the Salvation of Libya (NFSL), it concurrently alleged that the United States, Britain, and Sudan had acted behind the scenes, determined to politically eradicate Qaddafi. The Front, set up in 1981 under the sponsorship of Sudan, was the most important of the Libyan opposition groups then in existence. The violent assault in Bab al-'Aziziyya caused Qaddafi concern, as it signified a growing threat by radical Islam. Due to internal security constraints and logistics, the high tide of opposition was manifested mainly abroad, but the attack at home reflected the perilous interactions between domestic and expatriate opposition activists.[35]

The intensified pressures on Libya at home and in its relations with the Reagan administration were reinforced by rising tensions with Britain and France. In 1983 and 1984, the Libyan opposition, with strongholds in Britain and other European capitals, became a serious political problem for Qaddafi. This was already evident in September 1983, when a large group of Libyan exiles staged an anti-Qaddafi demonstration in front of the Libyan embassy in London. As tempers flared outside the embassy, its zealous, loyal staff hurried out of the building to confront the demonstrators. The level of hostility rose and eventually the police had to intervene to disperse the crowd. Turmoil among pro- and anti-Qaddafi circles in Britain continued to simmer, spreading to Libya itself, as evidenced by particularly violent domestic actions against the regime, including the attack on the Bab al-'Aziziyya barracks in Tripoli in November 1983, which may have been an attempt on Qaddafi's life; and the explosions at military installations near Benghazi in March 1984. Qaddafi appeared determined to crush both domestic and expatriate opposition no matter the cost. The public hanging of two students at the university in Tripoli on 16 April 1984 should be viewed within this context.

The hangings infuriated the expatriate opposition in London. A day after the event, a rally was held in front of the Libyan embassy to draw world attention to Tripoli's "policy of terror." The demonstration quickly escalated into violence, culminating in the death of a British policewoman and the injury of eleven Libyan demonstrators. Britain blamed Libya for the policewoman's death, but Libya denied any responsibility and pleaded self-defense. Libya perceived itself as the victim of "a horrible terrorist act" perpetrated by British authorities and accused the British police of "storming" the Libyan embassy and opening fire on its personnel. Relations between Tripoli and London promptly deteriorated, culminating in Britain's announcement on 22 April 1984 that it was severing diplomatic ties with Libya.

Concurrently, relations between Libya and France hit rock bottom, revolving mainly around their rival aims in Chad's politics and conflicting military positions in the Chadian War. Tensions reached a peak in late January 1984 when France blamed Libya for the attack on Ziguey, an outpost at the northern edge of the government-controlled part of Chad where a French military force of 3,000 had been stationed since the summer of 1983. France also held Libya responsible for the reported shooting down of a French Jaguar fighter plane by a SAM-7 missile in the course of that attack. Libya denied the accusations and repeated the call for immediate withdrawal of French troops from Chad, a demand the French government in turn made of Libya. Aggravated by the conflict of their interests in Chad, tense relations between Libya and France persisted into the second half of the 1980s.[36] Meanwhile, increased US pressure on the Libyan regime in a wide range of areas, including the conflict in Chad, only served to reinforce the anti-Qaddafi atmosphere in the international arena. Of course, with his belligerent policy toward Chad and his persecution of Libyan dissidents in Britain and elsewhere, the Libyan leader did plenty to stir up resentment himself, thus playing into the hands of the United States.

The Writing on the Wall: Toward an Explosion?

Distressed by the growing bellicosity against his regime and fueled by his renewed military intervention in Chad's civil war after a lull designed to enhance his chances for the OAU chairmanship (which, however, failed), Qaddafi turned to a new tactic. He made somewhat naive efforts to influence US politics by exerting pressure from within the United States to urge the Reagan administration to ease its hostility toward Tripoli. This new tactic served as a safety valve, allowing Qaddafi to let off steam. He established friendly relations with Louis Farrakhan, head of the Chicago-based Nation of Islam and a supporter of Jesse Jackson's presidential candidacy. The basis for these relations had been established in the fall of 1979 when a delegation of African Americans visited Tripoli and conferred upon Qaddafi a decoration in memory of slain civil rights leader Dr. Martin Luther King, Jr.

Seizing the occasion of Farrakhan's visit to Tripoli in February 1985 to speak via satellite to the annual convention of the Nation of Islam in the United States, Qaddafi declared his willingness to aid African Americans in what he portrayed as their "struggle for freedom" against their "white oppressors," namely the US administration. The Libyan leader further urged African American Muslims to revolt against "racist" America by renouncing the US armed forces and forming their own army, which he offered to help train and arm, to fight for a separate, independent state. Qaddafi also granted a standing loan of US$5 million to Farrakhan, expressing his hope that "our joint struggle will be crowned with final victory." "Trust us," he further addressed the conventioneers, "racism and imperialism are our common enemy [and] we shall fight together, shoulder to shoulder."[37]

Qaddafi's appeal to African American Muslims should also be viewed in the context of his self-assumed championship of the cause of not only Muslims but "oppressed" minorities throughout the world. While his gesture toward Farrakhan primarily reflected Qaddafi's trouble with and fear of the United States, it was but one expression of his declared sympathy for "subjugated minorities"; he also addressed Native Americans, who suffered treatment by the US government that was "intolerable . . . both from the human point of view and from the position of international law."[38] In late July 1985, Qaddafi hosted a delegation of the American Indian Movement in Tripoli, thereby strengthening his connections with militant circles in the United States. Notwithstanding the relative prominence Qaddafi gave to his connections with African American Muslims and Native Americans, however, they were only marginally useful in influencing Libyan-US relations, but rather, reflected Qaddafi's own political and ideological outlook.

Far more important were the new suspicions raised by Washington about Tripoli as an indirect result of the military coup in Sudan in the spring of 1985, which toppled Numayri's pro-US, pro-Egyptian, and anti-Libyan regime. Though the overthrow appeared to be entirely Sudanese-led, with no Libyan (or Soviet) complicity, the United States became apprehensive about the subsequent political rapprochement between Tripoli and Khartoum and the new Sudanese regime's declared policy of "balanced international relations." Washington had long regarded Sudan as an important political and strategic asset, which helped safeguard the important pro-US government in Cairo and curb further Soviet expansion into the Middle East and the Red Sea region, the Arabian Peninsula, and Africa. Although Qaddafi was aware of the United States' apprehension, he was also concerned over the measure of Soviet support Libya would receive following Mikhail Gorbachev's rise to power in March 1985. Qaddafi feared that Washington might not only torpedo Tripoli's new alliance with Khartoum but also decrease Libya's political attractiveness to the Kremlin. "Reagan's nose will be cut off if the US interferes in [Libya's relations with] Sudan," Qaddafi sternly warned. "Reagan has nothing to do with Sudan. Sudan is ours, not an American matter."[39]

Meanwhile, mutual suspicions continued to flare. The United States accused Libya of involvement in the hijacking of a TWA jet en route to Beirut with some US nationals aboard in the summer of 1985 as well as in the hijacking of the Italian cruise ship *Achille Lauro,* during which a wheelchair-bound US citizen was murdered in the winter of 1985. Libya was also implicated in two attacks on civilians in airports in Rome and Vienna on 27 December 1985. Concurrently, there was a wave of Palestinian terrorism against Israeli targets, apparently planned and carried out by the Abu Nidal group, which allegedly operated with backing from Tripoli. Qaddafi was aware that he posed a serious obstacle to Washington's policy in the Middle East, yet he continued to actively promote what he considered his country's legitimate positions.

The US Use of Power to Curb Libyan Threats

In fact, Libya endangered all of Washington's objectives in the region: combating terrorism across the Middle East, minimizing Moscow's influence while maximizing its own, consolidating stability against radical forces to safeguard pro-US Arab regimes, advancing the Arab-Israeli peace process, and ensuring the supply of oil at reasonable prices.

As Reagan ended the first year of his second term in office, his administration marked Libya as an ideal testing ground for an antiterrorism crackdown. It estimated that tough measures against Tripoli could be implemented without risking a confrontation with the Soviets, who were still bogged down by the war in Afghanistan and who were not particularly active in the Middle East in the mid-1980s in any case. In fact, at that juncture Libya's relations with the USSR were relatively cool, making Qaddafi more vulnerable to pressure from Washington. Tensions between Tripoli and Moscow were heightened due to Libya's transfer of Soviet-supplied missiles and arms to Iran for use against Moscow's ally, Iraq; Libya's inability to repay its Soviet debts in cash; and the USSR's revocation of its offer to build Libya's first nuclear power station.

The United States counted on Libya's military engagement in Chad, which in the fall of 1985 was entering its sixth year, to drain Tripoli's coffers and minimize its ability to retaliate. Even harder on the Libyan economy, however, was the dramatic decline in oil revenues following a price collapse in the world oil market, falling from a peak of about US$20 billion in 1980 to about US$7 billion in 1984. This slump definitely weakened Libya's ability to trade, resulting in financial shortages and the necessity to curtail spending on consumption, development, and defense.[40] It also undermined Qaddafi's posture at home and abroad, giving the US administration more room for maneuvering.

Libya also appeared to be largely isolated in the Arab world, plagued by various conflicts. Chief among these was the Iran-Iraq War, which broke out in 1980 and was still intense in 1986. The Arab-Israeli conflict, the related peace process, and the role of Egypt in pan-Arab affairs also exacerbated inter-Arab divisions. Compounding the hostile positions some Arab countries took toward Qaddafi, these cleavages lessened the possibility that any actions taken by the United States against Libya would raise an effective pan-Arab response.

Moreover, one of the Reagan administration's highest priorities was to break the United States out of the so-called Vietnam Syndrome. Reagan believed in the utility of limited military force as part of a coercive strategy for bringing political pressure to bear on America's adversaries. Reagan was also crucially affected by the unprecedented wave of terror that hit US targets in the mid-1980s. At that stage, the general international impression was that terrorism had become "a growth industry." Of more than 800 terrorist incidents in 1985, 177 targeted US citizens or facilities overseas. Among the 2,333 casualties, twenty-three Americans were killed and 139 were injured. There were also "unconfirmed reports" of Qaddafi's plans to launch a major terrorist campaign within the United States proper, which would include the assassination of Reagan.[41] This accusation should be viewed in the context of claims that the Reagan administration had made repeated attempts on Qaddafi's life.[42]

Aware that Libya was a potential target of the United States' antiterrorism actions as well as its broader foreign-policy strategy, Qaddafi's anxiety about a US assault steadily intensified. In early 1986, he declared "a state of maximum alert," warning the United States of his willingness to turn "the waters of the Gulf of Sirte into blood [and Libyan soil into] a graveyard for any invaders."[43] The United States added fuel to the fire by declaring Libya a threat to its national security and foreign policy. Subsequently, it ordered any remaining citizens (estimated to be between 1,000 and 1,500) to leave Libya immediately and froze hundreds of millions of dollars of Libyan assets in US banks and their subsidiaries.

Tightening the noose, Reagan imposed economic sanctions on Libya on 1 February 1986, commenting that Qaddafi "is not only a barbarian but he is [also] flaky." The next day, Qaddafi responded, "I had not heard that Reagan is a doctor or psychiatrist. [But] I know that he was a bad actor" who "has arteriosclerosis due to old age."[44]

The public exchange of insults, followed shortly by the reinforcement of US military strength in the Mediterranean, converged with a reduction in the attention the USSR paid to Libya. Frightened, Qaddafi vented his frustration through verbal barbs, referring to the "power mania" of the United States, which he portrayed as "a moth that cannot keep away from the flame until it is completely burnt up." He warned Washington not "to play with fire."[45] On 25 January 1986, during one of the peaks in this war of nerves, Qaddafi boarded a missile boat and sailed into the Gulf of Sirte, where he told the Libyan media that "Libya is not going to be content to live under international terrorism forever. I am now going on board this patrol boat to parallel 32° 30' to stress that this is the gate to the Gulf of Sirte . . . the death line where we shall stand and fight with our backs to the wall."[46] It is not clear to what extent this particular spate of militancy was leveled at the United States or tailored for domestic audiences in order to enhance his standing at home.

Tensions reached a new zenith on 24 March 1986. According to the Libyan version of events, US Sixth Fleet fighter planes violated the airspace over the Gulf of Sirte. Libya's air force then used long-range SA-5 missiles and "shot down" three aircraft, "which fell into the sea." Exploiting these alleged military achievements to the full for its propaganda war and resorting to particularly forceful rhetoric, Tripoli announced its determination to "teach the US a lesson worse than the lesson of Vietnam."[47] The United States, however, did not report the loss of any aircraft; on the contrary, it reported the bombing of missile batteries and radar installations at the Ghardabiyya air base and the sinking of one Libyan missile boat.[48] All in all, the incident appeared to be a failed attempt by the United States to draw Qaddafi into a broader armed confrontation, possibly in order to test the Libyan and Soviet responses to a full-blown air operation against Libya. Libya had now clearly become the site where Washington revealed its strategy for securing its Middle East interests by the use of force.

The bombing aboard a TWA jet on 2 April 1986 in Karachi elicited an announcement that the White House viewed Qaddafi as "a suspect." Libya immediately released an official denial. Three days later, La Belle, a West Berlin discotheque frequented by US soldiers, was bombed; 230 people, 79 of them Americans, were wounded and two US servicemen were killed. The administration accused Qaddafi of being linked to that event as well, claiming that the incident indicated Libya's "pattern of indiscriminate violence" against US citizens. Tripoli promptly protested what it called "the American state of hysteria" over and "obsession" with Qaddafi, letting fly virulent arrows at the US president's "frail body," which, it asserted, was plagued by "a cancerous tumor." Tripoli also repeated its denial of any connection with the "recent wave of [terrorist] attacks."[49]

At that point, the United States deepened its resolve to act forcefully against Libya, as was evidenced by its initiative to galvanize European countries into collective action against Qaddafi, who had become synonymous in Washington with terrorism. Toward mid-April 1986, its efforts proved successful. Britain secretly permitted US F-111 aircraft to fly from bases in the UK toward Libyan targets, and the European Economic Community (EEC) agreed to take measures aimed at restricting Libya's ability to sponsor terrorism. These measures included a reduction in the size of Libya's embassies and restrictions on the movement of Libyans in European countries as well as the imposition of stricter visa requirements on Libyans. The option of joint military retaliation against terrorism, and more specifically against Libya, became central to the US agenda during the first months of 1986. These successes, underscored by military exercises off the Libyan coast, were, however, merely harbingers of a major strike aimed at putting an end to what Washington persistently termed Libyan terrorism.

The Climax of the Drama: The US Air Strike on Libya

On the morning of 15 April 1986, Qaddafi's long-feared military assault by the United States, which dubbed it Operation El Dorado Canyon, took place. US aircraft bombed key installations in the Libyan power structure, including Qaddafi's headquarters and residence in Tripoli's Bab al-'Aziziyya barracks and the Sidi Bilal port military complex west of Tripoli, which the United States considered a terrorist training site. Simultaneously, there was a series of strikes against signal and radar installations and surface-to-air-missile sites. Qaddafi himself, who was presumably a target of the operation, escaped physical harm. This was an exceptional operation, not only in light of bilateral relations but also in comparison with past US conduct in the Arab world.

The shocked Libyan head of state disappeared from public view for nearly forty-eight hours following the US air strike. The rumor mill offered various explanations for his disappearance, including that he had been relocated temporarily to the PDRY to protect him from further US threat as well as from the Libyan opposition—especially the army—and in order to consult with Soviet officials. Tripoli eventually denied all these "stories."[50]

Although it later became known that, shortly before the attack, Malta had warned Libya that unidentified aircraft were heading toward it, the Libyans seemed to have been caught completely off guard by the raid. According to official data, the air strike resulted in thirty-seven dead—including Qaddafi's adopted daughter—and ninety-three wounded. It also lent a great measure of credibility to Qaddafi's perception that his regime was being persecuted by the United States.[51]

In Qaddafi's absence, Libya's state-controlled media stepped in the first day after the air raid to fiercely condemn the United States and give voice to the people's rage, inciting them to take revenge. By providing this outlet for the expression of genuine pain and anxiety, the authorities kept the public from turning against the regime, inflaming patriotic sentiments in a particularly florid style: "Every drop of blood . . . must be avenged. We here are drinking [American] blood. But every one of you [Arabs] can in his own place also drink the blood of the Americans. There are their embassies . . . companies, offices . . . [and] there are Americans living in the Arab capitals. . . . Oh Arab[s], slaughter [the Americans] like sheep." By broadcasting martial and national anthems, Tripoli's media also tried to boost morale. The repeated announcements of the "heavy damages" that Libya's "brave sons" inflicted upon the "enemy" should be viewed in this context. "At least twenty F-111 US aircraft were shot down by the Jamahiriyya's armed forces," Radio Tripoli announced on the day of the attack, further claiming the "total destruction" of a US-manned communication installation on the Italian island of Lampedusa in retaliation for the raid.[52]

On 16 April 1986, Qaddafi appeared for the first time since the attack in a television address to the nation. While strongly condemning "the barbarous American attack," he emphasized that he would not stop inciting "revolution, whatever raids [the United States] carried out." Wishing to minimize the traumatic effect of the raid and to project national resilience, Qaddafi urged his people to dance in the streets: "Turn on the lights [and] dance. . . . We were not afraid of America. . . . We have Allah on our side and Allah is stronger than America." Acting to calm the people, the Libyan media implored them on the same day to "stick together against the American savages" and "stress our unshakable, firm faith in our principles and aims . . . , [and] our insistence on our leader, thinker, teacher, and guide Qaddafi." The authorities' endeavor to strengthen patriotic feelings and Qaddafi's political position was also illustrated by the introduction of new terminology: the word *al-'Uzma* ("the Great") was added to the official name of the country "because the Great Jamahiriyya has withstood the biggest power in the world."[53]

Qaddafi continued to mobilize his people against the United States, inflaming their nationalistic and revolutionary fervor and increasing their motivation to support his leadership. In so doing, he hoped to check increasing public discontent over economic difficulties caused by the the continuing drop in world oil prices and increasing resentment among the Army Command, mainly over the prolonged war in Chad and financial hardships. In 1985 alone, the government canceled more than US$700 million in military construction projects, froze most promotions, and ended housing and travel privileges for soldiers. The bleak economic atmosphere was further darkened by the curtailing of Libya's most ambitious infrastructure project, the Great Man-Made River, construction of which had begun in 1983. The project aimed to transport water over 1,000 miles from an inland reservoir in the south to the densely populated coastal region of the country.[54]

Though definitely troubled by the growing social and political unrest in the wake of the air strike, Qaddafi, convinced that the United States was targeting him, attempted to romanticize Libya's victimization and to use it domestically as a public relations asset. Thus he stated that "in reality, the American aggression did not aim at anything but the demolition of the stronghold of freedom and the struggle against imperialism, Zionism and racism in the world and the [destruction of the] frontline of resistance in the Arab homeland as represented by the Libyan jamahiriyya." At the same time, Tripoli vehemently dismissed the notion that "the issue of terrorism was the basis of the attack," portraying the US president as the "Hitler of the twentieth century, wanting to destroy the world." Reagan was repeatedly called "Hitler Mark II" and "a new Nazi" by the Libyan media as well as Qaddafi in the period following the April attack.[55] The United States argued that the raid was in "self-defense."[56]

Qaddafi was concerned about the possible repercussions of the attack on the regime's political status and about further US aggression toward him personally. Foreign sources noted the Libyan people's "striking apathy and lack of support" for their leader following the attack, claiming that there were more anti-US demonstrations in other Arab capitals than in Tripoli, "where foreign journalists outnumbered the Tripolitanians" at the protests that did take place. This may partially explain Qaddafi's distress at that sensitive stage.[57] Other sources, however, negated the claims that domestic instigation against Qaddafi had increased in the wake of the US attack.[58]

Beginning in mid-1986, Qaddafi exhibited a high level of political nervousness but mobilized his considerable rhetorical talents and charm to strengthen the people's reliance upon his leadership, thus making the best of a bad situation. "We are ready to . . . die defending our land," he stated, and noted that if US aircraft carriers landed on Libyan shores, they would be annihilated "because we and the fish are waiting for them."[59]

Luckily for Qaddafi, the United States' antiterrorism policy suffered grave setbacks in the fall and winter of 1986 as a result of two public relations disasters. The first was the exposure of a plot against Qaddafi, thought up by the US administration and coupled with manipulation of the US media to enhance the prospects of his political elimination. The US media reported that the US National Security Council had launched a disinformation campaign aimed at further blackening Qaddafi's image, stating that he was planning to launch a new wave of terrorism. The purpose of this manipulation was to foster an anti-Qaddafi atmosphere within Libya and, subsequently, to enhance the prospects of a coup against him. The second was the revelation that, despite its own formal arms embargo against Iran, Washington was supplying weapons to Tehran with the aim of bringing home US nationals held hostage by pro-Iran terrorists in Lebanon. The publicization of these affairs heavily damaged the moral standing of the United States as a champion of antiterrorism, and, in turn, benefited Qaddafi's Libya.

Shifting its anti-Libyan pressure mainly to the war zone in Chad in early 1987, where its interests conflicted with Libya's, the Reagan administration equipped the government in Ndjamena with sophisticated weapons. Libya's fears of being attacked again by the United States, this time from the south through "Chad as the starting point," increased and elicited a vitriolic response against the "Yankees who have no morals [nor] conscience . . . [and] who constitute a threat to the future of mankind."[60] The assistance the United States provided the Chadian army, which totaled US$32 million and included Redeye anti-aircraft missiles as well as shoulder-fired Stinger missiles, eventually helped ensure the withdrawal of Libyan troops from most of the country later in the spring. Furious and humiliated, Qaddafi resorted to a new wave of recriminations against the US administration, alternately calling it the "Black House," a "modern-day Dracula," and "the world's policeman."[61]

Libya Accused of Manufacturing Chemical Weapons

Having scored successive achievements in its war against the Qaddafi regime, the United States closed in on Libya with fresh impetus, this time attacking from quite different quarters. In late 1988 and early 1989, the United States claimed for the first time that Libya was manufacturing chemical weapons in the "largest chemical weapons–production plant the CIA ha[s] detected anywhere," located in Rabta, southwest of Tripoli. Libya insisted that the plant was used solely for the production of pharmaceuticals.[62] Whatever its actual objectives, there was no doubt that the plant had the potential to produce chemical weapons.

Libya's fears of a new US attack were substantiated on 4 January 1989. US Navy fighters shot down two Libyan MiG-23 jet fighters over the Mediterranean off the Libyan coast. Qaddafi branded the incident an act of "terrorism." The United States claimed its pilots were acting "in self defense."[63] It is unclear, however, whether the United States initiated the attack, directly or by provocation, or whether the Libyans, who were very nervous, had instigated it in order to thwart a more damaging assault on targets within the country.

In addition to Libya, the Reagan administration was also beginning to focus on Iran and Syria, which it considered radical states. The United States had become increasingly concerned with the spread of chemical weapons and long-range delivery systems, a concern that threatened to affect its relations with NATO allies, in particular Germany (on the grounds that private German firms were supplying Libya with technology and assistance) as well as the Soviet Union.[64]

Qaddafi viewed the inauguration of George Herbert Walker Bush in early 1989 as an opportunity to ease tensions with the United States, but, to his disappointment, Washington rejected Tripoli's diplomatic overtures. In early 1990, when Washington renewed the accusation that Libya was manufacturing chemical weapons in Rabta, Tripoli reiterated that the plant was only manufacturing medical items. Insisting that Libya was producing chemical weapons, the United States called on the international community to stop it, lacing the appeal with a covert threat to bomb the plant if necessary.[65] On 14 March 1990, a fire broke out in the plant. It remains unclear whether the blaze was the result of sabotage or an accident. Libya accused the United States, Israel, and Germany of sabotaging the plant. All three unequivocally denied any involvement. The United States and the aforementioned NFSL—the strongest of the Libyan expatriate opposition groups— suggested that the fire was a hoax perpetrated by Qaddafi.[66]

Deeply concerned with what he viewed as unceasing US persecution, in the spring of 1990 Qaddafi reverted to his portrayal of the United States as a "satanic country" ruled by an "imperialist gang" who was launching yet "another crusade against Islam." Focusing with renewed emphasis on militant terminology employed by the Islamist regime in Iran and by the installation of an Islamist regime in Sudan in the summer of 1989, Qaddafi declared that Muslims "have only one choice if they want to survive: confronting the US Satan, which is manipulated by the force of evil." Qaddafi called on Arabs to develop a "deterrent force," which would include nuclear bombs, in order to defeat the United States: "If we had a deterrent force of missiles able to reach New York, we would have directed them at that very moment against it."[67]

Early in the summer of 1990, there were reports that Libya was planning to build a second, underground chemical-weapons facility in a remote desert location in Sabha, south of Tripoli. While denying these reports, Qaddafi urgently reiterated the "right and duty" of Libya and the entire Arab world to acquire "weapons of total destruction." If Libya had been able to manufacture such weapons, he stated, it "would not have hesitated and would not have hidden the fact." He promised to pay "one billion [currency not specified] to anyone who could build a chemical factory for Libya." He also encouraged the Arab world to develop a nuclear bomb "in defiance of America."[68] It seems that, at this stage, Qaddafi was reviving earlier plans to acquire nuclear technology. His enthusiasm for promoting the nuclear armament of the Arab world, however, did not elicit any significant response from the United States, whose concern with Libya was overshadowed in the summer of 1990 by the collapse of the USSR and the invasion of pro-American Kuwait by Iraq.

Not only did 1990 mark a historical turning point in Middle East politics and beyond, but it was also a landmark in Libya's political direction and its position in the regional and international arenas. For the first time since independence, Libya faced a dramatically changed global scene and an entirely different relationship with the United States. The dissolution of the Soviet Union represented a strategic crossroads that threatened all Libyan interests, both domestic and foreign. The Libyan leader expressed his anxiety about a new world dominated by one superpower that was particularly hostile toward Libya, stating, "The countries of Eastern Europe were friends of ours [but] now they handed over all our files to the US. They used to stand with us against imperialism and against Zionism [but] now they have said: the Israelis, Arabs, the Cubans and others are all the same."[69] Indeed, a new era had begun for Libya.

Notes

1. B. Davis, *U.S. Attack on Libya*, p. 33. On p. 113 of *Pariah State*, Sicker reports that the United States gave Libya US$222 million in aid during Sanusi's reign.

For more details on Libya and its relations with the United States during this period, see, for instance, Shaked and Webman-Souery, "Libya"; J. Wright, *Libya: A Modern History,* pp. 77–118; and Vandewalle, *Libya Since Independence,* pp. 41–63.

2. Britain's involvement in the Middle East considerably predated that of the United States, which began around World War II and intensified as the Cold War heated up. As British influence in the region waned, the US presence increased. For an overview of this transformation, see Kedourie, "Transition," and Pedaliu, "Truman, Eisenhower and the Mediterranean Cold War." For British and US involvement in preindependent Libya, see Sabki, "International Authority." See also Kelly, "Britain, Libya and the Start of the Cold War," and Mattes, "The Maghreb States," p. 13.

3. Radio Bayda (Tripoli), 16 October 1969 (British Broadcasting Corporation, BBC), and Libyan News Agency, 30 October 1969 (BBC). For the US position toward the new Qaddafi regime, see the series of secret documents declassified by Washington after thirty years and published in *al-Mushahid al-Siyasi* 5, issue 202 (23–29 January 2000): pp. 10–15. See also Mattes, "The Maghreb States," pp. 14–19.

4. In fact, the regime had already faced an attempted coup in December 1969, launched by Interior Minister Lieutenant Colonel Musa Ahmad and Defense Minister Lieutenant Colonel Adam al-Hawwaz. In May 1970, the authorities exposed a new plot, allegedly planned by a group of royalists. Prince 'Abdallah 'Abid al-Sanusi, King Sanusi's cousin, was said to have been one of the leaders of the plot.

5. See Gera, "Libya and the United States."

6. Nasser, who seized power in Egypt in 1952, died on 28 September 1970, leaving a huge vacuum in the leadership of the Arab world. For Qaddafi's admiration and active support of Nasser's ideology and the two leaders' common outlook on various issues pertaining to the Arab world and the West, see chapter 5; see also Ronen, "Personalities and Politics," 2001.

7. In 1971, Qaddafi still faced political difficulties, standing down from office in January and again in September under unclear circumstances. In addition, a coup attempt planned by 'Umar al-Shalhi, a close associate of former King Sanusi, was reportedly thwarted in early 1971. For Qaddafi's unionist initiatives, including the "Federation of Arab Republics," see Sela, *The Continuum Political Encyclopedia,* pp. 162–163.

8. For more details, see "Libya," *Arab Report and Record,* 16–31 March 1973, p. 173.

9. Korn, *Assassination in Khartoum,* pp. 193–194, 197–198.

10. "Libya," *Arab Report and Record,* 1–15 June 1973, pp. 251–252. For 1972 Libyan population data, see Nyrop, *Area Handbook for Libya,* p. vii.

11. B. Davis, *U.S. Attack on Libya,* p. 35. On the verge of the October 1973 War, Libya was exporting about 200,000 barrels of crude oil daily to the United States, or 2.7 percent of US imports. *Arab Report and Record,* 16–31 October 1973, p. 496. For more on Libya's oil industry during the first years of Qaddafi's revolution, see, for example, Vicker, *The Kingdom of Oil,* pp. 224–257; Waddams, *The Libyan Oil Industry;* Allan, *Libya: The Experience of Oil;* Cooley, *Libyan Sandstorm,* pp. 42–79; Bearman, *Qadhafi's Libya,* pp. 79–95; and Vandewalle, *Libya Since Independence,* pp. 74–81.

12. *The International Herald Tribune,* 29–30 January 1977. See also Haley, *Qadhafi and the United States,* pp. 35–55.

13. Radio Tripoli, 7 October 1977 (BBC). For more on Libya's armed conflict with Egypt and Libya's Cold War dimension, see chapters 4 and 5.

14. Al-Qadhafi, *The Green Book,* Part 1, p. 42. For the four points of People's Power, among them the use of the Quran as the code of society, see Arab Revolution

News Agency, 3 March 1977 (BBC). Libya's official name was declared on 3 March 1977 as The Arab Libyan People's Socialist State of the Masses *(al-Jamahiriyya al-'Arabiyya al-Libiyya al-Sha'biyya al-Ishtirakiyya)*. In 1978 and 1979, Qaddafi formulated the second and third parts of his Third Universal Theory. See *The Green Book,* Part 2, "Socialism," and *The Green Book,* Part 3. See also St. John, "The Ideology of Mu'ammar al-Qadhafi"; Ayoub, *Islam and the Third Universal Theory,* pp. 26–59; Vandewalle, "The Libyan Jamahiriyya Since 1969" in Vandewalle, ed., *Qadhafi's Libya: 1969–1994,* pp. 17–26; Burgat, "Qadhafi's Ideological Framework" in Vandewalle, *Qadhafi's Libya: 1969–1994,* pp. 47–63; Habiby, "Qadhafi's Thoughts on True Democracy," pp. 29–35; and "Mu'amar Gadhafi's New Islamic Scientific Socialist Society," *Middle East Review,* Summer 1979, pp. 33–39.

15. Muhayshi, together with two other members of the Revolutionary Command Council, Bashir Hawadi and 'Awad Hamza, were accused of responsibility for the coup plan. The affair duly distressed the regime, shaking the foundations of its top echelon and hence Qaddafi's confidence in its coherence.

16. *International Herald Tribune,* 6 April 1978; *New York Times,* 24 June 1978.

17. Radio Tripoli, 4 March and 19 June 1978 (Daily Report, DR).

18. For Libya's pan-Islamic calls, see Jamahiriyya Arab News Agency (JANA), 14 and 19 September 1979 (DR). For Libya's alleged involvement, see B. Davis, *U.S. Attack on Libya,* p. 37.

19. For the exchange of accusations, see *Financial Times,* 10 May 1980, and Radio Tripoli, 12 May 1980 (DR). On 14 October 1980, a Libyan student living in the United States who was known to be an opponent of the Qaddafi regime was shot. Libya admitted responsibility for the event. JANA, 17 October 1980 (DR).

20. For details on the uprising, see, for example, Agence France Presse (AFP), 18 August 1980 (DR); *Washington Post,* 19 August 1980; Middle East News Agency (Cairo), 19 August 1980 (DR). For Libya's denial, see 'Abd al-Salam Jallud, *The Jamahiriyya Mail,* 23 August 1980.

21. See Newsom, "U.S.-Libyan Relations Since 1969."

22. Quoted in the *Washington Post,* 22 October 1980.

23. *International Herald Tribune,* 9 May 1981; JANA, 7 May 1981 (BBC). For more details on the Reagan administration's policy vis-à-vis Libya, see Martin and Walcott, *Best Laid Plans,* pp. 315–321.

24. Haley, *Qadhafi and the United States,* p. 274. For more on US-Libyan relations throughout the 1970s, see ElWarfally, *Imagery and Ideology in US Policy Toward Libya: 1969–1982.*

25. For Libyan and US references to the aerial combat, see JANA, 19 August 1981 (DR); and *Washington Post,* 20 August 1981, respectively. For additional details regarding the conflict in the Gulf of Sirte, see Gunter, "Qaddafi Reconsidered," p. 123. For Libya's attempts to draw the USSR into the conflict, see William Safire's 23 August 1981 column in the *New York Times,* as quoted by Sicker in *Pariah State,* p. 117.

26. JANA, 21 August 1981 (DR).

27. For Qaddafi's statement, see *The Jamahiriyya Mail,* 22 August 1981, and Radio Tripoli, 1 September 1981 (BBC). For more details on Qaddafi's religious-political outlook, see L. Anderson, "Religion and Politics in Libya," and Marius K. Deeb, "Islam and Arab Nationalism." For more on the phenomenon of anti-Americanism, see Rubinstein and Smith, eds., *Anti-Americanism in the Third World,* and Faath, "The Problematic Topic of Anti-Americanism," pp. 1–11.

28. Radio Tripoli, 20 October 1981 (BBC).

29. Per a statement by Mubarak aired on *al-Ahram* (Cairo), 23 and 24 October 1981.

30. Radio Tripoli, 26 February 1983 (DR). For more on the Rapid Development Force, see B. Rubin, "The United States and the Middle East," pp. 33–35.

31. *Al-Zahf al-Akhdar* (Tripoli), 19 November 1982; *The Jamahiriyya Review* (London), May 1983.

32. *Al-Fajr al-Jadid* (Tripoli), 18 February 1983; JANA, 19 February 1983 (DR).

33. *Al-Zahf al-Akhdar,* 25 January 1983; JANA, 3 August 1983 (DR); *al-Zahf al-Akhdar,* 27 August 1983. The United States' pattern of dispatching AWACS planes to its Arab allies in hours of crisis was already apparent by the fall of 1980 at the outbreak of the Iran-Iraq War, when the US administration sent AWACS to Saudi Arabia.

34. For more on the Omdurman attack, see Ronen, "Sudan," 1986, p. 644. For Libya's response, see JANA, 18 and 19 March 1984 (BBC), and Radio Tripoli, 23 and 26 April 1984 (BBC).

35. The number of expatriate opponents was put at 50,000 in 1981. Most lived in western Europe, the Middle East, and the United States, but, fortunately for Qaddafi, they were weakened by divisions along ideological and political lines. For more details on the opposition, see also L. Anderson, "Qadhafi and His Opposition," and L. Harris, *Libya: Qadhafi's Revolution and the Modern State,* pp. 76–82. For the 8 May attack, see JANA, 9 and 16 May 1984, and *al-Zahf al-Akhdar,* 14 May 1984. The NFSL was established in 1981 under the leadership of Muhammad Yusuf al-Muqarayif, a former diplomat and lecturer at Benghazi University who a year earlier had defected with other Libyan officials, most noteworthy among them 'Izz al-Din Ghadamsi, the ambassador to Austria, and Anis Ahmad al-Shittawi, a former oil minister. The NFSL declared its main goal to be "liberating Libya . . . , saving it from Qaddafi . . . and then rebuilding a democratic state."

36. For Libya's disputes with Britain, see Ronen, "Libya's Conflict with Britain," 2006. For Libya's dispute with France, see Ronen, "Libya," 1986.

37. Radio Tripoli, 25 February 1985 (BBC); *New York Times,* 7 May 1985.

38. *Jamahiriyya Mail,* 27 November 1985.

39. *New York Times,* 11 April 1985, quoting Qaddafi during an interview with a US reporter in Tripoli.

40. *Africa Confidential* (London), 17 July and 4 September 1985; *Washington Post,* 15 June 1986; Miller, "North Africa's Oil Exporters"; Allan, "Libya Accommodates to Lower Oil Revenues."

41. Feldman, "The United States and the Middle East," p. 19; Jentleson, "The Reagan Administration," pp. 57, 63; Zilian, "The US Raid on Libya," p. 501; Woodward, *Veil: The Secret Wars of the CIA,* pp. 166–167, 181–187.

42. *Washington Post,* 3 November 1985 and 12 July 1987; Zoubir, "Libya in US Foreign Policy," p. 32. For a discussion on Libya and terrorism, see Blake and Abu-Osba, eds., *Libya: Terrorist or Terrorized.*

43. Radio Tripoli, 3, 4, and 5 January 1986 (DR and BBC).

44. Reagan, in a speech to the nation, *New York Times,* 8 January 1986; Qaddafi on Radio Tripoli, 9 January 1986 (BBC). For a discussion of the US sanctions policy in general and against Libya in particular, see Rodman, "Sanctions at Bay."

45. JANA, 24 January 1986; Radio Tripoli, 24 and 25 January 1986 (DR and BBC, respectively).

46. Tripoli TV, 26 January 1986 (BBC).

47. Radio Tripoli, 24 and 25 March 1986 (DR).

48. *New York Times,* 25 March 1986. According to Schumacher in "The United States and Libya," the United States sank "at least two Libyan patrol boats," citing

the number of drowned sailors as 72 based on a memorial list posted inside the Benghazi naval barracks.

49. For the US accusations, see *New York Times,* 4, 6, and 23 April 1986; for the Libyan denials, see Radio Tripoli, 7 April 1986 (DR), and JANA, 9 and 10 April 1986 (BBC).

50. *Daily Telegraph,* 22 April 1986; JANA, 24 April and 24 June 1986 (DR).

51. For the data on casualties and injuries, see Jallud in an interview with *al-Safir* (Beirut), 29 April 1986. According to Bearman, *Qadhafi's Libya,* pp. 287–298, "journalists in Tripoli" estimated that there were over 100 dead and twice as many wounded. For more on the attack, see B. Davis, *U.S. Attack on Libya,* pp. 133–180; Kaldor and Anderson, *Mad Dogs*; Bolger, "To the Shores of Tripoli," pp. 383–441; Stanik, *El Dorado Canyon: Reagan's Undeclared War with Qaddafi.*

52. Radio Tripoli, 15 April 1986 (BBC).

53. *Financial Times,* 18 April 1986; Tripoli TV, 20 April and 7 May 1986 (DR).

54. Middle East News Agency, 20 July 1986 (DR); *International Herald Tribune,* 14 and 15 June 1986; *al-Dustur* (London), 21 July and 15 and 22 September 1986.

55. Radio Tripoli, 15 April 1986 (BBC), 9 May 1986 (DR), 30 August 1986 (BBC); JANA, 22 April 1986 (DR); Tripoli TV, 7 October 1986 (BBC).

56. Gunter, "Qaddafi Reconsidered," p. 124.

57. F. Anderson, "Qadhafi's Libya," p. 76. See also Jentleson, "The Reagan Administration," pp. 68–79.

58. See, for example, L. Harris, "America's Libya Policy Has Failed."

59. From an interview published in *al-Ittihad al-Usbu'i,* 1 May 1986, and a speech quoted by JANA, 13 May 1986 (DR).

60. JANA, 12 January 1987 (DR); Tripoli TV, 2 March 1987 (BBC).

61. For the US$32 million in aid, see *The Guardian,* 11 September 1987; for Libya's reactions, see *al-Fajr al-Jadid,* 3 and 16 January and 4 and 16 February 1986; JANA, 24 October 1987 (DR) and 9 and 14 October 1987 (BBC).

62. For the US accusation, see *International Herald Tribune,* 27 October 1988, quoting CIA director William H. Webster. For the Libyan denial, see JANA, 14 November 1988 (DR). For a discussion of Libya's chemical weapons, see Wiegele, *The Clandestine Building of Libya's Chemical Weapons Factory: A Study in International Collusion.*

63. For the Libyan version, see Radio Tripoli, 4 January 1989 (DR); for the US version, see the United States Information Service (USIS), 4 January 1989, quoting Defense Secretary Frank C. Carlucci.

64. Spiegel and Pervin, "The United States and the Middle East," p. 28.

65. For the US accusations, see USIS, 8 March 1990, and the *New York Times,* 31 March and 9 June 1990. For the Libyan denials, see Tripoli TV, 12 February 1990 (DR), and an interview with Libya's ambassador to Rome by the Association Nazionale Stampa Associata, 20 March 1990 (DR).

66. *Al-Inqadh,* March–April 1990; *New York Times,* 31 March 1990.

67. JANA, 20 March 1990 (DR); Tripoli TV, 19 April 1990 (DR).

68. Radio Tripoli, 15 March 1990 (DR); *al-Sharq al-Awsat,* 25 May 1990.

69. Radio Tripoli, 21 November 1990 (DR).

3

Libyan-US Relations
in the New World Order

The demise of the USSR left the world under the exclusive domination of the United States, a country hostile to Libya. Qaddafi feared that the US administration would exploit the new international circumstances to inflict a fatal blow on his regime. The forceful US reaction to Iraq's invasion of Kuwait on 2 August 1990 and the prompt Russian alignment with the US-led anti-Iraq coalition considerably heightened Libyan anxiety. Qaddafi watched with deepening distress as deeply rooted Cold War patterns became irrelevant. Most disturbing for him was Moscow's total disregard of its 1972 friendship treaty with Baghdad, which stipulated that in case of danger to either of the two parties, they would coordinate their positions and neither would align itself against the other. The Russians not only ignored their commitment to their Iraqi ally in its difficult hour but, even worse, they adhered to a contradictory policy of "new political thinking" that relied on international bodies to achieve political resolutions to conflict before taking military measures. Indeed, in the UN Security Council, Moscow voted together with the United States and others for the condemnation of imposition of sanctions against Iraq in case of Saddam Hussein's refusal to respect Kuwait's sovereignty and withdraw. For the Libyan head of state as well as for the Iraqi president, this new Russian policy was a disastrous development, since his political and military strategies were still predicated upon the traditional Cold War format.

Moscow's halt of arms deliveries to Iraq further deepened the apprehension felt by Qaddafi, who drew appropriate conclusions regarding the possible consequences of military friction with the United States.[1] Drawing on the Iraqi case, Qaddafi may well have deduced that, following the US air raid on Tripoli and Benghazi in 1986, the critical military pressure the United States applied in 1987 to compel Libya's withdrawal from Chad, and the recent disappearance of the USSR from international politics, he

41

had now become easy prey for Washington. It was not surprising, then, that Libyan concerns were steadily exacerbated during the second half of 1990. Tripoli witnessed two developments: the shift in George H. W. Bush's attention toward the Gulf region and his consequent resolve to safeguard what Washington perceived as its vital interests in the Middle East on the one hand and the shift in Mikhail Gorbachev's attention away from the Middle East, accompanied by a dismissal of Moscow's Cold War–era commitments to its Arab client states, on the other.

At that juncture, Libya was troubled by other negative developments in its foreign affairs, the most noteworthy being the rise of radical Islam in its geographic environs—a phenomenon that was spreading into its territory and endangering Qaddafi's political position. Indeed, he became embroiled in a violent struggle against domestic Islamists who were determined to eradicate his "infidel" regime. The ascent to power of an Islamist regime in Sudan in 1989, the violent power conflict in Algeria that erupted in the late 1980s between the government and Islamist factions, and the growing violence of Islamists in Egypt—who, in an act that evoked Sadat's assassination, assassinated People's Assembly Speaker Rif'at al-Mahjub in the fall of 1990—frightened Qaddafi. This convergence of internal and external perils represented a major setback for Qaddafi's leadership—leaving it vulnerable to pressure from Washington.

Acknowledging these circumstances, Qaddafi adopted a relatively restrained stance toward the US role in the Gulf, wishing to avoid any dangerous aggravation. While reiterating Libya's wish to see the immediate withdrawal of "imperialist powers"—that is, US troops—from the Gulf region, Qaddafi expressed understanding for the US intervention against the "illegitimate" and "forcible" Iraqi annexation of Kuwait. Yet he considered the US military presence in the Gulf an act of "open aggression" aimed "at possessing the oil-rich Arab regions and the spiritual places in them." The United States, he stated, had "violated" the Arab nation, contaminating its earth with "the dirty boots of the Marines and the Yankees."[2] Referring to the US presence in Saudi Arabia—host to and principal partner in the US-led military coalition against Iraq—Qaddafi, like Saddam Hussein, portrayed himself as a champion of Arabism and Islam against what he termed Western imperialism.

Qaddafi's message reflected his anxiety about being attacked by the United States: "When [the United States] finishes destroying Iraq, it will turn its attention to Libya and search for anything to strike." The United States, he added, "waits for cheap opportunities [and wishes] just to satisfy its mad instinct to control the Arab arena . . . and its oil outlets."[3] Libya's fears intensified in late 1990 and early 1991 when the United States dispatched massive numbers of troops to the Middle East, proving that this region was the highest priority on Washington's agenda. By mid-September 1990, over 100,000 US soldiers had arrived in Saudi Arabia. Meanwhile, the UN Security Council passed Resolution 678, demanding the withdrawal of all Iraqi troops from Kuwait by 15 January 1991. This passage was accompanied by Secretary of State James Baker's militant announcement heard in Libya as well as Iraq, that "no nation should think it can devour another nation and that the US will somehow turn a blind eye."[4] A most convincing reminder soon followed as the US-led coalition against Saddam Hussein attacked on the night of 16 January 1991, defeating his military and liberating Kuwait.

The Lockerbie Dispute: A New Peak of Tension

Meanwhile, the end of 1991 saw mounting successes for US policy in the Middle East. Particularly noteworthy among them were the end of the US hostage crisis in Lebanon, which in turn led to the settlement of Washington's financial dispute with Iran, and the convening of the US-supported Madrid peace conference between Israel and the Arabs. Qaddafi worried that this series of achievements, crowned by the success of the Gulf War, would further motivate Washington to crack down on what it viewed as a Libyan threat to its essential interests.

It was not long before Qaddafi's anxiety proved justified. On 14 November 1991, following three years of investigations, the United States and Britain officially accused Libya of responsibility for the explosion of a Pan American aircraft en route from London to the United States (Flight 103), which crashed over Lockerbie, Scotland, on 21 December 1988. Washington and London demanded that Tripoli surrender to either US or British jurisdiction the two Libyan nationals suspected in the bombing, 'Abd al-Basit al-Maqrahi and al-Amin Khalifa Fahimah. The accusation coincided with the French charge that Libya was responsible for blowing up a French UTA DC-10 over the Sahara in 1989. Altogether, more than 400 people were killed in the incidents.

Tripoli flatly denied any connection with either of the explosions and refused to meet the US and British demand to extradite Maqrahi and Fahimah, "our compatriots," arguing that these two men "are us, the masses. You cannot take them and give them to another country." Tripoli perceived the extradition demand as a neocolonialist affront to its sovereignty since it had no extradition treaties with the US or Britain that would override the Libyan procedural law that prevented extradition of Libyans. Tripoli thus asserted its right to conduct an internal trial as prescribed by the 1971 Montreal Convention on airline terrorism.[5]

Beyond these arguments, however, lay more pragmatic considerations. Extradition of the two men would have signaled weakness to potential challengers within Libya's army, security forces, and the hard-line circles of the Revolutionary Committees established by Qaddafi in 1977 as a principal vehicle for propagating his revolutionary ideology and guarding the regime's interests. These powerful militant bodies and other radical Arab circles might have interpreted extradition as a humiliating submission to "Western imperialism." Moreover, were the suspects to stand trial in the West, they might link Qaddafi himself to the bombing or at least embarrass him personally and politically.

In addition, one of the suspects, Maqrahi, belonged to the pivotal Maqraha tribal group—as did other elites, including 'Abd al-Salam Jallud, one of Qaddafi's closest and most influential aides. From the autumn of 1986 onward, there were persistent reports of an ideologically tense power struggle between Qaddafi and Jallud, at that time his second in command. Extradition of the suspects might have further destabilized the fragile political and personal balance between Qaddafi and Jallud and threatened the already problematic relations between the regime and Libya's tribal system. Although undergoing tremendous social, economic, and political changes under Qaddafi's tenure, the tribal system continued to maintain some traditional patterns and loyalties.

Last but perhaps most important, Qaddafi was convinced that the West, particularly the United States and Britain, wanted him ousted and would exploit the Lockerbie dispute to that end. Thus, Qaddafi was clearly acting on his instinct for political survival when he refused to extradite the suspects. Mindful of earlier US military actions against him, Qaddafi denounced "official state terrorism" on the part of the United States and expressed his fear of another surprise attack "on a small peaceful country in the same way that Hitler attacked peaceful Poland."[6]

Reiterating Libya's innocence, Qaddafi offered his own version of the Lockerbie disaster. Given the prevailing bad weather over the area on the night of the explosion, he explained, the aircraft might have run into a storm that forced it to "land at a fuel depot at Lockerbie, setting fire to it and causing explosions aboard the aircraft." The Libyan head of state commented sarcastically, "the West insisted it was a bomb explosion. [Thus] it is a goat even if it flies."[7]

Whatever shaped Qaddafi's unequivocal rejection of the extradition demands, one cannot ignore the connection between his position and the significant improvement in Libya's economy in the early 1990s, when, largely due to the rise in oil prices in the world market following the Gulf War, it enjoyed the highest oil revenues since the oil boom of the 1970s. The increase in foreign exchange enabled the Libyan leadership to initiate a wide range of economic projects and revive many others that were suspended or canceled in the 1980s, when oil revenues had declined dramatically. This encouraging process was highlighted by the completion in 1991 of the first phase of the ambitious Great Man-Made River project, aimed at bringing water from an inland reservoir in the south to the densely populated, agricultural and industrial north. This achievement and the overall improvement of the socio-economic and political atmosphere in Tripoli instilled in Qaddafi new political confidence, affecting his position toward the United States.

UN-Imposed Sanctions

Swept up by the antiterrorism drive and encouraged by the success in the Gulf, the United States and Britain intensified the pressure against Libya to surrender the two suspects. A major move in this regard was the proposal on 21 January 1992 of UN Security Council Resolution 731, which called upon Libya to provide "a full and effective response so as to contribute to the elimination of international terrorism." This resolution, which coincided with an extension of the US-imposed, unilateral economic sanctions of 1986, warned Libya to hand over the two suspects for trial in the West or risk retaliation. Libya protested against the "wrongful" UN act, deeming it "incompatible with international law."[8] On 3 March 1992, in an attempt to gain time for diplomatic maneuvering, Tripoli asked the International Court of Justice (ICJ) in The Hague for legal redress against the US and British extradition demands. Concurrently, the United States and Britain persisted in their efforts to pass Security Council Resolution 731. Tripoli reacted nervously, seeking Arab support—particularly that of Egypt, with which it had improved relations and which had close access to Washington—to help contain the crisis, but it was to no avail.

On 31 March 1992, the Security Council adopted Resolution 748, a watered-down version of Resolution 731. It banned air travel and arms sales to Libya and reduced its diplomatic representation worldwide, a move that would take effect on 15 April 1992 unless the two suspects were turned over to the United States or Britain before then. The sanctions, however, included neither a blockade on oil, which accounted for almost all of Libya's exports, nor a freeze on Libyan financial assets in the West.

Qaddafi reacted by accusing the West of conducting a "crusade" against Libya and the Muslim world: "The battle has been transformed [now] into a battle between Christianity and Islam." If the West "harbors intentions of carrying out aggression," he warned, "we too must beat the drums, close ranks, sharpen our swords, and get ready for confrontation." He further declared that Libya would never let its two "sons" stand trial in "a hostile Christian state. . . . We will not surrender our sons to an enemy country." Moreover, in a sermon broadcast live by Tripoli television on the occasion of the feast of *'Id al-Fitr,* which marks the end of the holy fast of Ramadan, the state-appointed imam of Tripoli called for a jihad against the West. "Remaining silent against aggression . . . only leads to humiliation and disgrace," the imam concluded.[9]

On 14 April 1992, the ICJ ruled against Libya's appeal to bar the United States and Britain from forcing it to extradite the two suspects. A longer-term legal suit to determine whether Tripoli had the jurisdiction under the 1971 Montreal Convention on civil aviation to try the two suspects was still under deliberation. On 15 April 1992, the UN sanctions went into effect and air traffic to and from Libya ceased.

In response, Qaddafi increased his verbal assault on the "Christian West," accusing it of intentionally disseminating the AIDS virus and of "exporting twelve million rats to Egypt and Libya through the Israelis" in order to destroy their economies. The West, he claimed, had also exported a "virus or a bacteria to Iraq which rotted [its] missiles and aircraft" and distributed "hashish and narcotics to people around the world in order to annihilate them." Qaddafi went on to accuse the West of "being responsible for the First and Second World Wars" and of "killing 30 million innocent people." Yet at the same time, he released a statement renouncing terrorism in a "categorical way."[10]

Eschewing terrorism, however, satisfied only part of Security Council Resolution 748; Libya continued to ignore the demand to extradite the two suspects to the West. In any case, Qaddafi's perception of terrorism was quite different from that of the United States; though he condemned terrorist acts in general, he justified them for what he regarded as sacred causes, like the Palestinian and other "liberation" struggles across the world. Within this context, he supported what he perceived as the freedom struggle of militant African American and Native American movements in the United States.

The inauguration in January 1993 of Bill Clinton, who was replacing George H. W. Bush, the "tyrant and enemy of freedom," renewed Tripoli's hopes that the United States would display less animosity toward Libya. "Clinton's election," Qaddafi poetically stated, "is like a star shining in the dark." Signaling willingness to settle the Lockerbie feud, in early 1993 Libya offered what it perceived as a fair compromise: it would hand over the two suspects to stand trial in an Arab League member-state or any acceptable neutral country.[11] The United States and Britain were adamant, insisting on a trial on their turf. Launching a psychological war of attrition, Washington warned Libya on 13 August 1993 that if it failed to comply with the extradition demand by 1 October 1993, the United States would act to toughen the UN sanctions to encompass key oil-related, financial, and technological concerns.

Helpless to prevent what he portrayed as an arm-twisting US policy, Qaddafi tried to maximize political benefit from the crisis domestically. Portraying the Libyan jamahiriyya as a victim—a small country fighting for its existence—he acted to boost national pride and mitigate popular grievances. Achieving these goals was vital for the survival of his regime, which he attempted to absolve from responsibility for the growing socioeconomic hardships stemming from UN-imposed sanctions, putting all the blame on the "nuclear . . . and Christian countries." Aiming to galvanize the people against "the most powerful forces on earth" and instill in them the idea of a victimized Libya, Qaddafi declared, "We [and Westerners] do not have the same blood, religion, or language. . . . We are in a face-to-face confrontation with them. [The Lockerbie dispute] is not our fault at all, but rather 'an excuse,' envisaging that at any moment the Western sword is expected to strike."[12] In another inflammatory message, Qaddafi urged Libyans to address the United States "in the language of bloodshed and breaking bones [and to] return to our pre-Islamic tribal traditions and deal with them with the logic of revenge. . . . We must now . . . fight with our teeth and nails. . . . Let us take revenge and announce that the time for jihad has come."[13]

A Shift in Emphasis: The Diplomacy Track

But Qaddafi's harangue—which was mostly for domestic consumption—did not tally with discreet efforts to settle the dispute by Tripoli, which offered to allow the two suspects to stand trial in Scotland. Explaining his somewhat surprisingly favorable attitude toward Scotland, Qaddafi said in September 1993: "We look upon the Scottish people as different from the English people, and . . . as being colonized by the English. Because of that, they are suffering . . . from colonization . . . just like us." However, less than a month later, Ibrahim al-Ghawil, the Libyan coordinator of the defense panel for the suspects, announced that the panel had advised its clients not to stand trial in Scotland because of prejudicial pressures brought to bear on potential jurors.[14]

Arguing that such tactics aimed merely to reduce pressure and buy time, the United States ignored the new offer Libya made on 7 November 1993 to turn the suspects over to Switzerland for trial. Moreover, taking advantage of the post–Cold War era and enjoying the greatest leverage it had had in Middle East politics to date, the United States appeared determined to fight international terrorism, of which it perceived Qaddafi to be a major pillar. Presumably, the truck-bomb attack on New York City's World Trade Center on 26 February 1993, although it seemed to have no connection at all to Libya, served to reinforce Washington's resolve.[15]

This determination was clearly indicated by the US-sponsored UN Security Council Resolution 883, which was adopted on 1 December 1993 and which strengthened sanctions on Libya, freezing its overseas assets and banning sales of oil equipment. The exacerbation of its economic and diplomatic isolation notwithstanding, Libya seemed to be somewhat relieved by the resolution, since it stopped short of a total ban on oil exports (in contrast to the UN-imposed export ban on Iraq following the invasion of Kuwait).

Qaddafi's concern for Libya's hydrocarbon revenues, which amounted to US$9.5 billion in 1992—some 95 percent of the country's hard currency earnings—was clear.[16]

Nonetheless, Libyan authorities expressed their fury. Resolution 883, stated Foreign Minister 'Umar Mustafa al-Muntasir, "has brought the Libyan-Western crisis to a dead end and closed the door to dialogue. Even the threat of a nuclear bomb will not change this clear-cut decision." Qaddafi's furious response soon followed: "We have extended an olive branch . . . but [the United States] refused this and sought confrontation." He continued: "We are awaiting them; the fish await them too! The fish are awaiting the fair, soft flesh—American, British, French, and European flesh. . . . They are eager to taste their flesh, especially after having tasted it in 1986, when they tasted the flesh of the American pilots" Libya claimed to have shot down during the US air strikes on Tripoli and Benghazi in 1986. Libya, Qaddafi complained, was "facing an evil, arrogant, and unethical force [that] has no conscience."[17]

Meanwhile, the Libyan regime became even more beleaguered by the Lockerbie sanctions, which increasingly affected almost every aspect of domestic and foreign affairs. Qaddafi was concerned that mounting economic and social discontent would result in further growth of the already strong Islamist militancy against the regime, especially among the younger generation in the universities as well as the army. In 1987, Libyan authorities shot three soldiers and hung six civilians in Benghazi for alleged treason and acts of sabotage, identifying them as members of the radical group Islamic Jihad. This seemed merely to expose the tip of the iceberg of the Islamist threat. The swelling of Islamic extremism in Libya was only reinforced by flourishing Islamic radicalism in neighboring Sudan and Algeria. In Egypt, the radical Islamic movement was also gathering momentum, posing a serious threat to the stability of the regime of Hosni Mubarak, Qaddafi's sole foreign political backer. Qaddafi himself faced military uprisings in mid-October 1993 in Misurata, on the Mediterranean coast east of Tripoli, and in the Bani Walid area, a rural region southeast of Tripoli and the homeland of the Warfallah tribe, allegedly involving Islamic radicals.[18]

Against this backdrop, it was not surprising that in mid-February 1994 Tripoli put forth a new proposal for reducing the conflict with the United States: the two Libyans could stand trial in an Islamic court before an Islamic jury. Once again, the United States ignored the proposal. A short while later, Tripoli offered to allow the two Libyans to stand trial at the ICJ in The Hague before a panel of judges from Scotland. This proposal, too, failed to elicit any reaction from Washington. Annoyed by the complete disregard of what he perceived to be goodwill gestures toward the West and distressed by the apathy of the Arab world, Qaddafi channeled his frustration into even more vitriolic verbal attacks against "the number-one terrorist state in the world [and] the source of morbid diseases . . . like AIDS, through its CIA laboratories"—a state that "is more barbaric than Genghis Khan, . . . more Nazi than Hitler, and more fascist than Mussolini."[19]

Meanwhile, Libya's socioeconomic problems mounted further, compounded by a staggering foreign debt totaling US$1.353 billion including interest. These were in turn compounded by the ongoing activities of the opposition, mainly the violent Islamic militants. Paradoxically, then, in the mid-1990s Libya and the United States began to share an interest in curbing rising Islamic extremism in the Middle Eastern arena and beyond.[20] Yet this common interest did not spur either state to soften its antagonism toward the other. Neither likely imagined then that the Islamist phenomenon would reach the peaks of violence and destruction that it hit in the late 1990s and early 2000s. Moreover, Libya showed less initiative than its counterpart, not only because it was politically weaker but also because Qaddafi was not ready to collaborate with "American Christianity" against the Islamic extremists, even though they prospered as the UN-imposed sanctions tightened further and threatened his grip on power.

The sanctions exacted a grave toll on Libya between 1992 and 1995. According to Libyan data, the state's losses totaled US$19 billion and caused as many as 21,000 deaths. Most of the victims, the authorities explained, were patients in need of urgent medical treatment abroad or medications and vaccines at home, none of which was forthcoming due to the ban on air travel. Agriculture, the report said, was the hardest-hit sector, with losses of US$5.9 billion due to the export sanctions. Yet the difficult economic situation was not the product of sanctions alone. It was also a result of an ongoing decline in the country's oil revenues since the early 1980s—a problem faced by all oil exporters, mainly due to lower prices on the world oil market. Libya's estimated oil-export earnings in 1994 were US$7.39 billion, low compared to the US$11 billion earned in 1990, when the Gulf crisis triggered a temporary oil price hike. In a country where oil constituted the backbone of the economy and where, a decade and a half earlier, more than US$20 billion was being earned annually, the drastic loss of oil revenues would acutely affect the state's affairs and the people's daily lives as well as the regime's position.[21]

Libya's Activism: Sanction-Busting

In the spring of 1995, Qaddafi's fear of political strangulation as a result of the UN sanctions prompted him to shift his stance on the stalemated Lockerbie dispute from defensive to offensive. For the first time, he adopted the policy of sanction-busting. Championing the right of Libyan Muslim pilgrims to perform the *hajj* (pilgrimage) to Mecca by means of direct flights to and from Saudi Arabia—in clear violation of the UN-imposed air blockade—turned out to be a highly effective stratagem. "To go to the house of God and carry out the Hajj in direct flights," he pointed out, "is precisely jihad . . .

for God."[22] On 19 April 1995, a Libyan Boeing 727 filled with pilgrims left Tripoli without UN authorization, crossed Egyptian airspace, and landed in Saudi Arabia. Responding that same day, the UN sanctions committee, wishing to prevent an escalation of the nascent crisis, met in New York at Egypt's request and devised a compromise formula: Libyan pilgrims to Mecca were granted approval for future travel aboard Egyptian aircraft. In an attempt to minimize political damage while maintaining pressure on Libya, the United States promptly announced its support for the committee's decision "on humanitarian grounds."[23]

The event, which set a precedent and was the first political victory for Tripoli in its political war of attrition with the United States during the 1990s, made headlines both domestically and internationally. It clearly bolstered Qaddafi's self-confidence and prestige not only at home, particularly among the politically strong hard-liners, but also in the radical Arab world, contrasting his determination and brave Libyan spirit with the UN's helplessness and passive stance. By defying UN sanctions and emerging unscathed, the Libyan head of state showed himself to be a courageous Arab Muslim leader who could stand up to the "imperialist West" while projecting the image of a devoted guardian of Islam. "No American," he pointed out in his typically high-flown parlance, "can prevent us from reaching Mecca, even if we have to do it by swimming there in a sea of blood. The US should know this." Qaddafi's "great victory" over the United States in its attempt "to make us kneel" enabled 8,000 Libyans to travel to Mecca aboard Egyptian planes between 19 April and 3 May 1995.[24]

By justifying the sanction-busting as a matter of religious duty and using Islamic symbols and terminology, Qaddafi attested to his firm Islamic beliefs. These tactics also reflected well-calculated political considerations aimed at better managing the Lockerbie conflict; playing the cards of Islam against Christianity, Qaddafi hoped to extricate Libya from the UN's long-standing sanctions. What's more, they enabled Qaddafi to redefine the role of Islam in Libyan society and politics at a time of sharp tension with Jallud, his second in command, and along the tribal axis of the Qaddafa-Maqraha.

Gaining a political-religious boost, particularly by inflicting a blow on the "malicious and arrogant" United States, became increasingly important in the mid-1990s, when anti-Qaddafi extremists posited themselves as the sole genuine, dedicated Islamic force in the country and proclaimed that his regime was *kafir* (infidel) and no longer fit to lead the country. By resorting to increasingly pronounced Islamic rhetoric and framing his sanction-busting strategy in religious terms, Qaddafi tried to maneuver between the two dominant forces on the Middle East political scene: nationalism as embodied in the multitude of territorial states and their regimes on the one hand and political Islam, represented by various radical Islamic groups, on the other. The Libyan head of state thus hoped to accomplish two goals: to extricate Libya from the political and economic morass of sanctions and to undermine the monopoly of the Islamists as the standard-bearers of Islam in Libya. Achieving these goals would significantly improve his prospects for maintaining power.

Meanwhile, the United States was not sitting idly by. Acting to inject new measures of credibility into the faltering war against terrorism in the Middle East and against the Libyan state, Clinton reported to Congress in mid-July 1995 that Qaddafi "continues to pose an extraordinary threat to the national security and foreign policy of the US." Libya expressed anger and derision "at a superpower which has reached such a degree of aggression toward a peaceloving people."[25] Compounding its support for the UN sanctions, from late 1995 through early 1996 the US Congress debated a bill aimed at penalizing foreign companies that invested US$40 million or more per annum in Libyan (or Iranian) oil and gas industries. A company violating this law, the bill stipulated, could be banned from doing business with the US government or prohibited from exporting its goods to the US. The bill, known as the Iran-Libya Sanctions Act (ILSA), was finally passed on 23 July 1996 and was signed into law by Clinton two weeks later. ILSA was not related to any specific act by Qaddafi but rather signified the United States' determination to exert pressure upon what Clinton formally termed as the Libyan "rogue state."[26] At that stage, the most salient objectives of US policy in the Middle East were the isolation of radical regimes, the combat of terrorism, and the checking of the proliferation of WMD.

On 16 April 1996, Qaddafi once again defied UN-imposed sanctions. A Libyan aircraft, rather than a UN-approved Egyptian one, filled with Hajj-bound pilgrims flew from Tripoli through Egyptian airspace directly to Saudi Arabia. The violation elicited no response at all by the UN or the United States, which did not wish to face Arab-Muslim criticism for blocking the path to Mecca. Qaddafi then decided to go a step further and, in June 1996, flew directly from Tripoli aboard a Libyan plane to Cairo to attend the Arab summit. Flaunting his blatant violation of the air ban, he commented sarcastically: "Does it make sense . . . for the Americans to call [the summit's participants] to account and ask why this leader came by plane, why that leader came riding a donkey, and why a third leader came in a cart?"[27]

These violations coincided with such provocations against the United States as the hosting of Louis Farrakhan, the African American head of the Nation of Islam, in Tripoli on 23 January and 29 August 1996 and again in January 1997.[28] Farrakhan's visits, publicized by both the Libyan and the international media, contradicted the official US ban on travel to Libya, thus eroding its efficacy and embarrassing the United States, especially as Farrakhan's visits remained unpunished. This series of infractions gradually reduced the US- and UN-imposed sanctions to textbook cases of futility.

Apparently working under the assumption that further sanction-busting would be lightly punished if at all, Libya dispatched a Boeing 727 aircraft carrying a high-ranking delegation from the Foreign Liaison Ministry on a direct flight to Accra on 21 January 1997. Along with other African countries, Ghana had begun to actively promote Libya's efforts to remove the UN sanctions. In this case, Ghana excused itself for having granted the Libyan pilot permission to land on the grounds that he had sent out a distress call, claiming he was out of fuel.[29] This incident evoked no reaction and Qaddafi registered an additional boost to his prestige and sanction-busting policy. When, two months later, Hajj pilgrims flew to Jidda aboard a Libyan aircraft, the UN reacted with a mere reprimand and a warning to refrain from further violations, again demonstrating its limitations with respect to enforcing the sanctions.

Emboldened, the Libyan head of state soon defied the air embargo again, flying with a large entourage on four Libyan jetliners to Niger and Nigeria on 8 May 1997. The trip had pronounced Islamic overtones as Qaddafi addressed Muslim audiences on the occasion of the start of the Islamic lunar year, making it difficult for the UN to punish him. Once again, no penalty was forthcoming and, once again, Qaddafi scored a political gain, which meant a political defeat for the United States. Qaddafi had exposed the Achilles' heel of the sanctions, knowing he could defy them as long as he did so in the name of Islam.

Beginning in the summer of 1997, Libya mounted an intensive public relations campaign directed toward the West with the aim of resolving the Lockerbie crisis, again calling for holding the trial in a neutral court and for the lifting of sanctions thereafter. Libya contacted relatives of the Lockerbie victims by letter in order to argue its case, while Tripoli's UN mission ran a quarter-page advertisement in the *New York Times* that cited the case of Timothy McVeigh, whose trial for the 1995 Oklahoma City bombing was moved to a "neutral" location to ensure a fair hearing. When this effort was ignored, Qaddafi vilified the UN and the United States, which were in his view the same: "Ultimately," he argued, "the Security Council is America," and the United States is "a mad, irresponsible, irrational, and immoral state."[30]

A substantive turning point in the dispute eventually occurred as the result of a ruling by the ICJ on 27 February 1998 entitling Libya to request that the trial be held in a third country instead of in the US or the UK. To Qaddafi's satisfaction, a Security Council debate was held on 20 March 1998 at the request of Libya's African allies to discuss the fate of the sanctions in light of the ruling. The debate unfolded as a demonstrative show of support for Libya, although Qaddafi was unable to translate this backing into an immediate operational achievement.

Nevertheless, fortified by this diplomatic embrace, he adhered to his test policy, defying the air ban once again. On 29 March 1998, a Libyan Airlines aircraft carrying some 100 Libyan pilgrims arrived in Jidda for the Hajj. This latest violation of the sanctions likewise went unpunished. The UN sanctions and the United States' efforts at deterrence further eroded in the wake of the agreement signed in Tripoli in April 1998 by Jim Swire, spokes-man for the families of the British victims of Pan American Flight 103. The agreement called for the trial to be held in a neutral third country by a panel of judges under a Scottish chief justice in accordance with Scottish law.

A significant and gratifying milestone for Libya on the long, bumpy Lockerbie road was the decision the OAU made at its summit in Burkina Faso in June 1998 to call on all African countries to immediately suspend compliance with UN sanctions against Libya involving religious-, humani-tarian- or OAU-related Libyan flights. It also advocated ignoring all UN-imposed sanctions on Libya from September 1998 onward if the United States and Britain did not agree by then to Qaddafi's proposal to have the two suspects tried in a third country. This summit marked a breakthrough in moving the Lockerbie conflict toward a compromise.

The UN, the United States, and Britain could not afford to ignore the OAU decision or its implementation, as African heads of state soon turned violation of the air ban into an almost routine procedure, highlighting the powerlessness of the United States to stop them. In August 1998, the US and Britain found it politically expedient to agree to holding the trial in the Netherlands under Scottish law.

While mistrustful of the proposal, Qaddafi had, nevertheless, been worn down by the sanctions and like the United States and Britain sought a face-saving solution. While his resolve to end the Lockerbie standoff was pre-sumably reinforced by an assassination attempt that took place near Sidi Khalifa, east of Benghazi, on the night of 31 May 1998—which the opposi-tion group Islamic Martyrs Movement (Harakat al-Shuhada al-Islamiyya) claimed responsibility for and which left the leader wounded—it was not his primary motivation.[31]

The collapse of prices on the world oil market in 1998 had left Libya's internal affairs in disarray and the regime weakened. Libyan wages lagged behind inflation and unemployment was estimated at 27 percent, with even higher rates among the young. Moreover, Libya claimed that losses result-ing from the UN sanctions had risen to US$33 billion.[32] Libya was forced, therefore, to adopt a more conservative fiscal policy and to limit spending on public infrastructure to a few main engagements, such as the prestigious Great Man-Made River project. The completion of this project, a top prior-ity for the Libyan government, was vital not only for the development of the agricultural sector but also for daily life in the heavily populated coastal area. It was also important for Qaddafi's political standing, as he had long highlighted it as the flagship of the country's development projects, which were to turn Libya into the Garden of Eden. The 1998 US decision to con-tinue sanctions on Iraq for an eighth consecutive year, its firm show of sup-port for the Iraqi opposition, and its joint military attack with Britain on Iraqi targets in December 1998 and early 1999—which threatened the very foundations of the Baathist regime in Baghdad—all also affected Qaddafi's decision to reach a compromise over Lockerbie.

The Compromise: Suspension of Sanctions

In early 1999, Libya was attentive to foreign initiatives to advance a settlement of the Lockerbie dispute, most notably the plans proposed by South Africa and Saudi Arabia in coordination with the UN. These foreign mediations coincided with a debate raging within Libya's top echelon regarding the extradition of the two Libyan suspects. The hard-liners, led by the highly powerful Revolutionary Committees, rejected any compromise and advocated further militant defiance of the West. Particularly noteworthy among them were 'Abdallah al-Sanusi—a tough security veteran and Qaddafi's brother-in-law—and 'Abd al-Salam Jallud, once Qaddafi's most trusted aide. Although Jallud had disappeared from the center of power, his revolutionary aura remained intact and he maintained the political and ideological influence he had derived both from his earlier position in the regime and from his role in the powerful Maqraha tribe. Other, more pragmatic members of the Libyan elite pressed for some sort of compromise, hoping it would generate a better international atmosphere and a consequent economic boost for Libya. The two most salient figures in this camp were Energy Minister 'Abdallah Salim al-Badri and Foreign Minister 'Umar Mustafa al-Muntasir.

A series of articles published at the height of the debate by the state-controlled mouthpiece *al-Jamahiriyya* criticized the intransigence of the hard-liners and "their inability to recognize prevailing global realities," setting the stage for compromise.[33] It hinted at Qaddafi's pragmatic position, which manifested itself soon afterwards when the two suspects were handed over for trial in the Netherlands on 5 April 1999 with the proviso that their trial be limited to an investigation of their personal roles. As guaranteed by UN Security Council Resolution 1192, the move was followed by an immediate suspension of the UN-imposed sanctions.

Although the breakthrough was the result of a compromise, the Libyan head of state projected it as a personal and national triumph over the United States and Britain, thereby acting to prevent any further erosion of his image as a militant and nationalist Arab Muslim leader. The United States and Britain had suffered a "historic defeat," Qaddafi boasted, and should learn that the "Libyan people do not accept . . . submission and do not fear sanctions or warships." To avoid the impression of weakness, Qaddafi blustered: "I do not want a pardon from America. On the contrary, it is an honor for me to stay on the US blacklist forever." This message was mainly for domestic consumption; he released other messages for the international community, expressing hope that the compromise would herald a "new opportunity for forging equitable relations . . . , based upon mutual respect and noninterference in Libya's internal affairs."[34]

Tripoli's expectations of a tangible thaw in its relations with Washington following the handing over of the suspects soon proved unfounded. Qaddafi comforted himself with Libya's swift diplomatic reinstatement in Europe, a result of the suspension of the UN sanctions as well as a reflection of keen European interest in economic opportunities in Libya, among them plans for ambitious infrastructure development projects valued in the spring of 1999 at over US$14 billion. These European interests were matched by Libya's desire to promote its economic prospects. Indicative of this growing cooperation was the first-time attendance of a Libyan representative, albeit as an observer, at the European-Mediterranean partnership conference of foreign ministers in Stuttgart in mid-April 1999, which promised Libya full membership as soon as the UN permanently lifted the sanctions against it.[35] Also encouraging was Britain's decision to break ranks with Washington in order to reestablish full diplomatic ties with Tripoli on 7 July 1999, after a fifteen-year hiatus.

A rapprochement between Libya and France, accelerated by Tripoli's move to end the bilateral crisis engendered by the bombing of French UTA Flight 772 over Niger en route to Paris in 1989, further improved Libya's status in Europe. The plane had been downed in an attempt to eliminate a chief opponent leader expected to be on board as well as in revenge against France's active support of the Chadians who fought Qaddafi during the 1980s. Of the 171 casualties, 57 were French. In early July 1999, Libya paid France approximately US$31 million (f200 million) to compensate relatives of the passengers killed in the explosion—ignoring, as did the government in Paris, the verdict by a French court earlier that year giving the six Libyan suspects who were found guilty of the bombing life sentences in absentia.[36]

The US administration, meanwhile, continued to resist Qaddafi's repeated attempts to thaw the diplomatic freeze between Libya and the United States, although it admitted that Libya had "taken a number of important steps to reduce its support for terrorist groups and activities." Most notable among these steps, it stressed, was the expulsion of Palestinian organization Abu Nidal and all its members from Libya. The US described Libya's actions as no mere "window dressing" but rather as "serious [and] credible" steps and pointed out that Libya "shares the consensus [of the United States and of its Arab allies] about Islamic extremists, including Osama bin Laden and his associates." The United States also highlighted Libya's transfer of support from the anti–Yasser Arafat Palestinian camp to Arafat's Palestinian Authority in deference to mainstream Arab politics. Yet in spite of this improved performance, Washington remained firm in its reluctance to rebuild relations with Tripoli.

Even Qaddafi's efforts to bypass the administration and deal directly with the US business community and particularly oil firms in the hope that they would, in turn, exert pressure on their government failed to produce tangible results. In late 1999, Deputy Assistant Secretary of State for Near

East and South Asian Affairs Ronald E. Neuman argued that Libya had not yet fulfilled all the requirements set forth in the UN Security Council Resolutions regarding the Lockerbie affair. These included "the payment of appropriate compensation, cooperation with the Lockerbie investigation and trial, the acceptance of responsibility for the actions of [its] officials, the renunciation of WMD, and the end of supporting terrorism."[37] His statement was followed by a renewal of unilateral sanctions on Libya in early 2000. Echoing Neuman, State Department spokesman James Rubin added that in spite of its positive steps to end involvement in terrorism, Tripoli still "has a very, very long way to go before it meets the standards required to be removed from the terrorism list."[38] This position reflected conflicting pressures by various political and economic groups in Washington, which were grappling with the dilemma of how to handle a country that did not comply with all of its obligations to the UN but, nevertheless, did make a significant advance toward compliance by renouncing belligerence and by stopping sponsorship of terrorism.

Responding to some of these pressures, the Clinton administration permitted several US oil companies to send representatives to Libya in February 2000. This was followed by the dispatch of a four-member consular mission to Tripoli "to evaluate the security conditions" and decide whether to lift travel restrictions on US citizens to Libya. Libya seized the momentum to emphasize its desire to "normalize" relations with the United States, stating no preconditions "except respect for our full independence."[39]

Meanwhile, on 3 May 2000, the trial of the two Libyans opened in the Netherlands. About a month later, the US State Department changed Libya's status (along with that of Iran and Iraq) from a "rogue state" to a "state of concern." This change, however, was not followed by any substantial gesture of rapprochement, although oscillations in US policy toward Libya were discernible the following year, reflecting the political pressure felt in Washington in the lead-up to the presidential election of November 2000.

The Lockerbie Verdict: A Window of Opportunity

On 31 January 2001, less than two weeks after US president George W. Bush began his first term in office, the Lockerbie trial concluded with a guilty verdict and a sentence of life imprisonment for 'Abd al-Basit al-Maqrahi as well as an acquittal for his codefendant. Qaddafi was not implicated as the one who gave the nod, but, as the head of state, he was expected to accept responsibility on behalf of the Libyan officials. In an effort to reap political revenue despite the verdict, Libya's media hailed the "unprecedented, historic victory" the state had achieved thanks to the "civilized way" in which it dealt with the Lockerbie trial. Several days later came Qaddafi's own well-considered reaction. He denounced the verdict as "political" and based on "flimsy evidence," adding that it simply reflected the struggle between the "forces of liberalism and forces of enslavement, between justice and injustice, between good and evil, and between angels and Satan." This message was combined with massive demonstrations in the streets of Tripoli, particularly outside the UN building, where protesters expressed their rage and frustration over the "wicked" and "racist" victimization of Libya signified by the "disgraceful" verdict. Moreover, Tripoli reported that three demonstrators attempted to commit suicide by slashing their throats with razors in furious protest against the "unjust verdict."[40]

In maintaining the innocence of the Libyans, Qaddafi primarily aimed to prevent the possibility of his own political persecution. The fact that the prosecution had difficulty proving its case because there were no eyewitnesses, only circumstantial evidence, made it easier for Libya to unfurl the banner of victimization. Not only was Qaddafi worried about being directly implicated in the Lockerbie disaster following the verdict, he was also concerned by the mounting pressure to pay compensation to the relatives of the victims, fearing such a move might be interpreted as an acknowledgment of responsibility. Wishing to lessen the pressure, Qaddafi countered with a demand that the United States compensate the Libyan people for the damages and casualties caused by "failed Atlantic aggression"—namely, the US air raid on Libya in April 1986 and the "unjust" sanctions imposed on Libya by the UN at the behest of the United States from 1992 to 1999. In any case, Qaddafi stated that Maqrahi should be considered "a hostage" who had been "abducted in order to terrorize the Libyan people."[41]

In a defiant speech delivered three months after the verdict, Qaddafi again accused the CIA laboratories of creating the HIV virus and sending it to Libya. This mission, Qaddafi elaborated, was carried out by Bulgarian medical personnel working in Libya in conjunction with the CIA or perhaps Israel's Mossad, which, he alleged, had experimented on Libyan children at a pediatric hospital in Benghazi from the late 1990s.[42] In the same flood of wrath, Qaddafi further accused the United States of being behind clashes involving Muslims in Nigeria, Chechnya, and elsewhere: "I say, beware of the Americans. Do not allow them any influence in your countries."[43] Qaddafi's fury stemmed from the Clinton administration's refusal to formally lift the UN sanctions, against the advice of Russia, China, and many African countries, including South Africa.

On 3 August 2001, the Clinton administration extended the ILSA of 1996 for a further five years. Marking the occasion, President Clinton reiterated the US position that Libya must abide fully by UN Security Council Resolutions if it wished to move toward "a more constructive relationship" with the United States.[44] Although at that point the United States had enforced the ILSA only once (against a Ukrainian company that sold airplane parts to Libya),[45] Qaddafi perceived the extension as an act of bullying that reflected US determination to damage his regime. Of some consolation to him was the renewal of tension between the United States and the European Union (EU) over the extension. European countries had opposed the ILSA from the beginning, resenting the application of US law toward other countries. Fearing serious harm to its economic interests in Libya, primarily oil supplies, the EU passed a statute in late 1996 that made it illegal for European companies to comply with the extraterritorial measures of the act.[46]

Qaddafi continued his barrage of insults toward Washington. The United States, he railed, was the "weakest power" in the world and no "rational person should be afraid of it." It was so weak, he went on, that it was "unable to fight someone called Osama bin Laden. He is a tiny man, weighing no more than fifty kilograms. He only has a Kalashnikov rifle in his hands. He does not even wear a military uniform. He wears an Arab *jalabiyya* [robe] and a turban and lives in a cave. . . . [Yet] he has driven the US crazy, more than the former Soviet Union did!" Asserting that the United States had "failed to dominate the world by using force," Qaddafi further explained its weakness in terms of its failure to keep pace with changes in the technology of warfare. "War is no longer waged with aircraft carriers and cruise missiles but with electronic viruses," he claimed. He cited the explosion of the *USS Cole* in the Yemeni port of Aden on 12 October 2000, which was carried out by "barefooted and unclothed Yemenites" and killed seventeen sailors. Terrorism had seriously eroded the United States' power, he concluded, stressing that since war was "not against states or governments anymore," Washington "must sit down with people," clearly referring to himself.[47]

The 11 September Attack: A Turning Point

Qaddafi's rhetoric seemed almost prophetic ten days later on 11 September 2001, when terrorist attacks of unprecedented magnitude were perpetrated by Osama bin Laden's al-Qaida—the Islamic terrorist organization established after the Soviet Union withdrew from Afghanistan in 1989. The Libyan head of state was nevertheless quick to condemn the "horrifying attacks," express public condolences, and offer humanitarian aid, even starting a blood drive for the American people: "It is our humanitarian duty . . . to share this heavy, sad and horrible day."[48] Qaddafi appealed to the United States to exercise restraint in responding militarily to the terrorist attacks since retaliation would not end terrorism. Contradicting his recent statements to present the United States as "the most powerful state in the world," Qaddafi further argued that it could afford forbearance.[49] The potential reward for Libya's sympathy with the United States in its difficult hour might have been an advance toward improving ties, yet Libya hurried to reject any such motive: "Our position [is] not an opportunist but rather a humanitarian one."[50]

Nevertheless, reports emerged of a "sea change" in Libya's relations with the United States a short while later. This was mirrored in, among other things, the cooperation among US, British, and Libyan intelligence agencies in the hunt for members of al-Qaida. In early October 2001, Musa Kusa, Libya's intelligence chief, met with US Assistant Secretary of State for Near East Affairs William Burns in London in what was the highest-level meeting of public officials from the two countries since 1986, in the wake of the US bombardment of Libya. Kusa reportedly handed over a list of a dozen Libyan *mujahidin* (Islamic holy-war fighters) and members of other al-Qaida–related groups that had fought with bin Laden in Afghanistan. The United States reciprocated by adding to its list of terrorist groups the Libyan Militant Islamic Group (al-Jama'a al-Islamiyya al-Muqatilla), an opposition faction that had targeted the Qaddafi regime throughout the 1990s and continued to threaten it in the early 2000s, although with less force. The cooperation between Tripoli and Washington clearly reflected the latter's new priorities after 9/11, which placed combating terrorism and specifically al-Qaida at the top of its foreign policy agenda.[51]

Striving to capitalize on the improvement in communication, Qaddafi expressed his sympathy for the United States, which was facing a wave of anthrax attacks during the fall and winter of 2001. He strongly denounced the "cowardly, demonic, and irresponsible" use of this "worst and ugliest" WMD, portraying it as "the worst type of terrorism."[52] Qaddafi also intimated his desire to sign the Chemical Weapons Convention, clearly attempting to get back into the United States' good graces and project the image of a responsible leader who opposed terrorism.

Spurning his efforts, however, the United States alleged in mid-November 2001 that Libya—along with a number of other states in the Middle East and elsewhere—was developing biological weapons, effectively precluding any diplomatic rapprochement with Tripoli. Moreover, according to an early 2002 CIA report on nonproliferation, Tripoli had not renounced its goal of establishing an offensive chemical-weapons program. Additionally, the report argued that since the suspension of the UN sanctions in 1999, Libya had acquired weapons from North Korea and Russia and sought components and systems for the construction of missiles with a range from 500 to 800 miles.[53] In light of this finding, the United States renewed unilateral sanctions on Libya in January 2002.

Simultaneously, in discrete, back-channel diplomatic efforts, US officials held meetings with their Libyan and British counterparts in London with the goal of examining the extent of Libya's acceptance of responsibility for the Lockerbie bombing and the payment of reparations to victims' families. They also discussed a trilateral rapprochement and the possibility of removing Libya from the roster of states sponsoring terrorism. In addition, the United States demanded that Libya abandon WMD. In May 2002, Undersecretary of State John Bolton delivered a speech entitled "Beyond the Axis of Evil," in which he accused Libya (as well as Syria, Cuba, Iraq, Iran, and North Korea) of pursuing WMD. He noted that there was "no doubt that Libya continues its long-standing pursuit of nuclear . . . , chemical, and biological weapons as well as ballistic missile capability." Tripoli denied the "false accusations."[54]

Meanwhile, Libya continued to present itself as a friend of the United States, supplying Washington with intelligence on al-Qaida and other groups, including Abu Sayyaf, a Moro militant Islamic group in the Philippines with which Qaddafi and his son Saif al-Islam had enjoyed good ties. Its efforts were further evidenced in the late summer of 2000 by its role in the release of the Western hostages whom Abu Sayyaf had kidnapped in April. (Libya's ties to the Philippines were formed in the late 1970s when Qaddafi, then a self-declared champion of minority and particularly Islamic causes world-wide, allegedly financed and militarily backed the Moro National Liberation Front, later known as the Moro Islamic Liberation Front, which was fighting for independence in the southern Philippines.) Libyan-US talks coincided with the normalization of Libya's relations with France. While on a working visit to Paris in late February 2002, Saif al-Islam, who increasingly appeared to be an influential figure in his own right, asked the French authorities to lobby in Washington to close "the Lockerbie brief."[55]

On 14 March 2002, a Scottish appeals court in the Netherlands upheld Maqrahi's conviction and life sentence for the Lockerbie bombing. The verdict was unanimous and Maqrahi was airlifted the same day to a prison in Glasgow. Qaddafi dismissed the decision as political and referred to Maqrahi as no less than "the Jesus Christ *[Masih]* of the modern time."[56] Thousands of Libyans took to the streets in what appeared to be a government-orchestrated protest against the UN outside its offices in Tripoli—one that avoided, not inadvertently, specific reference to the United States and Britain.

Meanwhile, Libyan, US, and British representatives continued their negotiations over one of the major hurdles to ending the Lockerbie conflict—the compensation of the 270 victims' families. A breakthrough was achieved in late May 2002, with Libya's offering a total of US$2.7 billion or US$10 million for each bereaved family, subject to three conditions as follows: 40 percent of the compensation would be delivered when the suspended UN sanctions were lifted, another 40 percent when the United States lifted its unilateral sanctions, and the remaining 20 percent when the United States removed Libya from the State Department's list of sponsors of terrorism. The United States, while describing the offer as "a step in the right direction," continued to insist that Libya comply with the UN demand to accept responsibility for the explosion before sanctions could finally be lifted. Libya rejected this demand.[57]

At the commemoration of the thirty-third anniversary of his ascent to power, Qaddafi, still courting the United States diplomatically, declared Libya's commitment to never again becoming a rogue state and to yielding to international legitimacy, "although it is a distorted US legitimacy." He announced that no political prisoners except those affiliated with al-Qaida remained in Libya's jails. He also stressed that a campaign was underway in Libya to bolster human rights and curb torture and violence. This "effective" campaign, he pointed out, had led to the "resignation of officials in security, military, and civil departments" and brought about an atmosphere of respect for human rights. To lend credibility to this "new era" of improved civil and democratic rights—which, he was aware, was important to the United States—Tripoli released sixty-five Libyans who had been imprisoned for "political transgressions" since the 1980s.[58] The US administration was also anxious to place relations with Libya on a formal footing provided that the terms were acceptable, in order to benefit from the trade and oil opportunities there as well as to show that the tough war on terrorism was paying off.

However, in January 2003, the United States applied further pressure on Qaddafi. While renewing unilateral sanctions against Libya for the seventeenth successive year, Washington also unequivocally opposed Libya's first-time candidacy for the chair of the UN Human Rights Commission. The US explained its opposition on the basis of Libya's record as "an abuser of human rights" and "a country [still] under UN sanctions." The United States "cannot reward such terrible conduct," stated State Department spokesman Richard Boucher.[59] To block Libya's appointment, the United States insisted upon a vote rather than the usual method of decision by consensus that had been used since the inception of the commission in 1946. The ploy was unsuccessful: the vote on 20 January 2003 resulted in the election of Libya to the chairmanship of the commission for one year (thirty-three countries voted in favor; seventeen, including Britain and other European states, abstained; and three countries—the US, Canada, and Guatemala—opposed). As Washington expressed disappointment at the result, Tripoli portrayed the new appointment as "a great victory."[60]

This diplomatic success was masterminded by a coalition of South African–led African states following heavy lobbying by Tripoli in late 2002. Since it was Africa's turn to occupy the post and because European countries were eager to speed up Libya's diplomatic rehabilitation and consequently take advantage of the economic opportunities it offered, Libya found its path to the position smooth. The appointment of Libyan ambassador Najat al-Hajaji as the UN's chief human-rights watchdog clearly indicated Libya's improved diplomatic standing, formally providing Tripoli the moral status it needed to obliterate its image as a pariah. Tripoli's rehabilitated position in the West was further highlighted by the renewal of diplomatic relations between Libya and Australia in January 2003, after a hiatus of fourteen years.

Yet in early 2003, Qaddafi's desire to be "part of world peace"[61] and to establish diplomatic relations with the United States was still rejected by Washington, as George W. Bush's administration significantly sharpened its militant image via uncompromising policies toward the pursuit of WMD in the Middle East.

Fears of Becoming the "Next Iraq"

On 20 March 2003, US missiles hit targets in Baghdad and US armed forces invaded Iraq, marking the start of a crackdown on Saddam Hussein's regime. The military invasion followed a series of threats demanding that Iraq uncover all of its WMD stockpiles and programs or face war. Soon afterwards, the toppling of the bronze statue of Saddam Hussein by joyful Iraqis in Baghdad's Firdaws Square symbolized the defeat of the Iraqi regime. In addition, the disbanding of the Iraqi armed forces and the elevation of the de jure status of the US-led Coalition Provisional Authority to de facto status in May 2003 as a result of the passage of UN Security Council Resolution 1483 marked the end of Hussein's regime. Moreover, the killing of his sons and potential heirs Qusai and Udai, the capture of a growing number of key members of his ancien regime in the summer of 2003, and the reward of US$25 million offered for information on his whereabouts all clearly attested to the United States' political determination and military ability to uproot a government that Washington perceived as dangerous to its national interests.

Qaddafi was aware that Libya, like Iraq, could fall into this category. The memories of the 1986 air attack, the role the United States played in compelling Libya to pull out of Chad a year later, and the crushing US military victory that forced Iraq to withdraw from Kuwait in 1991, elevated Qaddafi's anxiety. The Libyan head of state definitely did not want to follow the Iraqi regime into the hell occupied by the "axis of evil." In the spring and summer of 2003, aware of the uncompromising US demand on Libya to fully agree to UN weapons inspections, Libya focused its diplomatic efforts on defusing US militancy and resolving the issue of WMD. In a letter in the US academic journal *Middle East Policy,* Saif al-Islam stated that "whatever some Americans may say, Libya has no weapons of mass destruction, neither nuclear nor chemical nor biological." Moreover, he added, Libya neither possessed the means to deliver WMD nor had plans to obtain such weapons. This indirect appeal, "recognizing America's special role as a superpower" in order to open a new era in relations between the two countries, was certainly an unusual attempt to influence US foreign policymaking in Libya's favor.[62] The Bush administration, however, disregarded the Libyan assurances, stressing that "Iraq is an important lesson for Libya," which "must put an end to its pursuit of WMD and long-range ballistic missile delivery systems."[63]

On 15 August 2003, Libya accepted "full responsibility" for the 1988 bombing of Pan Am Flight 103 over Lockerbie. This coincided with the fulfillment of Libya's compensation obligations of US$2.7 billion for the families of the victims. This breakthrough heightened Libya's desire for the formal lifting of sanctions. Yet the unilateral sanctions remained in effect, with Libya's pursuit of WMD still a key barrier to normalizing ties with the United States.

The Oil Factor

Meanwhile, both Libya and US oil companies exerted pressure on the Bush administration to end the dispute between the two countries and thus enable the companies, which had run much of Libya's oil sector until forced out by their government in 1986, to return to Libya. Qaddafi was in urgent need of new investments in oil and gas technologies; Libya's oil reserves were declining at a rate of 8 percent a year, falling to fewer than 10 billion barrels from a high of over 30 billion in the 1970s. Some of the larger oil fields were even more depleted and some gas fields that had produced liquefied natural gas were now completely exhausted.[64] While he preferred the US oil technology, Qaddafi's drive to put its oil companies back in business in Libya may also have reflected other motives, such as a desire to rehabilitate his wounded pride and a wish to involve an influential sector of US business in his complex relations with the US administration. This would provide Tripoli with a security net by making it difficult for Washington to order US oil companies to leave Libya again should another hour of crisis arrive.

In any case, the fact that Libya honored its lease agreements with US oil producers, despite attractive offers from European and Asian competitors, increased the US companies' determination to reclaim their interests in Libya. They argued that access to Libyan crude oil would enhance US energy security by reducing dependence on Gulf reserves.[65] In addition, Libya ranked as a top exploration market in the Middle East in the 2000s due to the presumed volume of undiscovered reserves, the ease of production, the quality of the crude oil, and the proximity to European markets. In 2002, total undiscovered reserves were estimated at 16.5 billion barrels, some two-thirds of which were in the Murzuq basin.[66]

Dropping the WMD "Bomb": Libya's Act of Renunciation

In 2002 and 2003, the United States became increasingly concerned with Libya's accelerated pursuit of a nuclear program and of long-range missile delivery systems in the context of the race for nuclear-related technology in

Iraq, Iran, and North Korea. Therefore, it made the issue of WMD a top priority on its Middle East agenda. Concerns about Libya were shared by other countries in the Middle East and beyond, since Qaddafi was still perceived as an unpredictable and dangerous leader driven by deep enmity toward the West and especially toward the United States and Israel. Not surprisingly, as preparations for Operation Iraqi Freedom, to combat the threat of WMD in Iraq progressed, so did US tension over WMD in the broader Middle East.

In the fall of 2002, Israeli prime minister Ariel Sharon sounded the alarm that Libya was on its way to becoming "the first Arab state to acquire nuclear weapons." Sharon noted that "Iraqi scientists are working in Libya on a nuclear project with aid from Pakistan, North Korea, and perhaps even from Saudi Arabia."[67] Qaddafi responded by labeling Sharon "crazy" and stressed that "Libya did not have enough money to manufacture WMD," which were "of no use to us" in any case.[68] A concerned Saif al-Islam, who spearheaded the reconciliation process with the US, added his voice to the diplomatic campaign aimed at convincing Washington that Libya did not possess any WMD whatsoever. He stressed that his country had signed the Nuclear Non-Proliferation Treaty (NPT) and the Comprehensive Test Ban Treaty (CTBT), as well as the Biological Weapons Convention (BWC).[69]

The unequivocal denials that Libya possessed or had attempted to acquire WMD contrasted, however, with Qaddafi's emphasis, well-publicized throughout the 1980s and 1990s, on the importance and legitimacy of acquiring WMD, whether through production or procurement abroad. The Libyan leader noted that no one had objected to Israel's acquisition of WMD and insisted that, therefore, not only Libya but the entire Arab nation had the right and the duty to acquire them as well, particularly since, as he further claimed, Israel also had nuclear capability. This perception spurred Qaddafi's efforts to acquire "off-the-shelf" nuclear weapons from the 1970s onward. He approached the People's Republic of China, India, France, the United States, and the Soviet Union, to no avail. Libya also appealed to Argentina for uranium extraction and purification technologies as well as the required equipment. It even sought to acquire nuclear weapons on the black market. Since these efforts bore no fruit, the importance of securing a source for the requisite technology, materials, and components to manufacture nuclear weapons domestically became Tripoli's top priority. Subsequently, Qaddafi stridently called on the Arab world to develop deterrent forces, including nuclear bombs. He also encouraged university students and faculty members throughout Libya "to work day and night" toward the manufacture of a nuclear weapon in defiance of the United States and Israel. In addition, Libya became a prime beneficiary of the illicit proliferation network established by Pakistani scientist Abdul Qadir Khan, as it spent "millions of dollars in return for significant infusions of nuclear technology and expertise."[70]

Against this background, Qaddafi's announcement on 19 December 2003 of Libya's decision to dismantle its WMD, halt its drive to develop long-range missiles, and open all weapons stockpiles and programs up to international inspectors in order to prove their elimination shocked the world. In doing so, Libya not only acknowledged for the first time that it had WMD, including a nuclear program, but also declared its willingness to abide by the rules of the international community. This act of renunciation clearly reflected Qaddafi's perception that the quest for nuclear weapons had become a strategic liability for his regime, which in turn resulted in a dramatic reversal in Tripoli's conduct of affairs. The Libyan authorities viewed their act as "a win-win deal" and a "courageous" step toward building "a green, peaceful, and stable planet free of WMD." Libyan prime minister Shukri Ghanem even described it in terms of Isaiah's vision of the last days, saying the decision was, in fact, "the turning of our swords into ploughshares."[71]

A leading Arab source dubbed the Libyan move "the mother of all surprises," ironically echoing Saddam Hussein's reference to "the mother of all battles." Other Arab sources referred to the "bomb of renunciation of the dream of the bomb." Some criticized the United States for having compelled Libya to give up its WMD, a move that had political significance for the wider Arab world.[72] Washington, the target of Libya's endeavor, was pleased at having eliminated WMD through a mixture of force and diplomacy and subsequently praised Qaddafi, calling his move "an example" to others, presumably Iran and North Korea. Bush declared that Libya had "begun the process of rejoining the community of nations," though the United States was still keeping a tight grip on Tripoli.[73]

The announcement raised an international debate on the actual scope of Libya's weapons store. At least there was a broad consensus on Libya's possession of mustard gas—estimated to be 23–100 tons—and other chemical agents used in the manufacture of sarin and other toxins at Libya's Rabta and Tarhuna production facilities.[74] While a broadly circulated assessment trumpeted Libya's weak economic and military infrastructure and drew attention to its sole, aging, Soviet-made 10 MW nuclear reactor in Tajura near Tripoli, other allegations warned of a collaboration between Libya and other countries as well as private Asian and European firms active in the nuclear technology black market. Aforementioned Pakistani scientist Abdul Qadir Khan was reported to have assisted Libya with a centrifuge-enrichment program and provided it with an actual nuclear weapon design.[75] The International Atomic Energy Agency (IAEA) stated in early 2004 that Libya was years away from producing a nuclear weapon. In the words of IAEA head Muhammad al-Baradai, although its nuclear capability was at "a very nascent stage," Libya had acquired "a great deal of high-technology equipment needed to enrich uranium," including 20 preassembled P-1 centrifuges and the components for another 200, as well as constructed enrichment cascades. The United States expressed surprise that Libya's nuclear-weapons program was "much further advanced" than it had assumed.[76]

When we analyze the motives behind Qaddafi's strategic shift, the first to suggest itself is fear of undergoing the same death-dealing "treatment" that the United States had administered to Saddam Hussein's regime in 2003. Conventional wisdom suggested that Qaddafi was alarmed by both the war and the humiliating capture of Iraq's president on 13 December 2003, as they signaled the very real possibility that similar drastic measures might be leveled against Libya. The Libyans, however, disavowed this theory, noting that their renunciation of WMD was merely one component of a broader endeavor to end hostility and normalize ties with the United States. Moreover, top Libyan leaders claimed that although it was announced only at the end of 2003, the decision had been made nine months earlier during secret trilateral negotiations among Washington, London, and Tripoli. The "Iraqi effect" was thus entirely "irrelevant," concluded Saif al-Islam. Rather, he expounded, the decision was the result of Libya's yearning to end the dispute with the United States and gain security, political stability, and economic prosperity. Whatever considerations shaped Tripoli's decision to renounce the nuclear program, they included the argument that a normalization of ties with Washington would remove the US security threat and thus cancel out Libya's need for such deterrents.

In addition, Libya indeed urgently needed foreign investments and a substantial influx of technological equipment and know-how for its oil-based economy. Having just celebrated his thirty-fourth anniversary in office, Qaddafi needed to recapture a sense of political and economic dynamism in order to reinvigorate his hold on power and thwart challenges from Islamists or other quarters.

Although the "Iraqi case" and Qaddafi's renunciation of WMD were linked in international opinion, the deathblow the United States dealt Afghanistan's Taliban regime in 2001 and the tightening of the military vise on the Afghan state from then on may also have affected Libya's decision. Not only had both Hussein and the Taliban been ruthlessly overthrown but, subsequently, catastrophic civil wars had plagued Iraq and Afghanistan since the installation of US-controlled governments. Qaddafi anxiously watched these events unfold and drew his own lessons. To these could be added the toughening position of the United States toward Syria in the last quarter of 2003, which saw the signing into law of the Syrian Accountability and Lebanese Sovereignty Restoration Act and the call for strict sanctions against Damascus due to its interventionist policy in Lebanon.

Saif al-Islam also explained the renunciation of WMD in terms of a shift in the reality that formerly had made these weapons a necessity. In the past, he explained, Libya wished to develop WMD "for the purpose of war with the enemy." Yet since the Palestinians "had given up the rifle and had taken the path of negotiations" and since the Arab world had betrayed Libya to the degree of "threatening Qaddafi with the American card"—that is, with full compliance with the US-led Lockerbie sanctions—Libya no longer needed recourse to such weapons.[77]

The Post-WMD Era

Qaddafi expected to reap rewards from the United States commensurate with his huge political and military sacrifice. He particularly wished to get urgent assistance in boosting his country's seriously eroded hydrocarbon industry, the backbone of Libya's economy. Following seven years of debilitating international sanctions together with eighteen years of unilateral US sanctions, the Libyan oil industry had been hard hit. Indications of its grave condition were its US$12 billion in oil sales in 2003 (compared to more than US$20 billion in 1980), when production was only half that of the annual average in the 1970s, and further exploration of oil reserves covered but a quarter of the state's territory.[78] The chronically sluggish global oil market prices, which had decreased since the beginning of the 1980s, only added to the decline of Libya's oil economy.

Qaddafi was aware of the implications of economic distress and social grievances for Libya's political conditions. In order to prevent popular unrest, Qaddafi's top priority in early 2004 was to modernize Libya's oil sector, extend exploration, and promote oil-export capabilities, thus maximizing foreign revenues and enriching the state's treasury. Libya's interests converged with those of the United States, which wished to diversify its oil sources away from the Gulf, strife-prone since the early 1980s. Moreover, the US oil industry was exerting strong pressure on the administration in Washington to remove all obstacles toward commercial oil opportunities in Libya, where European oil companies were already involved. Aware of this, Qaddafi put on hold the concessions acquired by the US oil companies before the 1986 ban in the hope that it would help lobbyists persuade the Bush administration to relent.

Qaddafi furthered overtures toward the US oil market by putting economic reforms at the top of his government's agenda during a significant cabinet reshuffle orchestrated in March 2004 by Prime Minister Shukri Ghanem, a trained economist and a prominent reformist. Ghanem, together with Foreign Minister 'Abd al-Rahman Shalqam—another reformist—acted to enhance Libya's political and economic attractiveness for the United States. Additional appointments during this reshuffle went to veteran oil experts Fathi bin Shetwan, now energy minister, and 'Abdallah Salim al-Badri, now chairman of the National Oil Company. These moves aimed to highlight Libya's effort to increase the political and economic openness of its oil industry to the United States. So did the appointment of Muhammad 'Ali al-Huwaiz, previously the head of the Libyan Arab Foreign Investment

Company, to the post of minister of finance. This series of new appointments was backed by Saif al-Islam, a major reformist who had already made a substantial contribution to fostering ties with the United States by increasing the economic attractiveness of Libya to its commercial sector.

In February 2004, Washington rewarded Tripoli by lifting the ban on travel to Libya. The following month saw a series of visits to Tripoli by US congressmen and political figures, including Assistant Secretary of State for Near Eastern Affairs William Burns. Following his visit, a US Interests Section was established in the Belgian embassy in Tripoli and a US diplomat was stationed there for the first time since ties with Libya were severed in 1986. These moves, Washington declared, reflected "step-by-step normalization in our bilateral relationship" with Libya.[79] As the US war on terror continued with no end in sight and as military and political events in Iraq and Afghanistan steadily deteriorated, tangible achievements in Libya were of considerable value to the Bush administration.

Europe's diplomatic and economic embrace of Libya continued, and relations with France were entirely rehabilitated early in 2004, after Libya paid a further US$170 million in compensation to the families of the victims of UTA Flight 772, who had earlier received a total of approximately US$31 million. Saif al-Islam administered the compensation deal through his charity fund, the Qaddafi International Foundation for Charity Associations, an informal state organ. In March, he visited Paris and met with President Jacques Chirac, thus ending a hostile era in the two countries' relations.

Other noteworthy indications of Tripoli's diplomatic rehabilitation in Europe were the visit of Britain's prime minister Tony Blair to Tripoli in late March 2004, which followed the official visits of Spanish prime minister José Maria Aznar in the fall of 2003 and Italian prime minister Silvio Berlusconi in January 2004. On 27 and 28 April 2004, Qaddafi visited the European Union headquarters in Brussels during his first official visit to Europe in more than fifteen years. When the media hailed him as "an apostle of peace," Qaddafi called on Europe and America not to waste "this opportunity for real historic peace."[80]

On 23 April 2004, aware of the need to reward Tripoli, the US administration lifted the sanctions imposed on Libya in 1996 under ILSA but still retained Libya's designation as a state sponsor of terrorism. Practically, this retention meant the continued prohibition of US exports that might be used for military purposes, the prohibition of direct air service between the two countries, and the continued freeze of Libyan government assets in the United States. On 13 May 2004, Libya announced that it would not deal in military goods or services with countries that it considered "of serious WMD-proliferation concern." Qaddafi soon reaped the benefits: on 28 June 2004, the United States renewed direct diplomatic ties with Libya, although without full representation. It opened a liaison office in Tripoli and Libya opened a similar office in Washington on 8 July 2004. Agreement on this was achieved during a second visit to Tripoli by Assistant Secretary of State William Burns, Coordinator for Counterterrorism J. Cofer Black, Assistant Secretary for Commerce William Lash, and others.

Meanwhile, in the summer of 2004, Saudi Arabia, a close ally of the United States, accused Libya of plotting to assassinate Crown Prince 'Abdallah bin 'Abd al-'Aziz Sa'ud and other prominent members of the Saudi government. Libya denied any role in what it described as fabricated accusations. Nevertheless, this crisis was a particular nuisance for Qaddafi because it erupted in the wake of successful efforts to gain worldwide diplomatic respectability and erase his image as a chronic enfant terrible. He again found himself accused of terrorism, this time by a state intimately linked to the United States despite having restored diplomatic ties with Washington—albeit before overcoming all obstacles to normalizing relations. The alleged Libyan plot was first outlined by US investigators in their case against a prominent Muslim American activist, 'Abd al-Rahman al-'Amudi, sentenced in July 2004 for conducting business dealings with Libya while it was still subject to sanctions. 'Amudi allegedly served as a go-between for Saudi dissidents and Libyan officials suspected of providing the plotters with "hundreds of thousands of dollars." The alleged plot unfolded against a background of rancor in Libyan-Saudi relations that stemmed from sharply conflicting ideologies and interests, with the most glaring source of division being Riyadh's political and military cooperation with Washington.[81]

Coincidentally or not, at the same time, the Libyans announced that they had uncovered the camp of a terrorist group with ties to al-Qaida in the desert in Chadian territory near Libya's southern border. This group, known as the Salafi Group for Call and Combat, (al-Jama'a al-Salafiyya lil-Da'wa wal-Qital), founded in 1998 under the leadership of Hasan Hattab (Abu Hamza), a veteran of the Afghan war, was striving to establish an Islamic state in Algeria. Along with other al-Qaida-related groups, it was threatening to turn the Sahara region into another Afghanistan, and the United States and Libya—along with other countries in the Maghrib and beyond—were anxious to stop them. Libya reported that it had killed two members of the group when they attempted to infiltrate Libyan territory.[82] This move reflected Qaddafi's resolve and ability to confront the Islamists, as he had already done in Libya's northern coastal area during the second half of the 1990s. Qaddafi hoped that by demonstrating just how valuable an asset Libya could be to the United States, particularly in combating Islamist-sponsored terrorism, he might offset the damage caused by the Saudi crisis.

On 20 September 2004, weeks before a presidential election, the United States lifted the trade and transportation sanctions on Libya that had been in place since the 1980s, unblocking some US$1.3 billion in Libyan financial assets. An executive order signed by President Bush documented the positive measures Libya had taken to dismantle its WMD programs and weapons systems and declared an end to the "national emergency" of US-Libyan relations as defined by Reagan. On 11 October 2004, the EU followed suit and lifted its arms embargo on Libya. This was a significant step because the EU produced 75 percent of Libya's imports and purchased 85 percent of Libya's exports, which went mostly to Germany, Italy, and Spain. In the same month, German chancellor Gerhard Schröder visited Libya, followed a month later by French president Chirac.[83]

George W. Bush was reelected in November 2004. Qaddafi was convinced that the Libyan "trump card" of renouncing WMD had "determined 50 percent of the election results." At the same time, he criticized Bush for reacting "with kind words—but nothing more concrete than that."[84]

Meanwhile, Libya closed the final brief from its terrorist period by agreeing to compensate the victims' families and other casualties of the 1986 explosion in the West Berlin discotheque La Belle. Libyan secret-service officials were convicted of the bombing in Berlin, and Libya paid US$35 million in order to remove this source of tension from its international agenda. Saif al-Islam, who sealed the deal through his charity fund, described the agreement as "historic," as it removed the last source of friction with the West, thus shaking off Libya's status as a pariah.[85] It appeared that Qaddafi had learned his lesson from the Lockerbie trauma.

In his address to the Arab summit in Algiers in March 2005, Qaddafi articulated his transformed perception of international politics, arguing that "nation-states" were no longer viable and that the fate of an individual state depended on becoming part of a broader "international bloc." Therefore, he elaborated, Arab states needed to engage in a dialogue with the West.[86] Unprecedented both in content and with respect to the venue in which it was delivered, Qaddafi's message was in diametric opposition to past statements that endorsed the ideological principles of pan-Arabism, the independent foreign policy of an Arab state whatever the price, and opposition to Western "imperialism." Qaddafi had changed his stand and publicly admitted it.

Whether this new message was a tactical move aimed at promoting his vision of an "Arab-African nation" in which he hoped to assume a central leadership role or whether it was a genuine reflection of his changed perceptions, Qaddafi appeared to have undergone a transformation from the belligerent, individualistic leader of old who was bent on fighting the hated West. It is likewise unclear whether his efforts to mitigate hostility toward Israel in 2004 and 2005 signaled a dramatic policy reversal or merely a tactical shift.[87] But there is no question that Qaddafi was convinced that the all-important road to the White House passed through Israel. His overtures toward Israel can also be viewed as an attempt to smooth the way toward acceptance into the Euro-Mediterranean Partnership, a result desired by both Libya and the EU.

Qaddafi's sharp turn toward the West is also striking when contrasted with bin Laden's ideology. Bin Laden held that the Arab world was relatively weak and backward because of the adoption of Western values, from the belief in US-style democracy to that in women's rights, as well as the failure to combat Western exploitation and even oppression of Arabs. Only Islam could provide solutions to Arab suffering, he argued, and only by means of jihad could Muslims overcome subjugation by the West. Qaddafi, who had barely extricated himself from this Islamist scenario, sided totally with the West against Islamism, hoping not only to achieve further cooperation with the United States but also to combat Islamist terrorism. The Arab Muslim dilemma was bluntly described by Libyan intellectual Muhammad 'Abd al-Muttalib al-Huni, who said that the Arabs had to choose between Western civilization and the legacy of the Middle Ages.[88] Yet as a devoted Muslim and a proud Arab himself, Qaddafi, it may be assumed, would reject this pronouncement out of hand.

The Grand Prize: Resumption of Full Diplomatic Ties

Libya was finally removed from the United States' list of states sponsoring international terrorism on 15 May 2005, just as Washington announced the resumption of full diplomatic relations. The development served both sides, yet its timing was decided solely by Washington. The United States, grappling with the refusal of Iran and North Korea to relinquish their nuclear weapons programs, could no longer withhold the reward Libya had sought to earn in relinquishing its own programs. Besides, embedded militarily in Iraq and Afghanistan, Washington sought any new positive turn in its foreign affairs.

The removal of this last hurdle enabled Libya to proceed apace toward its global economic goals. The resolution of its difficulties with France and Germany improved its position in Europe and even the quandary involving the Bulgarian medical personnel did not cast a substantial shadow on Qaddafi's regime, although it did hamper Libya's prospects of joining the Euro-Mediterranean Partnership.

At that juncture, Qaddafi encouraged the reformist camp under Prime Minister Shukri Ghanem to launch economic-modernization initatives with the aim of turning Libya into an attractive destination for foreign investors and technology experts, especially those in the oil sector. The steep rise in world oil prices as of early 2005 and the competition among foreign companies wishing to do business with Libya served as levers for boosting economic recovery and contributed to the political prestige of Qaddafi as well as that of his son Saif al-Islam, who increasingly albeit implicitly projected himself as his father's potential heir.

Domestic political reform was less successful. Facing a confrontation with the old-guard hard-liners affiliated with the leadership of the powerful Revolutionary Committees, Qaddafi was careful not to make a move that might endanger his hold on power. The influential antireformist camp aggressively warded off attempts at political and economic change and greater governmental transparency, acting to defend its privileges and vested interests. The reformist camp was led by Prime Minister Shukri Ghanem, Foreign Minister 'Abd al-Rahman Shalqam, and Saif al-Islam. The latter, as a product of the new media-savvy generation and of Western higher education, sought reforms involving both civil rights and the privatization of Libya's stagnant, socialist-oriented market. The conflict within the state's top echelon reached a new high in early 2006 and threatened to adversely affect Qaddafi's position.

In fear of being crushed in the collision between the two components of the state's top machinery, Qaddafi dismissed Prime Minister Ghanem in March 2006 and replaced him with Baghdadi al-Mahmudi, a less powerful political leader whose network of allegiances was narrower than that of his predecessor. This step reflected Qaddafi's wish to calm domestic pressures, appease the hard-liners, and gain more room to maneuver.

Thus, throughout 2006, Qaddafi invested most of his energies in securing his hold on power, letting foreign affairs—including those with the United States—take their natural course. Though the hanging of former Iraqi president Saddam Hussein on 29 December 2006 elicited his ire toward the United States, it did not affect the newly peaceful bilateral relations, which benefited Libya and were a source of comfort for Qaddafi. In any case, Qaddafi was the sole Arab leader to demonstrate sorrow for the death of the Iraqi ex-president, declaring three days of mourning throughout Libya.

Conclusion

From the moment Qaddafi took power, Libya's relations with the United States ran a troubled course. By 2005 or 2006, however, relations between the two countries seem to have settled down. It was the United States that broke off diplomatic relations at the beginning of the 1980s, and its initiative to restore them two and a half decades later ended a fierce cycle of enmity and terror.

From the Libyan point of view, no foreign-policy player affected the conduct of Qaddafi's regime on the local, regional, and international levels more than the United States. Yet the perception that the United States was the sole antagonist in this bilateral relationship, while Libya was merely a passive reactor, is distorted. The moment Qaddafi declared his all-out ideological, economic, and political war on the United States, he actually, if indirectly, shaped Washington's behavior toward what it perceived as the Libyan menace to its national security and, most discernibly, foreign policy goals.[89]

Not surprisingly, therefore, the confrontation between the United States and Libya highlighted their fundamental sociopolitical differences. The wide gulf separating the two states was often characterized in Libyan parlance as a built-in conflict between the "vicious, imperialist American enemy" and the "small, peaceful Libyan Arab state." The US air raid on Tripoli and Benghazi on 15 April 1986 and the US-spearheaded sanctions imposed by the UN on 15 April 1992—the two most traumatic challenges to political survival Qaddafi ever faced—clarified for the Libyan leader that the conflict was actually between a superpower and a small, isolated, vulnerable state.

The demise of the Soviet Union left Libya alone in the international arena and totally exposed to the US-dominated New World Order. The gravity of this development was further compounded by the drastic decline in oil prices throughout the 1980s, seriously shaking the foundation of Libya's economy. It seems that only at the turn of the millennium, in the wake of the devastating UN sanctions and the verdict in the Lockerbie trial, did Qaddafi finally realize that he would not be able to politically reshape his country's surroundings or force his visionary ideas upon them. Moreover, the growth of socioeconomic, political, and Islamist threats at home, culminating in serious challenges to his regime, motivated Qaddafi to make substantial changes in Libya's foreign-policy agenda. All these revelations eventually put an end to Qaddafi's Don Quixote–like struggle against the "imperialist" and "subjugating" West.

Internalizing the fact that the United States was the sole superpower in the post–Cold War era and thus exerted dominant influence on Libya and the wider Middle East during the 1990s, and aware of Washington's capacity to seriously harm him, Qaddafi confronted his earlier belief in his ability to undermine basic US interests. The United States had not deferred to Libyan aggression but rather, had counterattacked, causing a deterioration of bilateral ties. This circle of enmity encompassed a variety of conflicts fueled in no small measure by the Cold War, during which Libya had sided with the Soviet Union, and by the religious-cultural confrontation that Qaddafi termed "the war between Christianity and Islam."

Tightening its grip on Qaddafi's political and economic arteries and almost strangling his regime during the late 1980s and 1990s, the United States succeeded in bringing Libya back from the near-dead and in facilitating its integration into the international community in the early 2000s. From the US perspective, this was a great success—in fact, its sole tangible foreign-policy achievement in the Middle East or the broader Muslim world. Clearly, the disappearance of the Soviet Union from the global arena released the United States from earlier constraints and facilitated its unprecedented resolve toward Qaddafi. The United States compelled Libya to pay a high price for its long list of subversive and terrorist transgressions, foremost of which was the Lockerbie bombing. This resulted in Libya's renunciation of involvement in international terrorism and of its WMD programs and stockpiles, which in turn marked a watershed in Libya's relations with the West. Al-Qaida's attack on the United States on 11 September 2001, which underscored the Islamist nature of the new terrorism, brought about what in the 1980s would have been unimaginable: close Libyan-US cooperation in the struggle against Islamist-affiliated global terrorism.

The ebbing of the confrontation between the United States and Libya was significant for both sides, and the consequent rapprochement has produced extra dividends. For the United States, the reconciliation was a ray of light in the bleak night of its foreign affairs in the new millennium, as it grappled with outright refusal by Iran and North Korea to relinquish their nuclear programs. Washington viewed Libya's renunciation of WMD as the desired model for recalcitrant states that once craved nuclear capability. Its failure in Tehran and Pyongyang, however, together with its list of political-military entanglements—particularly in Iraq and Afghanistan—caused Washington to internalize a bitter lesson regarding a superpower's limitations in low-intensity warfare. The lesson was further driven home by Israel's failure to win a decisive victory against Hizballah in Lebanon in mid-2006 and compounded by Iran's efforts to replace the Lebanese government with Hizballah and turn Lebanon into an Islamic Shi'ite state. Tensions with Syria, which was helping Iran achieve its goals in Lebanon; the outbreak of violence between various Palestinian factions and the collapse of stability in the Gaza Strip; and Iran's support of Islamist Palestinian organizations, combined with its interference in Israeli-Palestinian peace efforts, all heavily burdened the United States' Middle East policy and presented wider implications for its foreign policy. Moreover, Iran's quest for hegemony in the Gulf significantly heightened US anxiety regarding its Middle East interests. Other issues of serious concern to the United States included rising oil prices, genocide in the Darfur region, and growing threats to the stability of the Comprehensive Peace Agreement (CPA) concluded between the north and the south of Sudan in 2005. The United States was also deeply concerned by the war in Somalia and by al-Qaida's presence in the Horn and in the broader Africa arena, where China was steadily gaining a strategic foothold, laying claim to the continent's energy resources in an attempt to achieve superpower status. For the US administration, then, its successful handling of Libya was a significant asset.

For Libya, the removal of the US stranglehold became critical to Qaddafi's survival and cast a positive light even on the issue of succession, as Qaddafi's son, Saif al-Islam, figures as a prominent candidate. Qaddafi acted not only out of fear for his political and personal future but also on the well-entrenched perception that he is the sole rightful leader of his country. Not only did he enjoy the power and splendor afforded by his position, but he also remained resolved to guard the unique, professedly revolutionary character he fashioned for Libya from the ideological vision he developed throughout the 1970s of the jamahiriyya, though it has gradually lost its significance. Indeed, Qaddafi and the old-guard leadership continue to adhere to the revolution's symbols and terminology, which have become part of their personalities and their raison d'être.

Yet Qaddafi, blessed with an excellent gift for political survival, seems to have been aware of the need for new ideas and dynamics, particularly in the economic sphere. In marshaling the state's energies in this direction, largely under Saif al-Islam's aegis and with the support of his reformist camp, Qaddafi clearly intended to placate Washington, expecting it, and the West in general, to assure his success in turn. It was Saif al-Islam who urged his father to view 9/11 as a turning point and act to rehabilitate Libya's position in the international community. As a leader who did not harbor adverse feelings or contempt for the West, Saif al-Islam seemed unlikely to make the same mistakes his father had made in his relations with the West, which ultimately damaged Libya's own interests.

From early 2000 onward, Qaddafi became more open to influence, taking his son's counsel seriously. He understood that his visionary ideas vis-à-vis the Arab world had been shortsighted and, in fact, that the Arab world had "betrayed" Libya by fully complying with the Lockerbie sanctions and thereby abandoning Libya in its darkest hour. Africa, where Qaddafi had tried to establish a leadership position during the 1990s, was beleaguered by failing systems and bankrupt economies, and its diplomatic potential had become less significant. Qaddafi knew that only by restoring relations with the West could he remain at the helm to see Libya flourish economically. For decades, he had insisted on calling the presidential residence in Washington the "Black House." Normalization of relations with the United States was the culmination of Qaddafi's decision to repaint the house white.

Notes

1. For Moscow's policy toward the Middle East and the crisis in the Gulf, see Golan, "Soviet Policy in the Middle East." For Iraq and the Gulf crisis, see Bengio, "Iraq," and B. Rubin, "The Gulf Crisis."

2. JANA, 18 August 1990 (DR); Radio Tripoli, 12 August 1990 (DR).

3. Radio Tripoli, 12 August 1990 (DR); *al-Zahf al-Akhdar*, 5 November 1990.

4. For details on US policy during the Gulf crisis, see B. Rubin, "The United States in the Middle East."

5. Tripoli TV, 2 March 1992 (DR). For more details on legal aspects of the case, see A. Rubin, "Libya, Lockerbie, and the Law," and Waller, "The Lockerbie Endgame," p. 74. For a discussion of the United States' right to assert jurisdiction over the suspects, see Kash, "Libyan Involvement and Legal Obligations." For the Lockerbie investigation, see Leppard, *On the Trail of Terror.*

6. JANA, 7 January 1992 (DR) and 3 February 1992 (DR). This was not the only time Qaddafi would compare the US leadership to Hitler; he reiterated the notion in an interview in late 1998: The United States, he said, "takes a racist and fanatical position [toward Libya], similar to the way Hitler treated the Jews. We feel that America is much like Hitler." See Viorst, "The Colonel in His Labyrinth," p. 66. For more details on the Revolutionary Committees, see Mattes, "The Rise and Fall of the Revolutionary Committees," pp. 89–112, and El-Fathaly and Palmer, "Institutional Development in Qadhafi's Libya," pp. 164–170.

7. JANA, 21 and 22 January 1992 (DR).

8. For Resolution 731, see *New York Times,* 22 January 1992. For Libya's protest, see Jallud, quoted in a statement made on a visit to Ankara, *Turkish Daily News,* 29 January 1992.

9. Tripoli TV, 3 and 4 April 1992 (DR); *al-Da'wa al-Islamiyya* (Tripoli), 8 April 1992. For the broader Libyan perception of the Lockerbie affair, see al-'Anan, et al., *Qadiyyat Lokerbie wa-Mustaqbal al-Nizam al-Dawli,* and Sabagh, *Muhakamat Sh'ab: Lockerbie.*

10. Tripoli TV, 4 April 1992 (DR); JANA, 14 May 1992 (DR).

11. According to interviews with Secretary for External Liaison and International Cooperation 'Umar Mustafa al-Muntasir in *al-Hayat,* 19 February 1993; with Ibrahim Bishari, Libya's representative to the Arab League, in *al-Wasat,* 8–14 March 1993; and with Qaddafi for Ankara TV, 29 March 1993 (DR).

12. From a speech marking the twenty-fourth anniversary of Qaddafi's ascent to power, Tripoli TV, 1 September 1993 (DR).

13. *Al-Shams,* 25 September 1993.

14. *Al-Musawar* (Cairo), 10 September 1993; Independent Television (ITV, London), 23 August 1993 (DR); and Middle East News Agency, 14 October 1993 (DR).

15. This terrorist attack, the first Middle East terrorist operation to be successfully carried out in the United States, resulted in six deaths and left many wounded. The operation was traced to a group of Islamic extremists residing in the United States, headed by Shaikh 'Umar 'Abd al-Rahman, an Egyptian spiritual leader of the radical Islamic Group (al-Jama'a al-Islamiyya). On 4 March 1994, they were convicted by a US federal jury, which claimed that the bombing was a part of a larger Islamist conspiracy against the West.

16. *Financial Times,* 13–14 November 1993.

17. From interviews with Muntasir in *al-Safir,* 17 November 1993 and *al-Hayat,* 19 November 1993; for Qaddafi's statements, see JANA, 29 December 1993 (DR), and Tripoli TV, 15 and 16 December 1993 (DR).

18. For more details on the uprising, see for example, *al-Hayat,* 20, 21, 30, and 31 October 1993; *al-Wasat* (London), 1–7 and 8–14 November 1993. On Qaddafi's Islam, see Mayer, "Islamic Resurgence or New Prophethood"; L. Anderson, "Qadhafi's Islam"; and Joffé, "Qaddafi's Islam in Local Historical Perspective." For the threat of Islamic extremism to Qaddafi's grip on power, which had been gathering momentum from the late 1980s onward, see Mary-Jane Deeb, "Qadhafi's Changed Policy," and Ronen, "Qadhafi and Militant Islamism," 2002.

19. JANA, 10 and 29 May 1994 (DR); Tripoli TV, 22 June 1994 (DR).

20. For the debt data, see *Financial Times,* 27 January 1994. However, Eljahmi, in "Libya and the US: Qadhafi Unrepentant," p. 17, rejects the assumption that Washington and Tripoli shared concerns about radical Islam. He termed this assumption naive.

21. "Country Report: Libya," nos. 1, 3 (1994), pp. 20–22 and 16–18, respectively; *al-Hayat,* 16 August 1994; *Africa Economic Digest,* 3 July 1995; *Middle East Economic Digest,* 10 October 1995; MSANEWS, 21 September 1996; *Africa*

Confidential, 17 July and 4 September 1985. For an analysis of the economic impact of the sanctions on Libya, see Niblock, "The Regional and Domestic Consequences." For a broader analysis of the sanctions and an assessment of their rationale, see Niblock, *"Pariah States,"* pp. 19–94.

22. Tripoli TV, 6 April 1995 (DR); *al-Jamahiriyya,* 13 April 1995.

23. Wireless File, 19 April 1995.

24. JANA, 19 April 1995 (DR); *al-Da'wa al-Islamiyya,* 3 May 1995; *al-Hayat,* 4 May 1995.

25. Wireless File, 12 July 1995; Tripoli TV, 19 July 1995 (DR).

26. As defined by US national security managers, rogue states are those that possess substantial military capability, seek the acquisition of WMD and violate what are seen as international norms. Thus, Libya, Iraq, and Iran were seen by Washington as rogue states in the Middle East. For various discussions of the definition of rogue states, ILSA, and Libya, see Zunes, "The Function of Rogue States," p. 150; Dhooge, "Meddling with the Mullahs," and Saunders, "Setting Boundaries." For more details on Libya's "rogue regime," see Tanter, *Rogue Regimes: Terrorism and Proliferation.* pp. 121–168.

27. Middle East Broadcasting Center TV (London), 23 June 1996 (DR).

28. Libya donated US$1 billion as well as an award of US$250,000 to Farrakhan as the 1996 recipient of a human rights prize sponsored by Qaddafi. He also appointed Farrakhan as his assistant in heading the World Islamic People's Leadership, a Libyan body formally aimed at promoting the position of Islam worldwide.

29. Radio Accra, 23 January 1997 (BBC).

30. Tripoli TV, 29 October 1997 (BBC).

31. *Al-Hayat,* 14 and 19 June 1998.

32. Between late 1997 and late 1998, the OPEC basket price fell sharply from nearly US$19 per barrel to under US$10 per barrel. For causes of the decline and its effects on Middle East oil-producing countries, particularly Libya, see Rivlin, "Economic Developments in the Middle East." See also Abi-Aad, "Libya: Effects of Sanctions on Petroleum Industry"; Siddiqi, "Economic Report: Libya"; Sandbakken, "The Limits to Democracy," pp. 144–146; and Mefarlane, "The Global Oil Rush," pp. 34–36.

33. Takeyh, "Qadhafi, Lockerbie, and Prospects for Libya" and "The Rogue Who Came in From the Cold"; Viorst, "The Colonel in His Labyrinth," pp. 70–71. For the negotiations between the United States and Libya on the eve of the surrender of the suspects in April 1999, see Ohaegbulam, "US Measures Against Libya."

34. Tripoli TV, 19 March, 5 April 1999 (BBC), quoting Qaddafi's first official announcement of the imminent surrender of the suspects and the anticipated suspension of sanctions.

35. *Middle East International,* 23 April 1999; *al-Hayat,* 22 April 1999. The Euro-Mediterranean body was established in 1995, composed of fifteen EU member-states aiming to open dialogues with Mediterranean states on political, economic, cultural, and security matters.

36. *Africa Research Bulletin,* 1 July 1999; *Le Monde,* 18 July 1999.

37. Neuman, "Libya: A U.S. Policy Perspective," a presentation by the Middle East Institute on 30 November 1999.

38. As reported at http://www.cnn.com, 25 March 2000.

39. *Al-Sharq al-Awsat,* 28 March 2000.

40. Tripoli TV, 31 January and 3 and 5 February 2001 (BBC); JANA, 8 February 2001; as quoted from a speech by Libya's representative to the UN, Abu Zayd 'Umar Durda, in *al-Wasat,* 12 February 2001. For more Libyan responses, see also *al-Hayat,* the entire first week of February 2001.

41. Tripoli TV, 5 February 2001 (BBC); *Middle East International,* 9 February 2001.

42. Tripoli TV, 27 April 2001 (BBC). Libyan authorities claimed in 2000 that almost 400 children were infected by the virus. The Bulgarian medics were charged with responsibility for the tragedy, allegedly knowingly using blood products contaminated with the HIV virus. The Bulgarian medics flatly denied the charges but were sentenced to death; the verdict was commuted later to life imprisonment, though they were subsequently resentenced to death in December 2006. They were eventually freed in July 2007. For a detailed analysis of the Bulgarian medics affair, see Ronen, "The HIV/AIDS Tragedy."

43. Qaddafi, addressing Muslims in Lusaka, Zambia, on 8 July 2001 on the eve of a pan-African summit, in *Middle East Times,* 14–20 July 2001.

44. USIS, 3 August 2001.

45. United Press International (UPI), 3 August 2001.

46. For details, see Smis and van der Borght, "The EU-US Compromise on the Helmes-Burton and D'Amato Acts," (the latter otherwise known as ILSA); Falke, "The EU-US Conflict over Sanctions Policy"; Takeyh, "Libya's Confident Defiance and ILSA."

47. Qaddafi, commemorating the thirty-second anniversary of his advent to power, on Tripoli TV, 1 September 2001 (BBC).

48. As reported at http://www.cnn.com, 12 September 2001; Pan-African News Agency (Dakar), 12 September 2001 (BBC); UPI, 13 September 2001.

49. Tripoli TV, 16 September 2001 (BBC).

50. *Al-Quds al-'Arabi,* 28 September 2001, from an interview with 'Ali 'Abd al-Salam al-Turayki, a senior Libyan official.

51. *Middle East International,* 12 October 2001; *al-Hayat,* 21 November 2001; *al-Suraqiyya,* 3 December 2001. For the changed US view of the Middle East in the wake of the 11 September terrorist attacks, see Mandelbaum, "President Bush and the Middle East."

52. JANA, 18 October 2001 (BBC).

53. Takeyh, "Post-Lockerbie Judgment."

54. *Middle East Times,* 11–17 May 2002; and *al-Quds al-'Arabi,* 9 May 2002.

55. *Al-Sharq al-Awsat,* 14 January and 25 February 2002; *al-Wasat,* 4 March 2002; Ronen, "Libya's Rising Star."

56. *Al-Quds al-'Arabi,* 15 March 2002.

57. US Secretary of State Colin Powell, quoted on the BBC News, 29 May 2002; *al-Quds al-'Arabi,* 8–9 June 2002; "Country Report: Libya," July 2002, pp. 7–8, 15. See also Qaddafi's interview in the *Washington Post,* 12 January 2003.

58. *Al-Hayat,* 2 September 2002; http://www.albawaba.com, 1 September 2002.

59. USIS, 13 January 2003.

60. For the US response, see USIS, 22 January 2003. For the Libyan response, see al-Jazira, 20 January 2003, quoting Foreign Ministry official Hasuna al-Shawish, and *al-Quds al-'Arabi,* 21 January 2003, quoting Libya's foreign minister, 'Abd al-Rahman Shalqam.

61. See Qaddafi's interview in the *Washington Post,* 12 January 2003.

62. Saif Aleslam al-Qadhafi, "Libyan-American Relations."

63. USIS, 16 April 2003 and 17 August 2003, quoting Undersecretary of State for Arms Control and International Security John Bolton and Secretary of State Colin L. Powell, respectively.

64. *Africa Confidential* 44, no. 8, 18 April 2003, pp. 4–5.

65. *Africa Confidential* 44, no. 11, 30 May 2003, p. 2.

66. "Country Report: Libya," July 2003, p. 26.

67. The subject of Libya's renunciation of WMD is dealt with here relatively briefly; for more on this issue, see for example, Hochman, "Rehabilitating a Rogue"; Alterman, "The Unique Libyan Case"; Shapir, "Libyan Weapons of Mass Destruction" and "Beyond the Axis of Evil"; Bowen, *Libya and Nuclear Proliferation*; Joffé, "Why Gaddafi Gave up WMD"; Squassoni and Feickert, "Disarming Libya: Weapons of Mass Destruction"; and Blanchard, "Libya: Background and U.S. Relations," Congressional Research Service Report for Congress RL33142, pp. 24–29.

68. Ronen, "Qadhafi's Christmas Gift."

69. Saif Aleslam al-Qadhafi, "Libyan-American Relations."

70. For a survey of Libya's efforts to acquire nuclear capability, see Bowen, *Libya and Nuclear Proliferation,* p. 8; Ronen, "Qadhafi's Christmas Gift." For Tripoli's appeal to Argentina, see L. Harris, *Libya: Qadhafi's Revolution,* p. 91.

71. From a CNN interview with Saif al-Islam, quoted in the *Jerusalem Post,* 21 December 2003; *al-Jamahiriyya,* 19 December 2003; Prime Minister Shukri Ghanem, quoted by *al-'Arab,* 20 December 2003.

72. See, for example, *al-Sharq al-Awsat,* 21 December 2003; *Ruz al-Yusuf,* 27 December 2003; and *al-Watan,* 12 January 2004.

73. As reported at http://www.cnn.com, 19 December 2003; see also Schweitzer, "Neutralizing Terrorism-Sponsoring States."

74. *Africa Research Bulletin,* 1–31 March 2004, p. 15692; http://www.cnn.com, 20 December 2003.

75. Hochman, "Rehabilitating a Rogue," p. 65.

76. As reported at http://www.cnn.com, 29 December 2003; see also Hochman, "Rehabilitating a Rogue," p. 65, and the *New York Times,* 29 December 2003.

77. From an interview with *al-Hayat,* 24 March 2004, and an interview of Secretary of the Libyan General People's Congress al-Zintani Muhammad al-Zintani with *al-Majalla,* 18–24 January 2004.

78. *Economist,* 3 January 2004.

79. Wireless File, 23 March 2004.

80. Qaddafi, quoted at http://www.cnn.com, 27 April 2004.

81. Ronen, "The Libyan-Saudi Diplomatic Rupture." See also *al-Ahram Weekly,* 17–23 June 2004.

82. *Al-Hayat,* 7 July 2004. For Islamic terrorist activities in the area, see Shinn, "Al-Qaeda in East Africa and the Horn."

83. Wireless File, 21 and 22 September 2004. For Libya's economic relations with the EU, see Joffé, "Libya: Who Blinked, and Why," and "The Status of the Euro-Mediterranean Partnership."

84. *Jerusalem Post,* 17 February 2004, quoting Qaddafi.

85. Saif al-Islam, in an interview with al-Jazira, 3 September 2004.

86. Algiers TV, 23 March 2005 (BBC).

87. For Libya's traditionally anti-Israeli position, see Ronen, "Libya's Qadhafi and the Israeli-Palestinian Conflict."

88. See http://www.memritv.org, no. 240, 12 September 2005.

89. For more general information, see Niblock, "The Foreign Policy of Libya"; L. Anderson, "Rogue Libya's Long Road"; Gilboa, "US Strategy in the Middle East"; and Richard A. Clarke, "While You Were at War . . . ," *Washington Post,* 31 December 2006, p. B01.

4

Strategic Alignment with the USSR: Balancing Against the West

This chapter analyzes the motives for Libya's alignment with the Soviet Union during the Cold War era and its implications for Tripoli's domestic and foreign agendas. Unequivocally rejecting the ideology of the Communists from Qaddafi's first years in power, his regime nonetheless increasingly relied upon the Soviet Union both politically and militarily from the second half of the 1970s onward. In effect, Moscow became Libya's sole foreign support and a counterweight to its enemies in the West, with which Tripoli was embroiled in a bitter conflict of ideas and interests.

The Soviet Union's disappearance from the international stage at the end of the 1980s and the beginning of the 1990s marked a milestone in Libya's foreign policy and substantially affected its internal affairs as well. This monumental global event is, therefore, an appropriate starting point for an a posteriori examination of the pivotal role the Soviets played in Libya's foreign relations. We will outline the high and low points in Libyan-Soviet relations mainly from Libya's point of view, and we will consider the external events and actors involved in shaping relations between Tripoli and Moscow throughout the Cold War era and its aftermath.

At the time of Qaddafi's military coup on 1 September 1969, a Soviet fleet was patrolling the Mediterranean Sea close to Libyan territory. The threatening presence of this fleet probably played a part in deterring Britain from acting forcefully to reinstate the deposed Libyan monarchy,[1] despite the fact that Britain had ruled Libya since the elimination of the pro-Nazi Italian colonial rule during the Second World War until the country's independence in 1951, and maintained numerous strategic and political ties to Libya and its new ruler, King Sanusi, ever since.[2] Thus, the Soviets' indirect contribution to Qaddafi's rise to power, as well as their recognition of his regime's legitimacy within four days—before recognition from the United States, Britain, or France—was engraved in Qaddafi's political memory.

As early as 1969, the Libyan leader was aware that alliance with the USSR was potentially a huge asset, politically and militarily, for his country's domestic and foreign interests. This potential was underlined by the Soviet Union's intervention on behalf of Egypt in its war of attrition against Israel—a move that earned Moscow a great deal of credibility in Qaddafi's view.[3] Nevertheless, he remained politically aloof from Moscow, primarily because of his belief in the Non-Aligned Movement but also because of his opposition to communist ideology. Qaddafi not only portrayed communism as "scientifically outdated" and "reactionary" but also accused the Communists of being "behind all plots against the Arab nation." He had a "deep psychological and religious hatred of communism," which had prevailed in Libya since its first years of independence, leading King Sanusi to reject proposed Soviet aid. Moreover, like the Sanusi regime, the new ruling elite perceived the Communists as *kufar*, or nonbelievers.[4] Rejecting Western capitalism as well, the Libyan leader gradually put forward his self-styled Third Universal Theory, which he regarded as superior to all other prevailing global ideologies. From the early 1970s, he set about implementing this agenda by establishing the jamahiriyya through which his unique, professedly revolutionary philosophy soon encompassed, at least formally, all facets of life in Libya.[5]

After Nasser's sudden death in September 1970, Qaddafi radicalized his country's foreign policy. First he abandoned his active endorsement of positive neutrality and nonalignment policies that he had adopted under the influence of charismatic Egyptian and pan-Arab leader Gamal 'Abd al-Nasser as irrelevant. He then dramatically reduced the hitherto dominant Western influence in Libya in keeping with the strong anti-imperialist and prorevolutionary slants to his national ideology and international agenda, thereby antagonizing the United States and Britain, both of which had essential interests in the country.[6]

Moreover, while distancing itself from the West, Libya edged closer to the Soviet Union. This shift in alignment, which gathered momentum toward the mid-1970s, was mainly the result of a pragmatic reevaluation by Qaddafi of his country's domestic and external affairs as well as of his regime's goals; it was notably devoid of any ideological considerations vis-à-vis the Cold War conflict per se. At the time, Qaddafi was mainly concerned with the pressure he was experiencing, largely as a result of his own policies, from the militantly hostile United States and its increasingly antagonistic allies Egypt and Sudan.

Tightening Ties with Moscow: Toward a Stronger Libya

In the mid-1970s, Libya and the USSR shared a strong desire to limit the scope and effectiveness of what both regarded as the threatening US buildup in the Middle East and Africa, particularly around the Red Sea and the Horn of Africa. In addition, they hoped to see the pro-US regimes of Anwar Sadat in Cairo and Ja'far Muhammad al-Numayri in Khartoum removed from power. Sadat, who had led Egypt since Nasser's death (1970), fatally damaged Moscow's strategic interests in Egypt and beyond by expelling thousands of Soviet advisers from his country in July 1972. He then added insult to injury by turning to the United States—"the worst enemy of the Arabs" in Qaddafi's mind—as his new military and political patron.

Sadat damaged Qaddafi's vital interests by undermining Nasser's legacy and thus Qaddafi's own pan-Arab ideology and political prestige, both at home and in the region. He not only thwarted Qaddafi's ambitions to establish union between Egypt and Libya and inherit Nasser's leadership role in the Arab world but also wounded the Libyan leader's pride by concealing (together with Syria's President Hafiz al-Asad) his preparations for the October 1973 War against Israel. This snub denied Qaddafi the opportunity to prove his dedication to the war against Israel and claim a slice of the victory over the Zionists that Cairo and Damascus sought for the Arab world, reducing his influence over the Arab-Israeli conflict—then a focal issue on the Arab agenda—and aggravating Libya's isolation in Arab politics. These blows were only reinforced by the diplomatic and strategic foothold the United States gained in Egypt and its environs after the war.

Libyan-Soviet relations were further boosted during the mid-1970s as a result of Libya's growing need for armament and political support in its military interventions in Uganda and Chad, as well as for the technological know-how and equipment to develop its oil industry and infrastructure and implement broader development plans. The dramatic rise in world oil prices after the 1973 war in the Middle East filled Libya's coffers and afforded the country a potentially prominent position in global affairs disproportionate to its actual geopolitical importance. Qaddafi set about to outfit his country with an army commensurate with Libya's newfound wealth and prominence.

The United States and Europe appeared increasingly reluctant to meet Libya's arms requests. In contrast, the USSR seemed enthusiastic about selling weapons and updated technological systems to Libya, aware of its valuable strategic position in the Mediterranean and on the seamline between the Middle East and Africa as well as its ability to pay in hard cash. Though Libya continued to adhere to its anti-communist ideology, the Soviets took the opportunity to increase bilateral cooperation by inviting a high-level Libyan delegation to visit Moscow from 23 to 28 February 1972. The delegation was headed by 'Abd al-Salam Jallud, Qaddafi's close associate and a highly influential member of the Revolutionary Command Council (the supreme executive institution in the country following the 1969 coup). Jallud, who was also minister for industry and economy, was the first top-level Libyan official ever to visit the Soviet Union.

The visit increased suspicion of Libya regionally and internationally and had a particularly adverse effect on Libya's already strained relations with the United States and Egypt. Moreover, the signing of the first Israeli-Egyptian disengagement agreement in early 1974—the result of intense US diplomacy after the October 1973 War—heightened Libya's ire. Qaddafi perceived the agreement, and indeed any form of political dialogue with Israel—the existence of which he refused to accept—as treacherous and the growing US influence in the Middle East as increasingly threatening.

These fears accelerated the pace with which Tripoli forged its relations with Moscow. The relationship was given a considerable boost after Jallud's second visit to Moscow from 14 to 25 May 1974, which culminated in the signing of a Soviet-Libyan arms deal worth US$1.2 billion, which included a supply of Soviet SAM missiles.[7]

From that point on, bilateral ties gathered steady momentum and were characterized in the mid-1970s by large arms supplies, including TU supersonic bombers—a particularly noteworthy breakthrough because, until then, the Soviets had provided them only to Iraq. Soviet prime minister Alexei Kosygin visited Tripoli from 12 to 15 May 1975, becoming the first high-ranking Soviet official to do so. A new arms deal soon followed, including antitank missiles, tanks, armored personnel carriers, MiG-23 aircraft, Scud surface-to-surface missiles, and submarines. This deal was accompanied by the dispatch to Libya of Soviet military advisers and technicians, whose numbers increased from 100 in 1974 to 300 in the late spring of 1975. The two countries also signed an agreement for the supply of a ten-megawatt nuclear facility to meet Libya's peaceful energy requirements,[8] which presumably explained Qaddafi's boast in early 1975 that Libya would soon possess a nuclear bomb.[9] Yet not everything in their military cooperation went smoothly. Not only did Moscow reject Tripoli's request for nuclear technology but it also registered friction between the Soviet advisers and the Libyan armed forces, caused largely by culture shock and language barriers.[10]

Still, Libya's strengthening relations with the USSR alarmed both the West and pro-Western regimes in the Arab region, especially Egypt and Sudan (and, behind the scenes, pro-US Saudi Arabia). The Western and pro-Western Arab media claimed that Libya was putting its land, air, and naval bases at the service of the Soviets and that the number of Soviet military advisers in Libya had increased to 700 by the fall of 1975 (later it was estimated to have been 2,000). Libya denied all such claims.[11] However, its ties to the USSR were clearly growing. The latest Soviet arms, including MiG-23 jets, SAM-3 missiles, and more than 100 T-55 and T-62 tanks, were displayed at a military parade in Tripoli on 1 September 1975, the sixth anniversary of Qaddafi's ascent to power—the central event on his revolutionary calendar.[12]

The Effect of the Dispute with
Egypt on Libyan-Soviet Relations

Following two abortive coup attempts aimed at overthrowing Numaryi's regime in Sudan in the fall of 1975 and the summer of 1976—which Khartoum claimed were backed by Libya and the Soviet Union—and the signing, with Saudi Arabia's blessing, of the Joint Defense Agreement between Egypt and Sudan, the political ties between Libya and the Soviet Union grew even stronger, as demonstrated by the military parade of September 1976, which displayed 25 Scud surface-to-surface missiles with a 160-mile range. The annual parades had become opportunities to show off the latest Soviet arms, publicize the strength of the Libyan regime, and underline the benefits of a close relationship with the USSR. Libya paid for the arms in hard currency, which it had in abundance thanks to the flow of oil revenues into its treasury. In 1976, Libyan oil production increased by about 30 percent from 1.5 to 1.9 million barrels a day—greater even than the general OPEC increase of some 12 percent. That year, Libya's oil production was approximately equal to the combined output of Kuwait, Iraq, Nigeria, and Venezuela.[13]

Qaddafi's first visit to the Soviet Union took place from 6 to 9 December 1976. At a Kremlin dinner, he declared that Libya's friendship with Moscow was "not ephemeral but . . . strategic."[14] Indeed, in the mid-1970s, Soviet-Libyan cooperation was at its zenith, affecting the Middle Eastern and African policies of both states. This was exemplified most prominently in Uganda, which, under anti-Western, pro-Libyan Idi Amin, became a significant theater in the late 1970s for the activities of Libya and the USSR due to their respective goals in the area. The Libyan-Soviet friendship was devoid of any Communist flavor, and Qaddafi's criticism of communism—albeit less emphatic than before—continued as he promoted his own Third Universal Theory.

Meanwhile, the Soviet Union took advantage of the escalating Libyan-Egyptian feud to secure its foothold in Libya with the added objective of enhancing its reputation as a dependable patron of the Middle East and beyond. Moscow therefore supported Libya in its four-day military conflict with Egypt (21–24 July 1977), which was initiated by Sadat and ended only after mediation by Algeria, Kuwait, and the PLO with behind-the-scenes diplomatic assistance from the United States and the USSR. At the height of this violent confrontation—unprecedented in nature and scope for the two countries—Egypt attacked military airports and radar installations deep inside Libya.[15]

Throughout the four days of conflict, the Soviets jammed Egyptian radar installations and provided reconnaissance of the Mediterranean area by naval helicopters operating out of Libyan bases.[16] Qaddafi subsequently portrayed the Soviet Union as "a sincere friend" that had fought "by our side against imperialism, colonial exploitation, and racism."[17] His praise of the Soviets was also intended to serve as a deterrent against further military aggression from Egypt or the United States. Although the Libyan leader had expected more substantial help from Moscow, the relationship between the two countries, essentially a marriage of convenience, remained intact.

Moscow's assistance, although limited, reflected not only commitment to Libya but anger toward Egypt, which had steadily been provoking Moscow ever since it abrogated the 1971 Soviet-Egyptian Treaty of Friendship in March 1976, thus publicly ending relations between the two countries. The loss of Egypt as the fulcrum of Moscow's Middle Eastern policy inflicted a heavy blow to the Soviet Union's prestige and interests in the region.

Although anchored primarily within the context of Egypt's growing strategic rapprochement with the United States and the USSR's support of anti-Egyptian forces in the region, Sadat's abrogation of the treaty of friendship also reflected his anger with Moscow's position on a wide range of issues. Most noteworthy among these were the Kremlin's refusal to reschedule Egypt's loan repayments, alleged support of subversive anti-Sadat forces within Egypt, and refusal to supply spare parts and sophisticated military hardware to the Egyptian army. In mid-1977, Sadat publicly disclosed that he had refused a proposed meeting between him and Soviet president Leonid Brezhnev to discuss drafting a new bilateral agreement or renewing the 1971 Treaty of Friendship.[18] Abrogating the treaty marked the culmination of the lengthy process by which Egypt switched sides in the Cold War. Sadat was in a particularly challenging position both domestically and externally, his fears of a Soviet-Libyan plot against him reinforced by the Soviets' increased interest in the Red Sea region. This position was mirrored in a statement by General Muhammad 'Abd al-Ghani al-Jamasi, the Egyptian war minister, during the Afro-Arab Summit Conference on 7 March 1977 in Cairo, which emphasized his country's determination to thwart the USSR's scheme to throw a hostile cordon around Egypt and the Sudan, embodied by Libya to the east and Ethiopia to the south.[19]

Russian interests in the Red Sea area and particularly in Ethiopia date back to the time of Peter the Great and were revived in the Soviet era. The Soviet navy sought strategic ports and facilities not only in the Red Sea but also in the Mediterranean and the Indian Ocean. This became more urgent in the late 1950s and early 1960s following the introduction of US nuclear submarines into Middle Eastern and African waters. Indeed, Soviet-Somali military cooperation in the late 1960s was primarily dictated by the USSR's need to establish a naval foothold at Berbera. Yet for various reasons, the USSR considered Somalia to be an unreliable ally. What's more, in the early 1970s, Moscow lost the use of the naval base in Alexandria, Egypt, and then its base in Sudan's Red Sea port when its naval forces were expelled after the Communist-led attempt to topple Numayri's regime was crushed in July

1971. Ethiopia was not an option either, being under the influence of the United States, which regarded Addis Ababa as an ally.

Ethiopia's emperor Haile Selassie lost his throne in 1974 and the Kremlin hastened to establish relations with what it termed the new progressive revolutionary leadership of Colonel Mengistu Haile Mariam in Addis Ababa. Soviet activities around the Horn of Africa gathered momentum in the second half of the 1970s and the area became a focal point of Cold War tensions as the United States and the USSR competed for influence there. An anti-Soviet bloc composed of Egypt, Sudan, and Saudi Arabia tried to fend off the Kremlin's attempts to ensconce itself politically and strategically in the area. The USSR, allegedly helped by its Libyan ally, doubled its efforts to bolster its influence around the Horn and gain access to the strategic waterways and naval bases of the Red Sea region.

While Sadat tried to fend off Soviet and Libyan threats, he also sought to thwart political subversion within Egypt itself. In early 1977, he faced the most serious antigovernment food riots of his term thus far in terms of mass participation, casualties, and material damage. Sadat accused the Soviets of complicity in the riots, which he perceived as, or, at least, he claimed was, an attempt by pro-Communist elements within Egypt to undermine his regime, thereby serving Libya's. Egypt's US-backed peace initiative toward Israel and Sadat's visit to Jerusalem in November 1977 only broadened the common ground between Moscow and Tripoli. Their animosity to Egypt, the United States, and the peace process reached new heights. Qaddafi and Brezhnev regarded Sadat's peace policy as a blatant betrayal of the Arab nation; by contrast, Libya objected to any dialogue with Israel and called for the annihilation of the Israeli state by military force.[20] Moscow was angered by the central role the United States played in the peace process and by Sadat's declaration that the USSR could not expect to play a similar role: "The Soviet Union has little in its hands [regarding the peace process]. This is the opportunity of those who hold 99 percent of the solution in their hands [namely the United States]."[21] It was not long before Qaddafi took a pivotal role in promoting an anti-Sadat, anti-Israel, and, in effect, anti-US Arab camp, engendering a fundamental shift in alliances among Arab nations. Libya, together with other anti-US, largely pro-Soviet forces in the region— namely Syria, Algeria, the PDRY, and the PLO—formed the Front of Steadfastness and Resistance. Meanwhile, the United States was attempting to recruit more nations, most notably Jordan, to the cause of Arab-Israeli peace while also trying to mobilize wider Arab support for Sadat's policies, particularly from Saudi Arabia and other Gulf states. The United States even kept a line open to Syria, although Damascus maintained its strongly anti-US stance. The Front worked to impede the diplomatic moves coming from Washington and Cairo while promoting its own rejectionist stance.

Despite their common enmity toward and denunciation of Sadat and his peace initiative, the USSR and Libya differed on some related issues and tactics. Most significant among these was the Soviet policy that aimed at securing a leading role in any Middle Eastern peace process, in contrast to Libya's rejection of such settlements. With the United States, the USSR cochaired an international symposium to encourage the reconvening of the Geneva Conference as a mechanism for negotiating a Middle East settlement—and it did so over the objections of Libya and Iraq, the two Arab regimes it favored most in late 1977. Eventually, however, the Geneva Conference did not reconvene and the Egyptian-Israeli peace process effectively pushed the Soviet Union to the margins of Middle East peace politics, leaving center stage to the United States and the "shame and humiliation accords of 'Stable David,'" as Tripoli called the September 1978 Camp David agreements. Consequently, in 1978 and 1979, Moscow and Washington stood firmly behind their Libyan and Egyptian protégés, which they regarded as spearheads for their own interests in the region and beyond.[22]

Meanwhile, hostility between Tripoli and Cairo steadily grew, reaching new heights in the wake of the peace agreement signed by Israel and Egypt on 26 March 1979. Both Libya and the Soviet Union portrayed the agreement as an anti-Arab plot and emphasized the importance of Arab unity. While Qaddafi's position was rooted in the ideology he had inherited from his mentor, Nasser, Moscow's position was tactical due to concern for its influence over the Front and to broader Cold War considerations. "It [is] now more necessary than ever to achieve unity of action among the Arab countries," stated Moscow, adding, "The future of the Arab nation is at stake. Will it fall victim to the strong influence of American imperialism and Zionist Israel?"[23] The USSR had an additional motive for promoting Arab unity: the hope that the oil-rich Arab states would pay for weapons ordered by their poorer brethren.[24]

Following the Egyptian-Israeli peace agreement, tension mounted along the Libyan-Egyptian border. Speculation about a possible Egyptian plot to invade Libya, overthrow Qaddafi, and seize the country's oilfields was nourished by a buildup of Egyptian troops along the border and by declarations of alert among the Egyptian armed forces. Concurrently, several reports pointed to heightened tensions in the tribal zones, which straddled the border, and to the reinforcement of Libya's defense system, probably with the active assistance of the Eastern bloc, Cuba, North Korea, Iraq, and Syria.[25] In May 1979, Libya reached a defense accord with Algeria, with which it shared strong opposition to Sadat's peace policy, and thus awakened further suspicion among its regional enemies. The United States and USSR stood firm behind their respective clients, causing tensions to mount further.

During this period of confrontation, Qaddafi was aware of the need to bolster Libya's army. Therefore, in May 1978, he announced the initiation of compulsory conscription for the first time in the country's history and increased the annual budgetary allocations for the armed forces (which constituted only part of the total military expenditure) as follows: from LD72 million (Libyan dinars; $1 = 0.296 LD in 1977–1978) in 1976 to LD80 million in 1977 and LD130 million in 1978. Moreover, on 20 June 1978, Libya formed the Higher Authority, which would establish the infrastructure of a modern armaments industry with an initial budget of LD150 million.[26]

At the same time, Qaddafi enlisted the Soviet Union's help in further modernizing Libya's armed forces. Moscow, considering such a prospect to be in its interests, signed a contract with Tripoli to build a 440-megawatt nuclear power plant in December 1977. This was followed by Tripoli's announcement, after Jallud's visit to Moscow from 14 to 22 February 1978, that it now had more than 1,000 aircraft, "including planes [that] only the USSR and Libya possess—long-range strategic bombers," namely, MiG-25 (Foxbat) supersonic fighters.[27] This acquisition highlighted the unprecedented nature of Libya's strategic-military cooperation with the USSR.

The Effect of the Invasions of Chad and Afghanistan on Libyan-Soviet Relations

Another major reason Libya stepped up arms acquisitions from Moscow in the late 1970s concerned its military interventions in Africa. In 1978 and early 1979, Libya was militarily active in Uganda—not for the first time, but with greater belligerence and political intent than before. Qaddafi acted to save the regime of Idi Amin, who had served Libya's wide-ranging interests. The Ugandan opposition, with military backing from Tanzania and Egypt, was no less determined to remove Amin from power. During this period, Libya was also militarily involved in Chad, with the primary aim of permanently annexing the uranium- and oil-rich Aouzou Strip on the Libyan border with Chad. Tripoli had long claimed the area, over which it had obtained de facto control at the beginning of the 1970s. Libya was interested in toppling the pro-Western, pro-Egyptian, and pro-Sudanese leadership in Ndjamena and replacing it with a government friendly to Tripoli, moves which would secure Libya's southern front and serve other essential interests.[28]

In these intensive efforts to strengthen its army, Libya extended its military relations far beyond the USSR to the broader Eastern European bloc. This was highlighted by Qaddafi's tour of Bulgaria, Czechoslovakia, Hungary, East Germany, and Poland in June 1978. A complementary series of high-level visits by officials from Eastern European countries followed, including that of Bulgaria's President Todor Zhivkov in early 1980. Nevertheless, Moscow pulled the political and military strings in the relations between its satellite states and Libya, as exemplified by its reported role in the transfer of Cuban troops and North Korean pilots to Libya from pro-Soviet Ethiopia and Angola in late 1978, presumably to reinforce the Libyan army at a time when many of its soldiers were fighting in Uganda and Chad, leaving the troops at home significantly weakened.[29] In spring 1979, there were reports that Libya had received two dozen Soviet TU-22 (Blinder D) reconnaissance aircraft. In short, the flow of sophisticated Soviet weapons and between 2,000 and 5,500 Soviet military advisers into Libya by the end of Qaddafi's first decade in power were a telling demonstration of the nature and scope of Libyan-Soviet relations.[30]

This strong political-military commitment was evident in Qaddafi's reaction to the Soviet invasion of Afghanistan in the final week of 1979. Afghanistan was already a Soviet satellite, but Moscow found the government insufficiently subservient and in danger of being overthrown by a rebellion led by nationalists and militant Islamists at a time when Khomeini's Islamic Revolution and its commitment to pan-Islamic solidarity reflected the rise of militant Islamic tendencies among the USSR's neighbors and even within its own borders. In particular, Moscow was deeply concerned that the Afghan army was in danger of disintegrating in the face of overwhelming tribal oppsition and that its control over the Afghan president, Hafizullah Amin, had diminished. Soon after the invasion, Amin was killed and the establishment of a pro-Soviet regime in Kabul became a fait accompli. The invasion marked a watershed in Soviet external affairs: it was the first time that Moscow had deployed ground forces on a large scale in a third world country.

Qaddafi remained silent in the immediate aftermath of the Soviet invasion. He avoided taking a clear stance, saying that it was "too early to judge" or that he did not have "enough information."[31] He knew that to do otherwise would be impolitic and would antagonize either the USSR or the many Muslim states resentful of the invasion.

The Libyan position gradually became clearer as international, Arab, and Islamic discussions of the Afghan crisis and its implications on the Middle East gathered momentum. As early as 14 January 1980, Libya abstained during a vote in an emergency session of the UN General Assembly, which overwhelmingly condemned the USSR. Algeria and Syria, pivotal members of the generally Soviet-oriented Front of Steadfastness and Resistance, also abstained, while the PDRY voted against the motion and the nonvoting PLO also took a strong pro-Soviet stance.

Two days later, at the conference of the Front of Steadfastness and Resistance in Damascus on 16 January 1980, Libya signed a joint statement expressing the participants' concern that Arab attention had been shifted away from the Arab-Israeli conflict toward Afghanistan. They declared that global opinion had been "fabricated by world imperialism led by the US" in collusion with Israel and Egypt, which aimed to "drive a wedge between the Arab nation and its friends," presumably the Soviet Union in particular.[32] While refraining from an explicit reference to the Soviet invasion, the statement enabled Libya to assert its fierce anti-Americanism, thereby indirectly paying its political debt to Moscow.

The next formally organized forum of Arab discussion of the Soviet invasion was the special meeting of the Conference of Islamic States in the Pakistani capital of Islamabad on 27 January 1980. Libya sent a low-level delegation, a move that implicitly reiterated Tripoli's anti-US position without explicitly backing the Soviet invasion.

In the summer of 1980, however, Qaddafi's position became even clearer. When asked by a British interviewer if he "sympathized" with the Soviet intervention, he replied, "I did not say this. What I said is basically that I am against interfering in other countries' internal affairs," but "in the case of Afghanistan I respect the will of the Afghani people." In the fall of 1980, he stated that "the Soviet forces entered Afghanistan at the official request of the Afghani government," implying that the Soviet military operation was legitimate.[33] Moscow itself had justified the invasion of Afghanistan by claiming that Kabul had made an "insistent request for urgent political, moral and economic help" and Qaddafi concurred, pointing to prior US interference in Afghanistan's internal affairs to further explain the invasion and Libya's position on it. At the end of 1980, Qaddafi sought to legitimate Libya's own highly controversial invasion of Chad by claiming that Tripoli had received a formal plea for help from the Chadian government and was simply responding to this request, just as the Soviets had done in Afghanistan.

It was clear that Qaddafi could not politically afford to criticize, let alone oppose, the Soviet invasion of Afghanistan. In 1980, Afghanistan and Iran were central foreign-policy issues for the Kremlin, and Moscow therefore expected firm support from its allies in the Arab world, including Libya. Qaddafi was careful not to let the Soviets down, especially not while Libya was in the midst of its invasion of Chad as well as increasingly tense interactions with Washington and thus had a sharply growing need for military backing from Moscow.

In November 1979, the tension stemming from the US hostage crisis in Iran and the attack on the Grand Mosque of Mecca exacerbated the relations between Libya and the United States.[34] Their antagonism peaked when a violent, state-instigated assault was made by a Libyan crowd on the US embassy in Tripoli on 2 December 1979, which was followed by suspension of US diplomatic activity with Libya. Bilateral animosity persisted and, in May 1981, responding to Tripoli's "provocations and misconduct," including "support for international terrorism," the United States reduced diplomatic relations with Libya to the lowest level short of complete severance.[35] This hostility, already marked by a near-clash between Libyan and US fighter jets over the Mediterranean in the fall of 1980, culminated in a full-fledged aerial confrontation the following summer.

At that time, the USSR was preoccupied with the military intervention in Afghanistan. The invasion reflected Moscow's disillusionment with dé-tente and lack of regard for Western opinion. Qaddafi was reassured by the assertiveness of the USSR, on which it relied to protect his country in the event of a US attack. At this time, Moscow was providing Libya with mil-itary support for its war in Chad and political assistance in fending off mounting Western pressure. Although Libya denied any connection between its interventionist policy in Chad and its ties with Moscow, critics—mostly hostile and non-Libyan—claimed that Soviet and East German military experts and technical staff were providing support to Libyan troops in Chad, including large quantities of military supplies and sophisticated weapons. Other sources claimed that thousands of military experts from Cuba and the Eastern bloc were actively engaged in military training in Libya itself.[36] As the world's tenth largest oil producer in 1979, when it earned an estimated US$16 billion in oil revenues,[37] Libya could readily pay for its purchases in the hard currency that was much needed by the Soviet Union and other East-ern bloc countries.

At the beginning of the 1980s, taking advantage of Libya's total depen-dence on the Soviet Union for political and military assistance, Moscow increased pressure on Tripoli to advance its interests both in Libya itself and in the broader Middle East. Moscow's intention was to strengthen its foothold in this geostrategically important region, from which it could encroach upon NATO's southern backyard and sustain a reinforced Mediter-ranean fleet, hitherto an Achilles' heel in the Soviet buildup of forces in the area. There were allegations that the USSR had gained access to Libyan ports as early as the mid-1970s and that the Soviets had established a naval base on the Libyan coast, northeast of Benghazi. Tripoli persistently denied it, declaring in late 1979 that "not a single Soviet military ship has docked in a Libyan port or anywhere on our shores." In early 1980, Egypt repeated the accusation and the Libyans again denied it. Moscow, however, continued to strive for well-established naval and land facilities in the Mediterranean.[38]

Meanwhile, the West, pro-US Arab states, and various African countries increasingly opposed Libya's intervention in Chad, on political and military grounds. This opposition, coinciding with that of expatriate activists in Western Europe and Arab capitals as well as with Libya's increasing isola-tion from both the Arab and African worlds, became more pronounced in the wake of the declared political union of Libya and Chad, announced on 6 January 1981.[39] This multidirectional pressure was believed to be one of the major topics discussed during Qaddafi's official visit to the USSR on 27 and 28 April 1981. Other issues Qaddafi wished to discuss with his hosts were "fresh Soviet arms, an agreement of a transfer of nuclear technology, assistance in the Libyan oil fields, and a public commitment to support Libya in case of a foreign attack. Instead of negotiating directly on these issues, however, Qaddafi and [the Soviets] 'bickered' over whether he could pray in the shuttered Grand Mosque of Moscow, whether the prayers would be broadcast from the minaret, and—after the [Soviets] had agreed to both demands—whether Qaddafi would reciprocate by laying a wreath at Lenin's mausoleum."[40]

The joint communiqué released at the end of the talks emphasized "solidarity with the Democratic Republic of Afghanistan in its struggle for independence and sovereignty" and the "normalization of the situation in Chad and the positive role [that] has been played by the aid that was given to Chad by Libya," thus reflecting not only the central issues on each of the countries' agendas but also the mutual nature of Soviet-Libyan interests.[41] Yet at the same time, the USSR refrained from further ties with Libya, perceiving it to be a problematic ally. In any case it was more concerned with consolidating its control over Afghanistan and keeping a close eye on the Gulf, where Iraq and Iran were locked in a bitter conflict that would have enormous consequences on Soviet interests in the region.

While the diplomatic aspect of his visit to the Soviet Union did not deviate, at least publicly, from the norm, Qaddafi accentuated its religious aspect in an attempt to enhance his position as an Islamic leader at home and in the wider Middle East. Indeed, the Libyan media celebrated his visit as "a triumph of the Faithful over the nonbelievers." Such press was especially important given the Islamist upsurge in Libya and its immediate vicinity as well as in the Soviet republics of central Asia following Khomeini's rise to power and attempts to export his revolution.[42] As for the military aspect of Qaddafi's visit, it was mostly kept secret, though word did spread that Moscow was examining the possibility of assisting Libya in the construction of an 800-megawatt nuclear power station.[43]

On 7 June 1981, the Israeli Air Force destroyed Iraq's nuclear reactor, Osirak, about 17 kilometers southwest of Baghdad. To a large extent, Qaddafi's confidence in the power both of his patron and of Libya's own armed forces, combined with his total denial of Israel's right to exist, motivated his appeal to Moscow on 26 June 1981 to "help him attack the Israeli nuclear reactor."[44] The Israeli destruction of the Iraqi nuclear reactor inflamed the Arab world. Moscow moved quickly to exploit the situation and enhance its position in the region, not only condemning the Israeli action but also highlighting the fact that US-supplied AWACS radar planes operating out of Saudi Arabia had been crucial to its success. Meanwhile, in Aden on 19 August 1981—the day two Libyan warplanes were shot down by the US Navy in the Gulf of Sirte—Libya signed a triple alliance with Soviet-aligned Ethiopia and the PDRY. The Libyans referred to this treaty as a defense-security agreement, although it appeared to be merely a morale-boosting exercise and a deterrent measure against the United States and its Arab allies, particularly neighboring Sudan and Egypt. Meanwhile, the dramatic assassination of Sadat on 6 October 1981 by the Egyptian Islamist Khalid Ahmad Shawqi al-Islambuli had no substantial impact either on Soviet-Libyan relations or on Egypt's foreign policy; Sadat's successor, President Hosni Mubarak, followed the lead in external and domestic affairs of his predecessor as the key player in US strategy in the Arab world, the leader of anti-Soviet forces in the region, and a sworn enemy of Qaddafi.

Whether in an attempt to expedite the construction of the nuclear power station or as part of an ongoing endeavor to acquire urgently needed supplies for maintaining the war machine in Chad, top Libyan political and military officials soon embarked on a spate of visits to the Soviet Union and Eastern Europe. These culminated in Qaddafi's own visits to Hungary, Romania, Yugoslavia, Czechoslovakia, Poland, and Bulgaria in 1982 and 1983. Earlier, during a lull in the fighting in Chad, Qaddafi had tried to enhance his prospects of convening the OAU summit in Tripoli with a view to becoming its chairman for the 1983–1984 session. After repeatedly failing to achieve this objective, however, he had resumed Libya's military activities in Chad and was therefore in need of military supplies.

Unstable Relations: Friendship in Decline

In the early 1980s, relations with Moscow suffered a setback, caused in part by Libya's growing inability to make cash payments for arms purchases, as Moscow badly needed hard currency. By the summer of 1982, Libya reportedly owed the USSR US$1 billion. Qaddafi's offer to pay Moscow in oil instead of hard currency was rejected.[45] Libya, whose economy was based almost entirely on oil, was more affected by the worldwide oil glut of 1981 and 1982 than were most Arab oil producers. Oil output plunged from over 2 million barrels a day in the late 1970s to about 600,000 barrels a day at the end of 1981 and fewer than 500,000 barrels a day in the spring of 1982. Accordingly, Libya's oil revenues fell from US$22 billion in 1980 to US$15 billion in 1981 and again to about US$10 billion in 1982. This drop was reflected in a decline of foreign-exchange reserves from US$13.5 billion in mid-1981 to US$8.7 billion by year's end and to less than US$6 billion in the fall of 1982. Not surprisingly, Libya experienced cash-flow problems of a severity unprecedented in Qaddafi's time as leader, and in July 1982 it owed more than US$2 billion to foreign creditors.[46] The USSR was also suffering from the drop in global oil prices, which triggered a drop in its own oil revenues from US$127 billion in 1980 to US$42 billion in 1986 (in 2000 prices). It was partly for this reason that Moscow now demanded cash for armaments.[47]

Libya's anger over Moscow's insistence on receiving hard currency was vented at a widely publicized meeting during which Qaddafi berated the Soviet ambassador in Tripoli for the USSR's lack of response to Israel's military invasion of Lebanon in June 1982 and the subsequent siege of Beirut. Despite the fact that Libya's response to the Israeli invasion was just as feeble, he warned Moscow that its friendship with the "Arab forces . . . was about to burn, as Beirut was burning."[48] For the first time, Libya openly called into question the credibility of the USSR as an ally of the Arabs. In retrospect, these recriminations were the first sign that the hitherto strong relationship between Moscow and Tripoli was waning.

Animosity toward Washington was also steadily mounting during this period. The United States had in effect made Libya a military target, appearing resolute in its goal of curtailing Qaddafi's activism, which Washington perceived as dangerous to vital US interests in the Middle East and beyond. Libyan and US aircraft nearly clashed over the Mediterranean off the Libyan coast in February 1983. A short while later, Sudan accused Libya of having attempted to overthrow Numayri's pro-US regime on 16 March 1983 with an air raid on Omdurman, one of three zones in Khartoum, Sudan's capital. Although Libya categorically denied any involvement, Sudan further alleged that the air assault was part of a broader conspiracy that was planned by the Kremlin, implemented in Havana, rehearsed in Addis Ababa, and financed by Tripoli.[49] Three days after the attack, the United States responded by dispatching two AWACS surveillance aircraft to guard the Sudanese-Libyan border, thus issuing a warning both to Libya and to its Soviet ally. On 16 to 18 March 1983, Jallud traveled to the USSR, now led by Yuri Andropov, with the aim of easing the recent strain in relations with the Kremlin and mobilizing renewed aid to counter the US threats and help Libya sustain its war in Chad.

Easing mutual tensions also suited the USSR. Aware that its inactivity during the Israeli invasion of Lebanon and the siege of Beirut had lessened its credibility as an ally of the Arabs, Moscow now sought to reinforce its position in the Middle East. The Soviet Union was also troubled by the diminished influence of its Arab friends—Libya, Syria, the PDRY, and the PLO—on regional politics due to a series of disputes among them, including feuds between Libya and the PLO and Libya and Algeria (to be discussed). As a result, during Jallud's visit, the Soviet Union agreed in principle to establish a treaty of friendship and cooperation with Libya.

What's more, concerned by Tripoli's growing confrontation with Washington, Moscow now agreed to take Libyan oil as payment for Soviet arms.[50] The reversal of policy on this point was critical because Libya's economic problems affected its domestic affairs and undermined the stability of Qaddafi's regime. During the early 1980s, foreign sources reported recurrent plots to end Qaddafi's rule, including assassination attempts. One of these allegedly occurred in March 1982 in Tobruk, which had already been the scene of an army uprising in August 1980.[51] The fact that circles in the armed forces were involved in these activities endangered not only Qaddafi's foreign-policy goals, notably the war in Chad, but his leadership as a whole. After all, the army was the only force in the country that combined the potential to carry out a coup with the ability to provide alternative leadership. Aware of the risk, Qaddafi took measures to ensure the loyalty of the officers or at least reduce the danger they potentially posed. He employed a corps of intelligence and security men from Eastern Europe to supervise security conditions within Libya and offered his military staff attractive terms of employment that required a great deal of extra funds. Without Moscow's agreement to accept oil as payment for Soviet arms, Qaddafi would not have been able to secure the requisite finances necessary to maintain his military's loyalty and to fulfill basic weapons requirements. US government analysts estimated Libyan arms purchases from the Soviet Union in 1983 at over US$20 billion.[52]

Other events accounted for Libya's move to tighten links with the USSR as well. On 8 May 1984, Qaddafi's headquarters and residence in the Bab al-'Aziziyya barracks in Tripoli were attacked. Qaddafi accused the United States of primary responsibility for the attack, although others—such as disaffected army officers or civilian members of the opposition—may have been involved. Collaboration between Libyan opposition factions and the United States could also not be ruled out (see Chapter 2). It is likely that the resumption of full diplomatic relations between the Soviet Union and Egypt in the summer of 1984 further prompted Tripoli to refresh its ties with Moscow. At the same time, Libya was ranged against France, as Paris had renewed its military involvement with anti-Libyan forces in Chad in mid-1983. Libya was also on uneasy terms with many African countries, mainly because of the war in Chad but also because of subversive activities on other parts of the continent. Throughout 1984, Libya's generally low-key relations with various Arab neighbors were strained. That fall, however, France under an agreement with Libya, withdrew troops from Chad, albeit temporarily. Concurrently, Qaddafi signed a unity agreement with Morocco, a Western-oriented country. Moscow welcomed both successes. The first reduced the danger of Libya's military entanglement with France and the second represented a chance to loosen the ties between Rabat and the West even as it took advantage of those ties to help further lessen tension between Tripoli and Paris.

Qaddafi continued to try to reinvigorate relations with the Soviet Union, visiting Moscow in October 1985, about six months after Mikhail Gorbachev had come to power. Qaddafi hoped to formally sign the friendship treaty agreed upon in principle during Jallud's visit two and a half years earlier, which would be similar to the Treaty of Friendship and Cooperation that the Kremlin had already signed with Syria, the PDRY, and Iraq. In addition, he wanted to convince the Kremlin to increase its supplies of arms and military equipment, which Libya needed to sustain the war in Chad (its agreement with France having collapsed), and to urge Moscow to build the long-promised nuclear power station. In Moscow, Qaddafi declared that "the defense of Libya's national interests is in full accord with the Soviet policy. That is why we are convinced that our multifaceted ties have by no means exhausted their potential and will continue to develop and strengthen."[53]

Gorbachev, stressing the need for a united Arab front, criticized Qaddafi's marred relations with his Arab neighbors, which hampered the effectiveness of the pro-Soviet Arab camp and strengthened US motivation to fight Libya. Nevertheless, the joint communiqué issued at the end of Qaddafi's visit was the strongest demonstration yet of the USSR's backing of Qaddafi against the explicitly anti-Libyan administration of President Ronald Reagan in the United States. Moscow declared its support "for the steps taken by the Libyan jamahiriyya to defend its sovereignty, independence, and territory." The communiqué emphasized the two countries' "similar views" on a wide range of international issues "of mutual interest."[54] Thus, the Soviets provided some measure of verbal backing for Libya's war in Chad.

This support was not backed with action. Moscow neither committed to advancing the nuclear power-station project nor signed a formal agreement of friendship with Tripoli, and soon it reverted to its earlier position of withholding weapons unless paid in cash—a condition that Libya was unable to meet. Although Moscow's insistence on receiving cash was motivated mainly by economic considerations, it was also shaped by the diminishment of Libya's political and strategic value. Moscow's relations with Khartoum had improved after the fall of Numayri and the rise to power of General 'Abd al-Rahman Muhammad Hassan Siwar al-Dahab in April 1985. Elected in the spring of 1986, Sudanese prime minister Sadiq al-Mahdi, who visited Moscow from 11 to 15 August 1986, declared that his visit had removed "the effects of the defunct era's stupid policy" toward the USSR, opening "a new chapter within the framework of nonalignment and balance."[55] The new regime in Khartoum distanced itself from a decade and a half of pro-US policies as well as from Egypt to take a more balanced position in East-West affairs. This turn somewhat diminished Libya's attractiveness to the Soviets, who now thought they had an additional springboard for their policies toward the Middle East, the Red Sea, and the Horn of Africa.

What's more, Tripoli had allegedly angered Moscow by transferring missiles and other arms bought from the USSR to Iran for use against Iraq, an ally with which the Soviets had signed a friendship treaty in 1972.[56] However, Soviet arms were also sent to Iran by East Germany, Bulgaria, North Korea, and other third parties, perhaps as part of a Soviet attempt to hedge its bets on the war due to vital interests in both countries. Indeed, these arms shipments coincided with the dispatch of 1,000 Soviet military advisers to Iraq, which owed Moscow US$5 billion.[57]

At the end of 1985, the Soviet Union reversed its policy again and sent SAM-5 anti-aircraft missiles and 2,000 military advisers to Libya to create an air umbrella that would protect against a possible US air raid. Until then, only Syria had received such weapons. The consignment strengthened Tripoli's position at a time of extreme tension with "the Black House" in Washington.[58] This reversal may have been a reaction to the recent exposure of a US plot to undermine the Qaddafi regime, which Moscow denounced in the strongest terms.[59] However, it may also have been part of the Soviet plan to provide Iran with arms, using Libya as a conduit. Relations between Tripoli and Tehran were not amicable. Iran had reservations about the fact that Qaddafi presented himself and his regime as the model for a revolutionary Islamic state, while the regime in Tehran perceived itself as the paradigm of the same. Despite this, the two countries shared a common enmity toward the United States— "the Great Satan"—and Israel, its "illegitimate son" in Iranian parlance.

When Tripoli praised and, according to US sources, assisted terrorists who attacked airports in Vienna and Rome in December 1985, it put Moscow in an embarrassing position. Soviet apprehension increased in March 1986 when US warplanes bombed Libyan military installations, including Soviet-made SAM-5 missiles, near the Gulf of Sirte on the Mediterranean coast. The USSR ran the risk of either confrontation with the United States or a loss of face if it failed to respond to an attack on its ally. According to one assessment, at the close of 1985, the Soviets may have felt that the United States—which had never before taken any substantial military action in Libya—would oppose Qaddafi only verbally.[60] If so, they were wrong. On 15 April 1986, some two weeks after the bombing of a Berlin discotheque frequented by US military personnel, US warplanes attacked the Libyan mainland. Ronald Reagan accused Qaddafi of responsibility for the attack in Berlin as well as other acts of international terrorism, including the hijackings of a TWA jet and the *Achille Lauro* in late 1985.

The US attack was not followed by any substantive response from the Soviet Union. According to various sources, the USSR may even have known in advance about the attack yet neglected to inform Libya. According to another source, Moscow had indeed warned Tripoli but only one hour in advance.[61] This uncooperative stance was further illustrated by the fact that Soviet military advisers in Libya remained in their underground bunkers during the attack, despite the Libyan government's request for help in erecting new launching pads. Yet another foreign report claimed that Moscow had pulled several hundred military advisers out of Libyan missile bases and had withdrawn its ships from Tripoli's harbors only two days before the attack.[62]

It was evident that Soviet interests were coming into conflict with those of Libya, particularly as the Kremlin was now keen to ease tensions with the United States. Gorbachev was much less concerned about angering Qaddafi than endangering the nascent US-Soviet rapprochement at a time when the Kremlin sought to sign a major arms-control agreement. The absence of a mutual defense agreement with Libya (like those Moscow had with Iraq, Syria, and the PDRY) further facilitated Gorbachev's decision. All in all, Moscow maintained diplomacy in its response to the air raid, depicting it as "barbaric" and "piratical" but doing nothing more.[63] The decline in support seriously damaged the deterrence Libya had enjoyed under Soviet patronage. In this light, the threat Qaddafi made three days before the attack to call on the Soviets for assistance appeared naive.

Qaddafi publicly criticized the Soviets' new stance but continued to threaten Washington that Libya would join the Warsaw Pact and "become another Cuba."[64] Libya's official decision, announced in May 1986, to "end the teaching of English at all educational stages and to begin teaching the Russian language instead"[65] aimed to give further credence to these threats but did not reflect any significant developments. In fact, by the summer of 1986, relations appeared to be deteriorating even further. Moscow increased pressure on Tripoli to pay the US$5 billion it owed and to get its economy under tighter control while continuing to refuse to build the nuclear plant in Libya.[66] On 26 May 1986, Jallud arrived in Moscow for an official five-day visit—his second that year—but it did not herald improvements or yield any significant arms deliveries, despite Tripoli's dire need for assistance in the war in Chad. Throughout the first months of 1987, Libyan troops in Chad suffered a series of defeats. The war consumed much of the Libyan arsenal and inflicted a serious blow to Qaddafi's prestige. Libya's distress further increased as the United States began to support Chadian military campaigns against Libya. At the beginning of 1987, Moscow suspended shipment of 100,000 barrels of oil a day from Libya to the USSR, both because it was anxious to disassociate itself from Qaddafi's fiasco in Chad and because it faced growing financial pressure. Between 1975 and 1990, the USSR received only 56 percent of the payments its allies owed for arms deliveries, and some of these payments were made in barter.[67] Libya had now lost its supply of high-quality Soviet weaponry.

At that juncture in the late 1980s, Moscow was preoccupied with other issues. The UN and the Islamic world were pressuring it to withdraw from Afghanistan; riots in the Republic of Kazakhstan were blamed on Gorbachev's policy of perestroika; the war in the Gulf between Iran and Iraq continued; and instability in the PDRY was spilling over into the broader Arab peninsula. In addition, Moscow was still trying to achieve an arms-control agreement with Washington. The relationship with Libya had turned from a strategic asset into a political liability. Gorbachev's multifaceted "new thinking" included, among other things, a desire for closer ties with pro-Western states in the Middle East, such as Egypt and Israel.[68] The change in policy clashed with Tripoli's own foreign-policy principles.

At the same time, Libya had serious domestic and foreign difficulties of its own, which jeopardized Qaddafi's hold on power. Most perilous among these was the rising tide of Islamist dissidence as well as growing pressure from the United States regarding Libya's alleged production of chemical weapons.

Conclusion: The Soviet Union's Collapse and Libya's Isolation on the International Stage

The Gulf War in January and February 1991, which ended with the military defeat of Iraq by a US-led coalition, marked a historical turning point as the first major post–Cold War conflict in which Moscow cooperated with Washington against its former client. Both before and after the crisis, Qaddafi openly criticized the impotence of what he continued to refer to as the Soviet Union, both as a superpower and as a supporter of the Arabs: "Why did the Soviet Union not say it was not permissible to crush Iraq and annihilate it once it left Kuwait, despite the fact that there is a treaty of friendship and cooperation" between Moscow and Baghdad? Such a treaty, he argued, "compels the Soviet Union to stand by Iraq if . . . aggression is waged against it." Qaddafi's conclusion that the Arabs "have no ally apart from themselves"[69] was, in effect, a public declaration that the Soviet Union had ceased to be a reliable patron.

The 1990s saw the beginning of a US-led New World Order, which arose in the aftermath of the USSR's collapse and compelled Libya to focus on the Lockerbie dispute. In November 1991, the United States and Britain officially charged two Libyan agents of bombing Pan Am Flight 103 over Lockerbie, Scotland, in late 1988. Initially, Libya refused to hand them over to "the enemy." However, there was no longer a Soviet counterweight to US hegemony, and in 1992 the UN imposed sanctions designed to force Libya to extradite its citizens. In September 2003, after a prolonged crisis, the Lockerbie dispute was finally resolved (see Chapter 3).

Aware that the balance of power in the region entirely favored the United States, Qaddafi was suddenly eager to normalize relations with Washington. On 19 December 2003, he announced Libya's decision to dismantle its WMD and allow international inspectors to monitor the process. This about-face was the most dramatic sign of Libya's acceptance of an international order dominated by a single superpower, one far removed from that of the Cold War era, when Qaddafi enjoyed the luxury of belligerence in the international arena.

In retrospect, the breakdown of the Soviet Union was crucial to Libya's sea change in foreign policy and, in turn, to its diplomatic rehabilitation in the international community. This resulted in renewed economic growth and the reinforcement of Qaddafi's power. With the elimination of its superpower ally from the global stage, Libya found itself in an entirely new situation. The close political and military relationship with the USSR, which had shaped Libya's foreign and, consequently, domestic policies, had been one of the main factors in Qaddafi's international isolation for almost two decades. In keeping with the New World Order, the West had now forced Libya to gradually relinquish its belligerent Cold War–era foreign policy. It is reasonable to ask, however, whether Libya would have returned to favor with the Western community and rehabilitated its respectability worldwide had the USSR not disintegrated.

Notes

1. Qaddafi's own assessment, quoted in Sicker, *Pariah State,* p. 102.

2. For Britain's roles in ending Italian colonial rule and in pre- and postindependent Libya, see, for example, J. Wright, *Libya: A Modern History*; Blackwell, "Saving the King"; and François de Lannoy, *Afrikakorps, 1941–1943.*

3. Ginor, "'Under the Yellow Arab Helmet.'" For details on the war of attrition, which Nasser called a prelude to the next phase of an all-out war for the liberation of Sinai, see Sela, *The Continuum Political Encyclopedia,* pp. 88–89.

4. See, for instance, *Arab Report and Record,* 1–14 February 1973, and *al-Jundi* (Tripoli), 13 February 1971. Qaddafi's perception of the subversive nature of communism in relation to Arab governments was reinforced after the failed Communist coup in Sudan in July 1971, aimed at toppling the Sudanese regime and reinstating a pro-Soviet one. For Sanusi's perception of the Communists, see el-Kikhia, *Libya's Qadhafi,* pp. 108–109.

5. For Qaddafi's ideology, see his three-part *Green Book.*

6. For a comprehensive survey of the relations between the United States and Libya after Libyan independence, see Chapters 2 and 3 and, for example, St. John, "The United States, the Cold War and Libyan Independence" and *Libya and the United States.*

7. *Washington Post,* 21 May 1974; *al-Diyar,* 26 May 1974. Another source claimed that the deal provided for the delivery of about US$1 billion of Soviet weapons. See Campbell, "Communist Strategies in the Mediterranean."

8. For details on the Soviet military deals and advisers, see Pajak, "Arms and Oil," p. 52; *al-Ahram,* 23 May 1975; *Arab Report and Record,* 16–31 May and 16–30 June 1975; and Arab Revolution News Agency (ARNA, Tripoli), 2 June 1975.

9. From an interview with Qaddafi in *Le Point,* 20 January 1975.

10. See el-Kikhia, *Libya's Qadhafi,* p. 134.

11. *Sunday Telegraph,* 21 September 1975. For Libya's denials, see for example, Qaddafi's interviews in *al-Diyar,* 28 June 1975, and ARNA, 2 May 1976. For the estimate of 2,000 advisers, see el-Kikhia, *Libya's Qadhafi,* p. 134.

12. *Arab Report and Record,* 1–15 September 1975.

13. *Quarterly Economic Review of Libya, Tunisia, and Malta,* 2nd quarter, 1977, p. 6.

14. ARNA, 7 December 1976.

15. For the origins and course of this armed conflict, see Chapter 5; also see Shaked and Ronen, "Simmering Tension." For more details on the two countries' relations in the mid-1970s, see Heikal, *The Road to Ramadan,* pp. 185–197.

16. Gera, "Libya," 1978, p. 541.

17. Qaddafi, quoted in *Le Monde,* 25–26 September 1977.

18. Radio Cairo, 16 July 1977 (DR).

19. Middle East News Agency, 2 August 1977 (DR). For more details on the Soviet strategic perception of the Middle East and particularly the Persian Gulf in the 1970s, see Ross, "Considering Soviet Threats to the Persian Gulf." For the Soviet Union's goals in Africa, see Bienen, "Perspectives on Soviet Intervention in Africa"; Ogunbadejo, "Soviet Policy in Africa"; and Grey, "The Soviet Presence in Africa: An Analysis of Goals."

20. Ronen, "Libya's Qadhafi and the Israeli-Palestinian Conflict," 2004.

21. *Al-Usbu 'al-'Arabi* (Beirut), 4 July 1977.

22. For differing inter-Arab positions on the peace process as well as the super-powers' respective postures, see Dishon, "The Middle East in Perspective."

23. Morison, "The Soviet Bloc and the Middle East," p. 38, quoting a Moscow broadcast in Arabic.

24. Rivlin, *The Russian Economy,* p. 19.

25. *Al-Mustaqbal,* 28 January 1978; Altman, "The Arab Republic of Egypt," p. 416.

26. Ronen, "Libya," 1979, p. 635.

27. Radio Tripoli, 11 June 1978 (DR).

28. For Libya's military intervention in Uganda (1972–1979) and Chad (from the 1970s to 1987), see Chapters 7 and 8 and Ronen, "Libya's Intervention in Amin's Uganda," 1992. For Libya's military intervention in Chad, see Lemarchand, "The Case of Chad"; J. Wright, *Libya, Chad and the Central Sahara*; Simons, *Libya and the West*, pp. 47–84; and Neuberger, *Involvement, Invasion and Withdrawal.*

29. *Foreign Report,* 2 May 1979. Because of limited space, this chapter does not discuss Libya's comprehensive relations with Soviet bloc countries.

30. *Défences Interarmées,* September 1979. For the delivery of TU-22 aircraft, see Sicker, *Pariah State,* p. 104.

31. *The Spectator,* 26 January 1980, quoting Qaddafi. For more details on the Soviet invasion of Afghanistan, see, for example, Becker and Fukuyama, "The USSR and the Middle East"; Behrens, "The Soviet Occupation of Afghanistan"; and Blank, *Operational and Strategic Lessons.*

32. Radio Damascus, 16 January 1980 (BBC).

33. JANA, 25 and 27 June 1980; Radio Tripoli, 5 September 1980 (BBC).

34. For details on both affairs, see Menashri, "Iran," p. 474, and J. Goldberg, "Saudi Arabia."

35. *New York Times,* 7 May 1981.

36. For Libya's denial that the Soviets were involved in its intervention in Chad, see for example, *Jamahiriyya Review* (London), March 1981. For reports on Soviet and Eastern-bloc aid, see for example, *Ruz al-Yusuf* (Cairo), 19 January 1981; *International Herald Tribune,* 26 February 1981; *Washington Post,* 10 March 1981.

37. "Libya," *Quarterly Economic Review,* 1980 Annual Supplement, p. 31.

38. *New York Times,* 11 December 1979; *al-Ahram,* 15 February 1980. For a survey on the USSR's Mediterranean interests at this time, see Campbell, "Communist Strategies."

39. For the decision to establish the Union, although it never materialized, see JANA, 6 January 1981 (BBC).

40. C. Wright, "Libya and the West: Headlong into Confrontation?" p. 38.

41. Telegraph Agency of the Soviet Union (TASS, Moscow), 29 April 1981 (BBC); *International Herald Tribune,* 29 April 1981.

42. For the Libyan press description, see C. Wright, "Libya and the West: Headlong into Confrontation?" p. 38. For Khomeini's Islamist Revolution and its impact on regional and global affairs, see Halliday, "The Iranian Revolution: Uneven Development and Religious Populism," in Halliday and Alavi, eds., *State and Ideology in the Middle East and Pakistan*; Halliday, *Nation and Religion in the Middle East*, pp. 155–167; Menashri, *The Iranian Revolution*; Taheri, *The Spirit of Allah: Khomeini and the Islamic Revolution*; and Esposito, *The Islamic Threat: Myth or Reality?* For the rise of Islamism in Libya, see Ronen, "Qadhafi and Militant Islamism," 2002, and Wharton, "'Between Arab Brothers and Islamist Foes.'"

43. *Financial Times*, 11 June 1981.

44. Grinevsky, *Stsenarii dlya tret'ey mirovoy voyny*, p. 103.

45. *Al-Watan al-'Arabi*, 1–10 October 1982; *Newsweek*, 16 August 1982.

46. Yitzhak Gal, "Economic Affairs Section," cited in Ronen, "Libya," 1983, pp. 751–752.

47. Rivlin, *The Russian Economy*, p. 27.

48. See Radio Tripoli, 26 June 1982 (BBC), and *Jamahiriyya International Report* (London), 9 July 1982. For an analysis of the Soviet response to the Israeli June 1982 invasion of Lebanon and to the Middle East in general during this period, see Freedman, "The Soviet Union and the Middle East."

49. For more details, see Ronen, "Libya," 1984, p. 714, and "Sudan," 1986, pp. 644, 663.

50. *Al-Nahar Arab Report and Memo* (Beirut and Zurich), 28 March 1983.

51. *Al-Sahafa* (Khartoum) and *al-Sharq al-Awsat*, 22 April 1982. Reports on coup attempts in Tripoli were almost exclusively reported by hostile sources. Libya systematically denied them.

52. L. Anderson, "Qadhafi and the Kremlin."

53. *Pravda* (Moscow), 13 October 1985 (DR).

54. *Pravda*, 13 and 16 October 1985 (DR); *Jamahiriyya Mail*, 23 October 1985.

55. From an interview with Mahdi in *Al-Siyasa* (Kuwait), 22 September 1986. For the Soviet-Sudanese rapprochement and its regional and international reverberations, see Ronen, "The Republic of Sudan."

56. *Foreign Report*, 17 October 1985; *al-Dustur* (London), 21 October 1985.

57. *Le Monde*, 13 March 1986; *Akhir Sa'a* (Cairo), 28 May 1986.

58. The term "Black House" was repeatedly used in the Libyan media. See, for example, Radio Tripoli, 2 and 10 January 1986 (DR) and 27 March 1986 (BBC).

59. *Foreign Report*, 31 October 1985; *Washington Post*, 3 November 1985; *al-Ahram*, 22 December 1985.

60. Freedman, "Moscow and the Middle East in 1985," p. 50.

61. *Ma'ariv*, 18 April 1986; *Jerusalem Post*, 27 April 1986.

62. *Guardian*, 23 April 1986; *International Herald Tribune*, 7 May 1986. For the figures on Soviet and Eastern European advisers in Libya, see Schumacher, "The United States and Libya," p. 346.

63. *Pravda*, 16 April 1986 (DR).

64. From interviews with Qaddafi in *al-Mawqif al-'Arabi* (Beirut), 30 May 1986, and *al-Ittihad* (Abu-Dhabi), 1 May 1986.

65. JANA, 22 May 1986 (DR); Qaddafi in an interview with the *Times of India*, 27 April 1986 (BBC).

66. *Guardian*, 17 June 1986; *Le Point*, 18–23 June 1986.

67. C. Davis, "Country Survey 16," p. 158.

68. For Gorbachev's "new political thinking," his preoccupations with regions other than the Middle East, and his policy in the Middle East in the late 1980s, see

Goldberg and Marantz, eds., *The Decline of the Soviet Union*; Hannah, "The Soviet Union and the Middle East"; and Golan, "Soviet Policy in the Middle East."

69. From Qaddafi's speech to military graduates in Benghazi, aired on Tripoli TV, 31 August 1991 (DR), and an interview with Libya's foreign minister, Ibrahim Bishari in *al-Wafd* (Cairo), 11 September 1991, respectively.

5

The Dynamics of
Inter-Arab Relations:
Courtship and Rejection

Immediately after his ascent to power, Qaddafi ventured into the Mashriq, the Arab-Muslim region east of Libya to make it the center of his foreign-policy agenda, waving the banner of allegiance to the pan-Arab cause and holding Arab unity as a central tenet of his ideological philosophy as he did so.

Following a series of failures in the region in the mid-1970s, however, Qaddafi shifted his focus. Exploring alternative opportunities for advancing Libya's interests and his own political prestige, Qaddafi turned to the Maghrib—the other key Arab-Muslim region in North Africa, this one lying to the west—as an area of considerable promise. He invested new efforts to bolster his country's position within this regional framework. It was not long, however, before his ambitions for Arab unity and leadership were stymied here, too, due to what he perceived as the blatant unresponsiveness of the Arab world to Libya's embrace.

Qaddafi's failure in both the Mashriq and the Maghrib caused him to broaden his foreign-policy spectrum beyond the Arab-Muslim world into the orbits of sub-Saharan Africa and the Soviet Union. Yet the Libyan leader did not relinquish his aspirations for these regions, zigzagging between them, at times using militancy, even violence, as a vehicle and at others employing more measured policies. This preoccupation became one of the defining characteristics of Qaddafi's inter-Arab relations. Tracing the chronology and nature of these relations throughout Qaddafi's rule, this chapter also analyzes their underlying motives and examines their connection to Libya's domestic and broader foreign affairs.

Center and Margin in Qaddafi's Arab Outlook

At the turn of the 1970s, Qaddafi sailed full steam ahead on his new revolutionary ship toward the heart of the Arab Mashriq, Egypt, striving to carve out a niche for himself from which to implement a political and ideological vision that included not only the Libyan people but the entire Arab nation.

Preceded as it was by a postcolonial, pro-Western, monarchial regime (1951–1969) that had never exhibited any particular interest in Arab nationalism or in current inter-Arab politics, the Qaddafi regime represented a new day in Libya as it wholeheartedly embraced Arab nationalism and pan-Arab interests. Having grown up under the influence of his father figure and mentor Gamal 'Abd al-Nasser, Qaddafi not surprisingly waved the Nasserist flags of Arab combat against Western influence in his country and its vicinity.[1]

Although Qaddafi did not entirely ignore the Maghrib during his first years in power, most of his efforts centered on the Mashriq in keeping with his firm perception of ideological and political center and margins in Libya's Arab orientation. Loyal to the idea of pan-Arab unity, Qaddafi initially attempted to achieve unification with Libya's closest Mashriqian neighbors. This goal, together with that of consolidating his political position at home and strengthening his influence on regional politics, were the highest priorities on his agenda at that juncture.

The Libyan leader focused his unionist drive on Egypt, led since Nasser's death in September 1970 by Anwar Sadat. Concerned with the potential of the pan-Arab legacy Nasser had left not least for enhancing his political position domestically and regionally, Qaddafi appeared determined to exceed his mentor by injecting uncompromising militancy into the ideology he had adopted. None of the unity plans Qaddafi initiated were successful, however. His initial attempt for Libyan-Egyptian-Sudanese unity, launched in late 1969, was soon thwarted by Egypt's lack of enthusiasm, as well as by Sudan's inability to join the planned union due to domestic constraints mainly relating to civil war and the political power struggle in Khartoum.[2] His next attempt was a unity framework composed of Libya, Syria, and Egypt. This new union, known as the Federation of Arab Republics, was formed in October 1971 but soon collapsed as well.[3]

Qaddafi's obsession with Arab unity soured Tripoli's relations with Cairo and damaged its prestige in other Mashriq countries, which were concerned about Qaddafi's increasing activism.[4] Egypt's fear of Qaddafi's preoccupation with Arab unity was not the only problem in Libyan-Egyptian relations. The differences between the two heads of state encompassed their personalities, ideologies, and regional and international political orientations. That the latter had become increasingly incompatible by the mid-1970s was reflected in Libya's increasingly vehement objection to the presence of "American imperialism" on the Arab scene and in Libya as well as in its overtures toward the Soviet Union.

It is not surprising, therefore, that increased US involvement in Egypt and Sudan toward the mid-1970s concerned Qaddafi, prompting militancy against the closely linked, pro-US regimes of Sadat and Numayri, who had dramatically turned their backs, for different reasons, on the Soviet Union. Cairo and Khartoum responded to Tripoli's hostility in kind. Their triangular relationship thereby entered a maelstrom of mutual acts of subversion. The October 1973 War, launched by Egypt and Syria against Israel, excluded Qaddafi from the core of the Arab-Israeli conflict. Qaddafi had persistently called for military struggle as the sole solution to the conflict, and his exclusion damaged his prestige both at home and in the wider Mashriq region. Nevertheless, he pledged Libya's oil and financial support to the warring Arab countries: "Now that the battle is taking place, we have no alternative but to give whatever we can to gain victory. . . . Nevertheless," he elaborated, "this is not my war. Sadat and Asad took their decision and worked out their plan without consulting me, without even informing me. . . . Even if Egypt and Syria were to defeat Israel, I cannot lend my name to a comic-opera war," he concluded.[5] Libya was reported to have provided some US$500 million in support of the war effort, which among other things financed the purchase of seventy replacement aircraft and other equipment.[6] In the aftermath of the war in 1974, Egypt signed a disengagement agreement with Israel under US sponsorship. Libya, perceiving this as a clear violation of the three *no*'s of the 1967 Khartoum Conference—no negotiations, no peace, and no recognition of Israel—had no further expectations from Egypt, hitherto regarded as the central pillar in Qaddafi's Arab edifice.[7]

The Soviet Role in Shaping Libya's Arab Politics

After failing to achieve unity in the Mashriq, Qaddafi revived his earlier idea of making Libya a "link between the Maghrib and the Mashriq with the aim of uniting all the Arabs from the Gulf to the Atlantic," thus, demonstrating that his pan-Arab ideology had not dissipated but only shifted to another geopolitical arena. This is supported by the argument that the demise of Arab nationalism in the pan-Arab sense seemed to be overstated, "not least because it is in the interests of states to sustain it, even as they manipulate it." This argument further claims that "there remains a coexistence of pan-Arab and state-centered nationalism: it is not a question of it being resolved one way or the other, in the direction of a full political *wahda* or, conversely, by the end of the pan-Arab dream, but rather by shifts from one plane to the other."[8] Subsequently, Libya and Tunisia proclaimed unity on 12 January 1974, a move that was greeted with surprise both in the Maghrib and in the Mashriq. It later became known that discussions had been underway between the two countries since Libya had initiated them in the autumn of the previous year.

Shortly afterward, Tunisian president Habib Bourguiba rescinded the pact over disagreements on two major issues. The first was Tunisia's pro-Western orientation versus Libya's anti-Western and increasingly pro-Soviet stance; the second was Tunisia's belief in a political solution to the Arab-Israeli conflict as opposed to Libya's refusal to recognize Israel's right to exist. As early as in 1965, Bourguiba had urged Arab countries to recognize Israel on the condition that there be a return to negotiations in the spirit of UN General Assembly Resolution 181 (1947), which recommended the partition of Palestine, and Resolution 194 (1948), which called for the return of Arab refugees to their homes. Qaddafi, by contrast, persistently called for the annihilation of Israel.

However, these sources of contention existed prior to the decision of the two countries to unite and, therefore, fail to provide a persuasive explanation. Rather, Tunisia's primary motivation for canceling the unity agreement was Algeria's threat to attack it if it refused to do otherwise—a threat backed by the amassing of Algerian troops along the border. As Algeria saw it, a Tunisian-Libyan bloc on its eastern border would further threaten the Algerian position in the region and adversely affect its foreign policy agenda. The abrogation of the unity agreement also reflected a power struggle among the top Tunisian leaders. For Libya, however, the reasons were unimportant compared to the hostility it created in Tripoli toward Tunis upon shattering Qaddafi's vision of Arab unity, humiliating him and damaging his prestige at home and in the broader Arab arena.[9]

The political echoes of this blow to Libya were amplified against the background of strained relations with Algeria and Morocco. Moroccan-Libyan relations in particular soured after a failed coup against King Hassan II's pro-Western regime on 10 July 1971. Although army forces were clearly responsible for the bloody coup attempt and Libya's role was unproven, Rabat's severance of ties with Tripoli reflected the widely held Moroccan belief that Libya had indeed been involved in active subversion.[10]

Thus experiencing stalemates on both Arab fronts, Libya made significant efforts to align itself with Moscow. This move exacerbated Libya's tension with the United States and its Arab allies, primarily Egypt and Sudan. Egypt, which since 1972 had gradually disengaged itself from its once-close Soviet ally while orienting itself toward the West, interpreted the growing political and military collaboration between Libya and the USSR as explicitly anti-Egyptian. Concurrently, Libya perceived Egypt as a dangerous US stronghold, accusing Sadat of "openly plotting" against Libya "at American behest."[11] Both Egypt and Sudan considered Libya to be a tool of Soviet interests that endangered their own, particularly after Haile Selassie's pro-US regime was overthrown in Addis Ababa in 1974.

Under Mengistu Haile Mariam, Ethiopia's new revolutionary regime increasingly aligned itself with Moscow, to Cairo's and Khartoum's growing alarm. The closely linked regimes of Sadat and Numayri, backed by the United States, tried to curb Moscow's expansion into the Middle East and the

Horn of Africa. They particularly feared Soviet penetration of the Red Sea region, whether directly or via Libya or Ethiopia, as they along with pro-US Saudi Arabia considered the "lake of peace" a "neutral zone." When the Suez Canal reopened in 1975, the Red Sea once again became one of the most important waterways of the world. Thus Ethiopia's burgeoning alliance with the Soviets goaded Egypt, Sudan, and Saudi Arabia to coordinate a defensive strategy under the slogan Arabization of the Red Sea.[12]

In the fall of 1975 and the summer of 1976, Libya, together with the Sudanese opposition, launched coup attempts in Sudan with the full support of the USSR—at least according to Khartoum, which severed diplomatic ties with Tripoli in the wake of a 1976 attempt that nearly toppled Numayri's regime and subsequently signed the Saudi-backed Joint Defense Agreement with Egypt. This move, signaling the alignment of pro-Western Arab countries against Libya, was also prompted by Libya's deepening political and military involvement in Chad, its southern neighbor and backyard to Egypt and Sudan. Khartoum and Cairo considered the Libyan intervention in Chad a Soviet plot to expand Moscow's influence in the Arab-African zone.

Meanwhile, Qaddafi's standing in the pro-Western Maghrib also faltered, as indicated by a heightening of tensions with Tunisia after Bourguiba granted political refuge to Qaddafi's most dangerous adversary, Major 'Umar al-Muhayshi. Until the exposure of his planned coup in summer 1975, Muhayshi had been an influential member of the Revolutionary Command Council, the leading political body in Libya, composed of close aides who had helped Qaddafi seize power in 1969.

After initially taking refuge in Tunisia, Muhayshi moved to Cairo. The Egyptians, aware of Muhayshi's importance in fighting the Libyan regime, granted him broad access to their media, which he used to launch a propaganda campaign against Qaddafi. Rumors of a Libyan plot to kidnap Muhayshi resulted in the detention of Tunisia's former foreign minister Muhammad Masmudi in Cairo. Masmudi was known for his close association with Qaddafi as well as his role as the architect of the 1974 Tunisian-Libyan unity agreement. Soon afterward, Tunis and Tripoli retaliated by arresting each other's citizens (who were finally released in the spring of 1977). Already involved in propaganda attacks and subversive activities against Bourguiba, Qaddafi increased his political pressure on Tunisia, provoking a dispute over the demarcation of the oil-rich continental shelf in the Mediterranean Gulf of Gabes in May 1977.

Tripoli and Tunis also held conflicting positions in the dispute over the Western Sahara, ruled by Spain until early 1976 and then handed over to Mauritania and Morocco. Polisario—that is, the People's Organization for the Liberation of [former Spanish colonies] Saquia al-Hamra and Rio del Oro—had proclaimed the establishment of the Saharan Arab Democratic Republic (SADR) and was attempting to realize its independence by military means. Libya supported Polisario both politically and militarily but, unlike Algeria, refrained from formally recognizing the SADR. Tunisia sided with Morocco and Mauritania in their claims of sovereignty over parts of the area.

It was not long before the Western Sahara dispute became the focus of inter-Maghrib politics. The confluence of the interests of Libya and Algeria, which also supported Polisario, established a new basis for rapprochement between Qaddafi and Algeria's Houari Boummedien. However, whereas Libya viewed the dispute mainly as a conduit by which to promote its political influence and interests throughout the Arab world, Algeria was primarily concerned with preventing the expansion of Moroccan territory and influence.[13]

Driven by a dramatic rise in oil revenues, a large arsenal, increasing entrenchment in Africa, and growing political and military cooperation with the Soviet Union in the second half of the 1970s—all of which strengthened his political self-confidence—Qaddafi's belligerence reached new heights. Egypt became a prime target. Cairo accused Libya of involvement in instigating the food riots that flared up in Egyptian towns on 18 and 19 January 1977. These were the most serious antigovernment protests since the 1952 revolution in terms of mass participation, loss of life and property, means used to restore order, and challenge posed to Sadat's hold on power.

Determined to "teach Qaddafi an unforgettable lesson," Egypt attacked Libya from 21 to 24 July 1977.[14] The main targets of the Egyptian Air Force were military—airports and radar installations—but civilian targets were also hit, including the town of Tobruk, 120 kilometers west of the Libyan-Egyptian border. Libya's reaction was limited to artillery shelling of the Egyptian border town of Sallum and the threat of future retaliatory strikes by surface-to-surface missiles. The brief war cost Libya 10 aircraft (destroyed on the ground), about 30 tanks (disabled), and some 300 casualties (including several Soviet advisers).[15] Ironically, Libya, which had once waved the banner of Arab solidarity, looking to Nasser's Egypt as the ultimate model of pan-Arabism, was now being attacked by Egypt, its "sister Arab state," albeit under different leadership.

Reshuffling Libya's Cards: In the Wake of Sadat's Peace Policy

Sadat's trip to Jerusalem from 19 to 21 November 1977—the first formal visit by an Arab head of state to Israel—and the ensuing Egyptian-Israeli peace process shocked Qaddafi. He rejected the "treasonous" Egyptian policy, repeatedly depicting it as a "crime against the Arab nation." In early December 1977, Libya, like other members of what was soon to become the rejectionist Arab front, severed diplomatic ties with Egypt. Libya perceived the flying of the Egyptian flag in Israel during Sadat's visit a desecration of an Arab symbol and, in protest, replaced its own national flag—hitherto identical to Egypt's—with a green one to honor the color of Islam. The act of choosing a new flag also symbolized the end of Libya's total identification with Egypt, the core of the Mashriq. Qaddafi called for a "revolution of revenge and liberation" against Sadat, while the latter referred to Qaddafi as a "lunatic," "a lost case," and "his own worst enemy."[16]

Slamming the door on Egypt, Libya assumed a leading role in inspiring the rejectionist Arab countries to fight Sadat's peace policy and regime. Within a short time, there was a major realignment of blocs in the Arab realm. Convening in Tripoli in early December 1977, Libya, Algeria, Syria, the PDRY, and the PLO formed the Pan-Arab Front of Steadfastness and Resistance. This new platform for rejectionism enhanced Qaddafi's political prestige both at home and on the broader Arab scene by connecting Libya to the radical Arab consensus. It offset, to some degree, the controversy surrounding the implementation of the People's Power System, with its particularly problematic socialist and economic reforms. These reforms, which were increasingly enforced during the late 1970s, alienated Libya's small urban propertied class, as well as members of the religious establishment and the army. They nourished domestic opposition, which was partially inspired and supported by Egypt. But Tripoli now had a new Arab platform for action against Egypt and, for the first time, was part of a coalition whose members shared its strong anti-Western, anti-Israeli, and anti-Egyptian sentiments.

In October 1978, Libya rejected the "shameful and humiliating" Camp David accords, which Qaddafi renamed "David's Stable."[17] The mounting tension between Libya and Egypt following the accords was reflected in increasing suspicion concerning military buildups, bordering on open hostilities. Without mentioning his name, Qaddafi accused Sadat of planning naval and air attacks on Libya's military forces and oil installations in October 1978. He did not explain why the planned attack never took place, but his accusation reflected the enmity between the two heads of state.[18]

Libya denounced the Egyptian-Israeli peace treaty signed in March 1979. Mutual fears of military retaliation increased, and both countries concentrated their troops along the border. At the same time, in spring 1979, Libya experienced a humiliating military and political fiasco in Uganda after a long-standing military intervention there. The debacle led to increased criticism of Qaddafi's foreign policy among Libyan army officers and deepened the rifts within the regime's top echelon.[19]

These crises, together with Moscow's shift in attention toward Afghanistan after the invasion in late 1979, spurred a growing disillusionment about the USSR among once staunchly pro-Soviet Arab countries, accompanied by fears of the encroaching US military presence in the Middle East. Libya and Syria thus sought a new political alignment in their region. On 10 September 1980, they issued a proclamation announcing a "forthcoming union."

Hafiz al-Asad was interested in strengthening ties with Qaddafi out of fear of being isolated by escalating tensions with his neighbors Iraq and Jordan, as well as out of suspicions that they, along with Saudi Arabia, Egypt, and Kuwait, were supporting the opposition in Damascus. Asad also feared that the United States was determined to impose its influence on the Arab region and further isolate Syria. Moreover, the militant Islamic wave following Khomeini's ascent to power in Iran in early 1979 posed a new challenge for the regimes in Tripoli and Damascus, each struggling to combat the rising Islamist tide in their own countries. Aware, however, of the merely symbolic significance of any unity framework with Libya—which was only at the conception stage in any case—Asad signed Syria's Treaty of Friendship and Cooperation with the USSR in October 1980. Concurrently, Libya expressed its own desire for such a treaty with Moscow, possibly in the hope that its Syrian ally would assist.[20]

At the turn of the 1980s, a considerable increase in the activities of domestic and expatriate opposition to Qaddafi further spurred him to mobilize support outside the country in order to bolster his position within it. Resistance manifested itself in the form of both increased unrest among expatriates in Europe, particularly London and Rome, and in allegedly sharp disagreements between Qaddafi and his second in command, 'Abd al-Salam Jallud. In addition, various reports claimed that the regime had foiled a series of coup attempts, the most serious planned by circles within the army, a major pillar of support for the regime.[21] However, it was not long before Qaddafi realized that the unity plan with Syria was an empty framework and, in any case, it was overshadowed by Iraq's invasion of Iran less than two weeks later. The Iran-Iraq War soon affected the inter-Arab arena, with Jordan and Saudi Arabia taking Baghdad's side and Libya, along with Syria, supporting Tehran.

The fact that Arab and international attention was diverted to the Gulf area, far from the core of the Mashriq, enabled Libya to intensify military operations in Chad unfettered by any moral or ideological commitments to its "Arab brothers." This unilateral action reflected Qaddafi's isolation within an Arab world that, only a decade earlier, he had dreamed of unifying, a feat tantamount to the jewel in the crown of Libya's foreign affairs. "A Bedouin visionary," noted a Western observer explaining Qaddafi's conduct of regional politics at that time, "has no real friends, only tactical allies."[22]

This was further illustrated when, in response to a Syrian request, Libya joined the other members of the Front of Steadfastness and Resistance in boycotting the eleventh Arab summit in Amman from 25 to 27 November 1980. In return, Qaddafi expected Syrian support for his invasion of Chad in September 1980. The Libyan and Syrian heads of state exchanged views during Asad's visit to Tripoli in mid-December 1980, but Syria never declared its support for the Libyan invasion nor did it promote the unity scheme with Libya.

Libya's relations in the Maghrib further deteriorated, culminating in what became known as the "Gafsa incident," an armed attack on the southern Tunisian mining town of Gafsa on the night of 26 January 1980. The Tunisian government held Qaddafi responsible for the attack and severed diplomatic ties with Libya a short while later. While Libya denied the accusation, portraying the event as a "popular uprising," Tunisia insisted that the attackers came from Libya's large community of Tunisian migrants, who had been mobilized, trained, armed, and dispatched on their mission by the Libyans. Libya retaliated by broadcasting propaganda that backed the attackers against Bourguiba's "lackey regime" and by expelling large numbers of Tunisian workers from Libya while concentrating Libyan troops along the border. Whatever the Libyan role in the Gafsa attack, Qaddafi had an explicit interest in seeing a pro-Libyan, anti-Western government in Tunis and particularly in bringing down Tunisian prime minister and heir presumptive Hedi Nouira, whom Tripoli held responsible for having aborted the Libyan-Tunisian unity agreement of 1974. The upheaval in Tunis accelerated internal turmoil that culminated in the removal of Nouira for "medical reasons" at the end of February 1980. His replacement the following spring was Muhammad Mazali, a veteran politician with close ties to Tripoli. In the summer of 1980, the Libyan-Tunisian crisis subsided, mostly as a result of the government reshuffle in Tunis, although the Arab League helped. Diplomatic ties were soon resumed, but relations remained reserved.

At the same time, tension in Libya's relations with Morocco was escalating further in light of Tripoli's formal recognition of the SADR, a move in line with the decision made by the Front of Steadfastness and Resistance. Significantly, the Carter administration's increased support for the Moroccan monarch exemplified in early 1980 by its decision to sell him reconnaissance planes worth US$232.5 million—a deal the Saudis helped finance—highlighted the growing US presence in the area. This furthered the split between Libya and Morocco, as did Morocco's commitment to the Israeli-Arab peace process.[23] Rabat's severance of diplomatic ties with Tripoli in spring 1980 provided further evidence of Tripoli's diminished status in the Maghrib. Relations with Algeria—where a new president, Colonel Chedli Benjedid, had ascended to power in early 1979—remained unchanged, as Algiers, like Tripoli, was preoccupied with its own agenda and had no urgent issues of common concern with Libya. When, in 1979, Mauritania relinquished its part of the disputed territory in the Western Sahara to the Polisario Front and Morocco annexed the Mauritanian zone to prevent a Polisario takeover, tensions in Tripoli's relations with Nouakchott subsided.

The Arab world witnessed a series of dramatic events affecting its conflict with Israel. Most noteworthy were the Israeli raid on the Iraqi nuclear reactor at Osirak on 7 June 1981, the assassination of Sadat on 6 October 1981, the Israeli invasion of Lebanon on 6 June 1982, and the Israeli-Lebanese agreement signed on 17 May 1983. These vicissitudes provided Libya with new opportunities to raise the activist profile of the rejectionist front under the banner of Arab solidarity and for the sake of Arab interests. Libya raised this banner high, arguing that Arab solidarity was critical in order to mobilize the resources necessary to effectively combat the "Zionist enemy."[24]

Following the signing of the 1983 Israeli-Lebanese agreement, Libya recalled its ambassador from Beirut in protest, appealing to the Arab League to penalize Lebanon as it had Egypt in the wake of the Camp David Accords in 1978. Libya also resumed calls to "confront the Zionist deathwagon threatening the Arab nation's existence," hoping to achieve new momentum for pan-Arab activism.[25] However, there was a credibility gap between Qaddafi's vocal support of military solutions to the Palestinian problem and his inaction when the Israeli army threatened Palestinians in Lebanon. Qaddafi had chosen not to intervene in the war in Lebanon because of "the impossibility of carrying out any direct military action from Libya on the northern front for geographical reasons"; he insisted that Libya would other-wise have taken part in transporting forces and would not have stopped until the Zionist enemy was destroyed.[26] Distance, however, did not prevent Qaddafi from taking military action in geographically remote Uganda when he so wished. Qaddafi's position vis-à-vis the Palestinians in Lebanon clearly attested to his trepidation in facing off against Israel as well as to his waning concern with regard to pan-Arab and mainstream Palestinian causes. Ironically, when a political settlement for the evacuation of the Palestinian combatants from Beirut was offered, Qaddafi advised PLO leader Yasser Arafat to "commit suicide rather than accept shame," claiming the evacuation was a "plot . . . to legitimate the Palestinian rifle." Qaddafi supported anti-Arafat dissidents in al-Fatah throughout 1983, sending them money and arms and thus undermining Arafat's leadership.[27]

Libya's foreign-policy failures on all fronts during 1982 and 1983—from escalating military confrontation with the United States and France in the Chadian war zone to two unsuccessful bids for the chairmanship of the OAU—combined with growing political unrest at home to heighten Qaddafi's urgent need to boost his political prestige. This came in the form of the Arab-African Federation Agreement Qaddafi signed with King Hassan II in the Moroccan town of Oujda on 13 August 1984. The agreement reflected Qaddafi's talent for pragmatic flexibility and his preference for political expediency over ideology. The Federation Agreement, initiated by King Hassan, followed an earlier thawing of tensions between the two countries. Still, it was somewhat surprising in light of still-prevailing mutual strain between the nations, stemming from conflicting interests on a wide range of issues. Characterized by a foreign analyst as "a marriage of necessity," Libya itself called the agreement "a landmark in progress toward a union of the Arab countries of northwest Africa, which itself will be a prelude to wider [Arab] unity."[28]

Libya gained tangible dividends, at least in the immediate term, from the Federation Agreement. In Paris, Morocco successfully mediated a French-Libyan arrangement for the simultaneous withdrawal of Libyan and French troops from the Chadian war zone. This was a great relief for Qaddafi, whose fourth year of full-scale war in Chad had overextended Libya's political and military resources and led to a simultaneous confrontation with the United States, France, Egypt, and Sudan. The war had also caused mounting domestic and expatriate opposition to Qaddafi's regime that culminated in an attack on Qaddafi's office and residence in Tripoli on 8 May 1984.

In return for its help, Tripoli promised to repay Rabat by ending its political and military support for Polisario. In a scenario typical of Maghribian politics, the declared tactical reversal soon affected other regional relationships, this time straining ties between Libya and Algeria, a patron of the SADR and Polisario. Thus, two rival camps existed in the mid-1980s: Algeria-Tunisia-Mauritania and Libya-Morocco. Their rivalry was not confined to Maghribian politics but affected Maghrib-Mashriq relations as well, suggesting a new link between Maghrib affairs and wider inter-Arab matters, as the growing political affinity between Algeria, Tunisia, and Egypt—all of which shared a mutual antagonism toward Libya—made apparent. To erode the effectiveness of this triple alliance without damaging Algerian interests, Qaddafi aimed at the other two members: in the summer and fall of 1985, Libya expelled 30,000 Tunisian workers and between 20,000 and 100,000 Egyptian workers, hoping to undermine the stability of the regimes in both Tunis and Cairo.[29]

Libya could afford to be tough thanks to the improvement in its relations with Sudan following the surprising overthrow of the pro-Egyptian, pro-US regime of Numayri on 6 April 1985, and the subsequent advent to power of a one-year transitional military regime friendly to Qaddafi, headed by General Dahab. Diplomatic ties between Libya and Sudan were immediately resumed, followed by an exchange of visits by top officials to Tripoli and Khartoum. Most noteworthy were Qaddafi's visit to the Sudanese capital on 18 May 1985 and the visit to Tripoli from 29 June to 7 July 1985 of Brigadier General 'Uthman 'Abdallah Muhammad, Sudan's defense minister and an important member of Dahab's Transitional Military Council. Subsequently, Libya withdrew its support for rebel camp the Sudanese People's Liberation Army (SPLA), which had been fighting the Sudanese government in the south since the renewal of the civil war in 1983. Sudan announced that it intended to "balance" relations with the superpowers and "preserve [its] neutrality and remove [its] independent decisionmaking from power blocks." In effect, this meant distancing itself from the United States, albeit without actively approaching the USSR.[30]

Libya's Inter-Arab Relations Following the US Air Raid

The dramatic US bombing of Libya on 15 April 1986 marked a watershed in Libya's foreign affairs, exposing its lack of any meaningful support from either the Soviet Union or the "brotherly" Arab world of the Mashriq and the Maghrib. Algeria was something of an exception, strengthening ties with Libya, although mainly in protest of the military action by a superpower against an Arab state. Nevertheless, Libya turned to its "Arab brothers," calling for an emergency Arab summit to discuss the "treacherous and barbarous air raid." In response, Algeria wavered, as did Sudan, while Syria and the PDRY supported Libya. Iran and Syria echoed Qaddafi's call to Arab countries to cut off diplomatic ties with "the American enemy." Their triangular alliance stemmed not only from their shared anti-US position but also from common anti-Israeli and anti-Iraqi sentiments and reflected the reciprocity between the politics surrounding the Libyan Gulf of Sirte and those of the Persian Gulf, where the Iran-Iraq War was in its sixth year.

Libya, in need of any political support it could muster, made overtures to the Maghrib, focusing on Algeria. It offered to create a unity framework for the two countries that would function as a "survival weapon for the Arab revolution, for Arab unity, and for pan-Arabism" and claimed that the combined human resources and industrial and agricultural capacities of Libya and Algeria would grant their union superpower status.[31] Yet bilateral relations did not develop despite even a series of top-level diplomatic contacts, including a visit by Algerian president Chedli Benjedid to Sirte—located "in the Gulf of Defiance" against the United States—on 3 December 1986, which, as Libya's media emphasized, signaled Algerian support for Tripoli against Washington.[32]

This new affinity between Tripoli and Algiers, though of a tactical nature, soon affected another aspect of Libya's Maghribian affairs, this time causing strain with Morocco over the Western Sahara dispute, in which Algeria, along with Syria and Iran, supported Polisario. In addition, Morocco had not supported Libya in the wake of the US attack. Further strain between Tripoli and Rabat was caused by the visit of Israel's prime minister Shimon Peres to Morocco from 22 to 23 July 1986, who attended a highly publicized meeting with King Hassan in the palace in Ifran.[33] Libya depicted the Ifran meeting as "treason" and a violation of the Federation Agreement. This reaction, although not unique in the Arab world, prompted King Hassan to abrogate the agreement on 29 August 1986, a move that reflected his country's divisions with Libya over broader issues, such as relations with the West and

Libya's ongoing war in Chad. In response, Qaddafi gave prominence to the attendance of a senior Polisario leader, Muhammad 'Abd al-'Aziz, at the 1 September 1986 Libyan Revolution Day celebrations for the first time since the 1984 signing of the agreement with Morocco.

In the meantime, the strain on Libya's relations with Tunisia was further aggravated when Tripoli accused Tunis of allowing US aircraft to overfly Tunisian airspace in the April 1986 attack. Tunis denied the accusation and counteraccused Libya of maintaining contact with the Tunisian opposition and of instigating anti-US and antigovernment unrest in the streets of Tunis.[34] Warning it against further subversion, Tunisia deported Bashir al-Gumgum, the Libyan representative to the Arab League headquarters in Tunis.

Meanwhile, the military fiasco in Chad in the spring of 1987 aggravated domestic dissent against Qaddafi, particularly within the army. At that time, the army was reportedly demoralized, contending with defectors and draft dodgers. One foreign source put the number of soldiers failing to report for duty in 1987 at 4,000. Reports of army officers who had made attempts on Qaddafi's life and of the infiltration of Islamists into the ranks of the military were also released.[35]

The US accusation that Libya had established a chemical-weapons industry was a new source of potential confrontation between Tripoli and Washington and prompted Qaddafi to try to improve his inter-Arab relations. He concentrated his efforts on the Maghrib, which he thought would be more responsive than the Mashriq at that time. Following Benjedid's visit to Tripoli on 11 January 1988 and Qaddafi's visit to Algiers on 6 February, the two leaders made a joint visit to the Tunisian-Algerian border village of Sakiet Sidi Youssef, west of Tunis, two days later to mark with the Tunisian head of state the thirtieth anniversary of its bombing by the French during the Algerian War of Independence, thereby highlighting the rapprochement among Libya and its two Maghribian partners. Other developments in the Maghrib throughout 1988—most notably the Moroccan-Algerian reconciliation process and an outburst of civil turmoil in Algeria unprecedented since independence—paved the way for the establishment of a wider political and economic framework in the region. Referred to as "the Greater Arab Maghrib," this framework was designed to enable its members to better deal with the threats and challenges of their surroundings. In the second half of 1988, Qaddafi proposed that the Greater Arab Maghrib be a step toward comprehensive Arab unity.[36] This proposal was particularly important for Libya in light of the rapprochement between Sudan and Egypt and the Palestinian uprising *(intifada)* against Israel in the West Bank and Gaza, which broke out in December 1987.

Qaddafi announced that he was channeling "all our resources" for the "tremendous Palestinian revolution," which "restores Arab dignity," and called on the Palestinians to extend the intifada throughout the region "from the [Jordan] river to the [Mediterranean] sea and from southern Lebanon to southern Palestine." However, he avoided offering any military support, thus exposing once again the wide gap between his ideology and practice as well as the emptiness of his reference to "our brothers, the Palestinians."[37]

To Libya's concern, the rapprochement between Egypt and Sudan was reinforced by Hosni Mubarak's visit to Khartoum on 1 March 1988 and his extension of military aid to Sudan's government, under the leadership of al-Sadiq al-Mahdi's Umma Party since the spring of 1986. Egyptian support bolstered the Sudanese regime and enabled the Sudanese army to recapture two strategic garrisons on the Ethiopian border, Kurmuk and Qaysan, from the SPLA. Sudan and Egypt, backed by Chad, France, and the United States, exerted strong pressure on Qaddafi to evacuate Libyan troops, as well as Libyan-backed Chadian rebel forces, from Darfur in western Sudan, which borders Chad. Darfur was an ideal base of operations for Libya at the time due to the area's geostrategic proximity to the Libyan territory, its lack of central authority, its distance from Khartoum's control, and its poverty, neglect, and instability. These conditions were particularly helpful for Libya's encroachment into this important region, particularly after Libya's enforced withdrawal from Chad that followed its military defeat in 1987. The establishment of the Arab Maghrib Union (AMU) during a summit of Maghrib countries in Marrakesh from 15 to 17 February 1989 thus marked a timely breakthrough for Libya. Not only did the AMU satisfy Qaddafi's goal of building the Great Arab Maghrib in partial fulfillment of his comprehensive vision of Arab unity but it also provided him with an urgently needed framework for Arab political affiliation and a legitimate instrument by which to affect the region's politics while primarily promoting Libya's. What's more, it did not require any compromises of Libya's essential interests.

The increased dynamism in Maghribian politics was exemplified by Qaddafi's visits to Morocco in mid-February and again on 13 and 23–26 May 1989, as well as by the role Morocco's King Hassan played in ending the Libyan-Egyptian dispute. The Libyans reciprocated by formally closing the Polisario office in Tripoli and by ending military aid to Polisario in the autumn of 1989. Concurrently, there was growing rapprochement between Libya and Tunisia, marked by the visit of Tunisian president Zayn al-'Abidin bin 'Ali to Tripoli on 22 May 1989 and the signing of a number of bilateral economic agreements.

Diminished tensions in the Maghrib between 1988 and 1989 coincided with important events in the Mashriq, among them the termination of the eight-year-long Iraq-Iran War in the summer of 1988 and the opening of the US-PLO dialogue at the end of that year. The Soviet pullout from Afghanistan in 1989 also affected Mashriq politics, and, at the turn of the 1990s, the Palestinian-Israeli conflict returned to the forefront of Middle East concern. Egypt was readmitted into the Arab League as Libya, Syria, and Lebanon agreed to renew diplomatic relations with Cairo, thus officially ending its ostracism. Rapprochement between Libya and Egypt was achieved through independent mediation by Algeria and Morocco that highlighted the linkage between Libya's Maghrib and Mashriq politics. The Arab League summit in Casablanca from 23 to 26 May 1989 served as the venue for a meeting between Qaddafi and Mubarak, the first since their prolonged estrangement in the aftermath of the Egyptian-Israeli peace agreement began a decade before. Although Qaddafi continued to oppose the peace agreement, he nevertheless agreed to Egypt's return to the Arab League and, by implication, to Egypt's preeminent role in the Arab world.

On 16 October 1989, Qaddafi visited the Egyptian city of Marsa Matruh for a meeting with the Egyptian president, and the two leaders met in Tobruk the next day. In turn, Mubarak came to Libya two months later. In March 1990, the Arab foreign ministers decided to move the Arab League headquarters back to Cairo after an eleven-year absence, thereby facilitating Qaddafi's return to the Egyptian capital. For the first time in more than a decade, Qaddafi visited Cairo on 1 June 1990. Egypt's growing political activity in the Arab Cooperation Council—the subregional group formed in 1989 that included Jordan, Iraq, and Yemen—made good relations with Mubarak even more attractive to Qaddafi.

Thus, in the mid-1990s, with the collapse of the USSR and the consequent dominance of the United States over Middle Eastern affairs, Qaddafi adopted a new pragmatic approach to his country's inter-Arab relations, determined to defuse tension even if it entailed relinquishing ideology for political interests. Once again, Qaddafi showed his talent for changing priorities and relinquishing principles in the name of political expediency.

Notes

1. For Egypt and Pan-Arabism, see Gershoni, *The Emergence of Pan-Arabism in Egypt,* and Podeh and Winckler, eds., *Rethinking Nasserism.* For the dwindling Nasserist ideology, see Shamir, ed., *The Decline of Nasserism, 1965–1970: The Waning of a Messianic Movement.*

2. See Dishon, ed., *Middle East Record 1969–70,* pp. 589–598.

3. See "Arab Unity," in Sela, *The Continuum Political Encyclopedia,* p. 162.

4. See Shaked and Ronen, "Simmering Tension."

5. See Shaked and Ronen, "Simmering Tension," p. 119. For the quoted argument, see Halliday, *Nation and Religion in the Middle East,* p. 50.

6. Pajak, "Arms and Oil," p. 51.

7. *Al-Fajr-al-Jadid,* 22 January 1974.

8. *Le Monde,* 15 February 1971, quoting Qaddafi's address to the Tunisian National Assembly three days earlier. For the quoted argument, see Halliday, *Nation and Religion in the Middle East,* p. 50.

9. See "Tunisia," *The Middle East and North Africa 1974–75,* p. 688, and Mary-Jane Deeb, "Inter-Maghribi Relations." For more details on Bourguiba's perception of the Arab-Israeli conflict, see Laskier, *Israel and the Maghrib,* pp. 192–193.

10. Legum, *Africa Contemporary Record,* 1973, pp. B43, B54–B55.

11. ARNA (Tripoli), 17 April 1975 (DR).

12. *Events* 6, 20 May 1977; Radio Riyadh, 1 November 1977 (BBC). For the Arabization policy of the Red Sea and the Ethiopian connection, see Erlich, *The Struggle over Eritrea, 1962–1978,* pp. 79–84. For background on Ethiopia, Egypt, and Sudan in the post-Nasser era, see Erlich, *Ethiopia and the Middle East,* pp. 151–164. For Ethiopia's oscillation from the Western to the Soviet orbit, see Petterson, "Ethiopia Abandoned? An American Perspective."

13. See Dishon and Ben Zvi, "Inter-Arab Relations," 1978, pp. 170–171, and 1979, pp. 243–245. For the Western Sahara dispute, see Maddy-Weitzman, "Conflict and Conflict Management"; Zoubir, "The Western Sahara Conflict: Regional and International Dimensions" and "The United Nations' Failure"; and Jensen, *Western Sahara.*

14. Radio Cairo, 22 July 1977 (BBC).

15. For a detailed analysis of the Egyptian-Libyan war, see Shamir and Segev, "Arab Republic of Egypt," and Gera, "Libya," 1978. See also Pajak, "Arms and Oil," p. 53, and a detailed discussion in Shaked and Ronen, "Simmering Tension," pp. 123–125.

16. Radio Tripoli, 18 November 1977 (BBC). See also Gera, "Libya," 1979, p. 637, and Reinich, "Arab Republic of Egypt," p. 391.

17. See his interview with *al-Anba,* 8 October 1978. For more on Camp David, see Shamir and Maddy-Weitzman, *The Camp David Summit—What Went Wrong? Americans, Israelis, and Palestinians Analyze the Future of the Boldest Attempt to Resolve the Palestinian-Israeli Conflict.*

18. JANA, 16 November 1978 (BBC).

19. For Libya's military intervention in Uganda, see chapter 7. For reports of escalating unrest, see *al-Anba* (Kuwait), 6 November 1978; *Sawt Libya* (Voice of Libya, a Paris-based organ of the Libyan expatriate opposition), May 1979; and Maghreb Arabe Presse (Morocco), 7 April 1979 (BBC).

20. Ginat, "The Soviet Union and the Syrian Ba'th Regime."

21. See, for example, *October* (Cairo), 7 January 1979; *al-Ahram,* 7 March 1979; and *al-Sharq al-Jadid* (London), 1 April 1979.

22. Dishon and Maddy-Weitzman, "Inter-Arab Affairs," p. 208.

23. Laskier, *Israel and the Maghrib,* p. 255.

24. *The Jamahiriyya Mail,* 4 July 1981.

25. JANA, 17 and 18 September, 10 October, and 17 December 1983 (DR); *The Jamahiriyya Mail,* 25 June 1983.

26. Rabinovich, "The War in Lebanon."

27. *The Jamahiriyya Mail,* 17 July 1982; Ronen, "Libya's Qadhafi and the Israeli-Palestinian Conflict," 2004, p. 89. For more details on the discord within the PLO, see Susser, "The Palestinian Liberation Organization."

28. For more on the partial thawing of tension, see *al-Majalla,* 27 June 1981, and *The Strategic Week,* 12–16 July 1981. For the text of the agreement and the motives behind it, see Radio Rabat, 20 August 1984 (BBC); Maddy-Weitzman, "Inter-Arab Relations," 1986, pp. 144–146; *The Jamahiriyya Mail,* 17 August 1985; and Henderson, "Libya and Morocco: Marriage of Necessity."

29. For more details on Arab affairs during that period, see Maddy-Weitzman, "Inter-Arab Relations," 1986, pp. 141–147, and 1987, pp. 129–132. On Libya's penalizing policy of expulsions, see *Africa Confidential,* 4 September 1985, and Middle East News Agency, 17 August 1985 (DR).

30. From interviews with Dahab in *al-Sharq al-Awsat,* 17 April 1985, and *al-Khalij,* 22 April 1985.

31. *The Jamahiriyya Mail,* 25 June 1986; Radio Tripoli, 25 July 1986 (BBC).

32. See, for example, *al-Fajr al-Jadid,* 4 and 6 December 1986.

33. For more on the meeting, see Tessler, "Moroccan-Israeli Relations," pp. 80–81. See also Laskier, *Israel and the Maghrib,* pp. 263–264.

34. See Maddy-Weitzman, "Inter-Arab Relations," 1988, p. 118.

35. For reports on the unrest, see, for example, *Africa Confidential,* 23 September 1987, and *al-Watan al-'Arabi,* 9 October 1987. The public executions of three soldiers by firing squads in Benghazi, which were shown on state television in early 1987, attested to the growing threat of the Islamists, whom Qaddafi portrayed as "the allies of Satan and the hirelings of imperialism and Zionism." Tripoli TV, 17 February 1987. For an analysis of the then-rising tide of radical Islam in Libya, see Ronen, "Qadhafi and Militant Islamism," 2002.

36. Tripoli TV, 6 September 1988 (DR).

37. Ronen, "Libya's Qadhafi and the Israeli-Palestinian Conflict," 2004, p. 89.

6

Abandoning Pan-Arabism: A Libyan Heartbreak

The collapse of Libya's sole international patron, the Soviet Union, and the consequent empowerment of the United States as the world's only superpower removed obstacles to Washington's handling of Middle East policies. The effect of this fundamental shift in international politics was evident in the aftermath of the US-led Gulf War that followed Iraq's invasion of Kuwait on 2 August 1990. The war restored the status quo in the region and strengthened the deterrent effect of the US position in the broader Middle East by early 1991. This successful US intervention in inter-Arab affairs made it clear to Qaddafi that the New World Order was to Tripoli's detriment.[1] Libya therefore adopted new tactics aimed at successfully coping with the changed balance of power in its international and regional affairs. Qaddafi feared the increasing "imperialist and hegemonious" influence of the United States in the Middle East, the possibility of another US attack on Libya, and the enhanced political status of the pro-US Saudi regime.

When the Arab League met in Cairo on 10 August 1990, it decided to dispatch a peacekeeping force to the Gulf region. Libya dissented, Algeria abstained, Mauritania expressed reservations, and Tunisia refused to attend the summit altogether. By contrast, Morocco, Egypt, Syria, and the six countries of the Gulf Cooperation Council—Saudi Arabia, Kuwait, Oman, Bahrain, Qatar, and the United Arab Emirates—agreed to deploy troops that would serve under a unified command headed by the Saudis as an international coalition force against Iraq. Libya's dissent did not indicate support of Saddam Hussein's invasion of Kuwait. Rather, Libya was responding to the situation through the prism of its animosity toward and fear of the United States and "reactionary" pro-US Saudi Arabia, which had played a central role in the summit's outcome. Qaddafi also wanted to avoid confrontation with the new militant Islamist regime in neighboring Sudan, which took power on 30 June 1989 and staunchly supported Iraq, having sent forces to fight alongside the regime in Baghdad.

Granted, at the same time, he was anxious neither to harm Libya's improving relations with Egypt nor damage his close ties with Syria.[2] Nevertheless, he was emotionally, ideologically, and politically unable to join the US-led coalition. When the war began, Qaddafi defined Libya's position: "We wish Iraq to triumph and America to be defeated. . . . That would be nice."[3] Qaddafi later stated that the war "is an imperialist mission and [an expression of] hatred against the Arabs" rather than a means to protect Kuwait's interests. Qaddafi called for an end to the war and championed "an Arab solution" to the Gulf crisis "away from any foreign interference."[4]

Yet by standing aside while one Arab state attacked another, Qaddafi had placed himself in an awkward position. He therefore resumed his prewar mediation efforts, urging the UN to forbid the anti-Iraq coalition to fight beyond the liberation of Kuwait, thus indirectly admitting the justification for freeing Kuwait from Iraqi control. He warned that his country would not "accept that Kuwait be delivered from one occupation to another"—that is, from Iraqi to US hands—and demanded that the UN Security Council supervise the Iraqi withdrawal to ensure that Kuwait was "effectively liberated."[5] Qaddafi frequently presented his country's position as one of concern with the welfare of both Iraq and Kuwait and the entire Arab nation against the "colonialist [US] military campaign in the Arab homeland."[6] In the face of the United States' military success in the Gulf and the postwar arrangements for installing peacekeeping forces, Qaddafi stated, "The Arabs must take responsibility for pan-Arab security. . . . There is no need for foreign [namely US] troops in the Gulf after the liberation of Kuwait."[7]

To maintain some measure of influence in the complex web of Arab politics, Libya mediated in the Egyptian-Sudanese dispute that erupted following the ascent to power of 'Umar Hassan Ahmad al-Bashir's militant regime in Khartoum in 1989. Bashir's strong Islamist bent worried Mubarak, who feared its effect on the Islamist opposition in Egypt, which he considered a serious threat to his rule. Qaddafi shared his fears.

In 1990 and 1991, Libya focused on the Gulf and on the Egyptian-Sudanese situation, almost completely ignoring the Maghrib. The euphoria over its establishment having largely subsided, the AMU proved an ineffective organ, paralyzed by individual state interests and bilateral divisions. The differing stances of individual AMU members toward the Gulf War, along with the eruption of political turmoil in Algeria after the victory of Algerian Islamists in the first round of municipal elections in 1990, prompted Qaddafi to break ties with the AMU and other states in the region.[8]

The Impact of UN Sanctions

By increasing its involvement in Mashriqian politics in the early 1990s, Tripoli aimed to combat the rising influence of Islamist militancy at home and in its immediate vicinity—Algeria, Sudan, and, to a lesser extent, Tunisia and Egypt. Qaddafi feared that it might spread to Libya and fuel the domestic Islamist opposition that was determined to overthrow his "heretic" regime.

In late 1991, the "sole policeman of the world,"[9] as Qaddafi sarcastically described the United States, together with Britain, accused Libya of responsibility for the explosion of a Pan Am Boeing 747 over Lockerbie, Scotland, three years earlier and demanded the extradition of the two Libyan nationals suspected in the bombing. Libya flatly rejected this demand, denying any connection to the incident. Not long after, the United States and Britain spearheaded UN sanctions on Libya, which went into effect on 15 April 1992 and were aimed at forcing Tripoli to comply with the extradition demand.[10]

The Lockerbie conflict soon dominated the state's life, adversely affecting its position on the Arab scene. Libya perceived the full compliance of "all Arab sister-states" and "brothers in Islam" with the UN-imposed sanctions as betrayal: "What sort of [Arab] nation and what sort of religion is it that prompts a brother to turn his back on his brother?" The conclusion was that "we must turn to our [Libyan] interests only. What we have given to Muslims—who have given nothing to us in our time of trial—is enough." Libya's petroleum, it was decided, should be reserved for Libya alone: "We sacrificed everything [for them], even our children's bread. . . . We exhausted our economy for their sake. [Now] the fig leaf has dropped and everything has been laid bare: The Arabs are these days reserves for the [US] Marines. . . . It would not be surprising if [the Arabs] were overcome with joy while listening to the [Security Council sanctions] resolutions. Pan-Arabism now means dollars and the Arab cause is now being sold at auction for dollars." The intensity of Qaddafi's sense of betrayal was echoed in the state media. Most typical was the statement that "we Libyans no longer trust the Arabs. The truth about the Arabs is that they were hypocritical toward us. They deceived us."[11]

The adherence of both the Mashriq and the Maghrib to UN sanctions infuriated Qaddafi not only because he viewed himself as the leader most devoted to Arab nationalist values since Nasser but also because he considered it proof of Arab disregard for Libya's diplomatic distress and domestic turmoil. The Libyan leader targeted the Arab League as the leading representative body of the Arab world, repeatedly threatening to withdraw from its ranks. These threats were alarming since no Arab state had withdrawn from the League since its establishment in 1945.

Libya's anger with AMU members prompted it to consider ending its membership in the AMU. Yet due to its need for an overland transit route as an alternative to the UN-imposed air blockade, Tripoli was careful to manage its relations with Maghribian states, particularly Tunisia. As for Egypt, though its dependence upon Cairo's mediatory efforts in Washington grew with the worsening of the Lockerbie dispute, Tripoli took concrete measures to punish

Egypt for complying with the UN sanctions. These included imposing strict controls at the border crossing of Masa'id and custom duties on Egyptian goods, as well halting remittance to Egyptian workers. In addition, Tripoli recalled its highest-ranking official in Cairo, Ahmad Qaddaf al-Damm, in the summer of 1992. Still, Libya remained cognizant of Egypt's utility with respect to overland transit routes, its connections in Washington, and its crackdown on anti-Mubarak Islamic militants. Preoccupied with his own subversive Islamist opposition, Qaddafi had a stake in the stability of the Mubarak regime and in maintaining cooperative efforts to combat Islamic militancy.

Within this context, Qaddafi was also relatively less aggressive toward the Algerian government, concerned that the Algerian Islamist tide might also intensify Islamist pressures within Libya. About 1,000 alleged Islamic radicals were jailed in Libya in late 1992. The need for regional cooperation in eradicating the Islamist danger tempered Qaddafi's resentment toward what he viewed as the Arab world's act of treason against Libya. Once again pragmatic, Qaddafi reverted to pan-Arabism, saying that "surrendering the flag of pan-Arabism is a mistake and would lead to the death of a nation. The flag of pan-Arabism must be hoisted."[12] Thus Qaddafi clearly projected himself as "the last of the Mohicans" with respect to pan-Arabism.[13]

The sanctions were renewed periodically due to Qaddafi's refusal to meet UN demands. In spite of his pan-Arab posture, the "treacherous" Arab world fully complied with the sanctions. The only state that hosted Qaddafi during the first shocking year of isolation under the UN sanctions was Egypt (from 18 to 23 January 1993). Mubarak's subsequent visit to Tripoli from 17 to 19 August 1993, was a politically valuable gesture—more so than those of other African heads of state with less status in the international community, including Tunisian president Zayn al-'Abidin bin 'Ali, who visited on 1 and 2 April 1993. The depiction in an Arab periodical of Egypt as Libya's *manfadh* (gateway) to the world was indeed apt.[14] Though Egypt was unsuccessful in its attempt to fashion a compromise between Libya and the West, Qaddafi, during a visit to Sidi Barrani in Egypt's Marsa Matruh region on 4 November 1993, praised Mubarak personally for playing a most important "pan-Arab role."[15] The Libyan leader was among the first heads of state to congratulate Mubarak upon his reelection to a third presidential term.

On 10 December 1993, veteran Libyan opposition leader Mansur Rashid al-Kikhya disappeared from his hotel room in Cairo. Kikhya headed the Egyptian-based Front for the Liberation of Libya, one of the expatriate groups determined to overthrow the Qaddafi regime. Political circles in Egypt, especially those close to Kikhya, held the Qaddafi regime responsible for his disappearance and alleged transfer to Libya. Although there was no proof, circumstantial evidence pointed to possible Libyan involvement. Since the Egyptians had guaranteed the safety of Kikhya as a trustee of the Arab Human

Rights Organization, which convened in Cairo at the end of 1993, his disappearance seriously damaged Cairo's relations with Tripoli. Egyptian uneasiness increased in the face of international interest in the affair, including that of the United States.

Another source of friction between Cairo and Tripoli was the hostile stance of Jallud, Qaddafi's second in command, toward Egypt and the United States. Jallud's scathing anti-US rhetoric irritated Cairo and hampered its efforts to defuse tensions between Tripoli and Washington. Moreover, while touring Iran, Algeria, Pakistan, and Turkey in 1992, Jallud had denounced Egypt as "defeatist" for signing the peace agreement with Israel. The Egyptians responded by calling Jallud "reckless" and saying that Qaddafi "should have gotten rid of Jallud a long time ago." An Egyptian editorial addressed Jallud, stating, "Be assured that had it not been for our esteem for the colonel [Qaddafi], we would have settled our account with you very roughly."[16]

After a two-month period of crisis, Libya took steps to remove at least the Kikhya problem from the bilateral agenda, issuing a series of statements reiterating its innocence in the affair, which was portrayed as "a conspiracy aimed against Egyptian-Libyan relations" that "would lead to the closure of the border between the two countries with a view to suffocating Libya and intensifying the embargo on it." Later Tripoli explicitly accused the "US intelligence and its Libyan [expatriate opposition] agents" of Kikhya's abduction.[17]

Seeking an outlet for his grievances against the Arab world in its compliance with the UN sanctions, Qaddafi channeled them toward the "impotence" of the Arab League. Once again, he threatened to leave the Arab League, which would "enable the Arabs to welcome their brother, Israel," instead.[18] By threatening to leave the League—a move that would primarily hurt Egypt, its traditional head—Qaddafi hoped to rally Arab leaders under Mubarak's leadership to help alleviate or end the boycott. Indeed, not long afterwards, Cairo and the Arab League's top echelon led a lobbying campaign. To some extent, Qaddafi's success in reactivating the League enhanced his image at home as a proud nationalist leader who bowed neither to the West nor to "submissive" Arab policies. This was effective both for releasing Libyan domestic pressure and for drawing Arab attention.

Hoping to encourage Mubarak further, Qaddafi contributed to the offensive against Islamic radicals in Egypt, which had positive implications for the comparable struggle in his own territory. On 11 January 1994, Libya handed over three suspected Egyptian Islamic militants to Cairo and permitted Egypt to search all Libyan cars crossing the border into Egypt, including those with diplomatic license plates. Then again, Qaddafi also announced his intention to reduce the number of Egyptian foreign workers in light of Libya's limited finances, a result of UN sanctions. Although Tripoli emphasized that the reduction did not aim "to touch Egyptian workers in particular,"[19] Cairo was justifiably alarmed, as Libya was a major market for Egyptian labor. Moreover, Egypt still remembered the massive expulsion of its workers from Libya in the mid-1980s. Although that expulsion had largely been justified by severe economic hardship due to the sharp decline in oil prices on the world market, Qaddafi politicized the expulsion by specifically removing workers from countries with which he was on bad terms. Wishing to appease Qaddafi through a gesture of friendship, Mubarak arrived in Libya on 26 June 1994, still the only important head of state willing to visit Libya under sanctions.

Qaddafi reciprocated by trying to mediate in Cairo's bitter feud with Khartoum over sovereignty of the Hala'ib border on the Red Sea coast, thus preserving Libya's role in trilateral relations despite its regional and international isolation. The Hala'ib dispute was not the source of the antagonism between Egypt and Sudan but rather a symptom of the their conflict of interests and mutual fears of subversion. Sudan was concerned by Egypt's rejection of its Islamist regime and consequent support of the Sudanese opposition, organized under the effective umbrella of the National Democratic Alliance. Egypt was alarmed in turn by what it viewed as Sudan's support of radical Egyptian Islamic movements. The Hala'ib dispute escalated throughout 1994 as Egypt and Sudan concentrated troops along their border while trading verbal attacks, acts of civilian harassment, and punitive diplomatic actions.

Qaddafi viewed the Sudanese regime of President Bashir and his right-hand man, militant Islamic ideologue and political hard-liner, and, in fact, the power behind Bashir's "throne," Hassan 'Abdallah al-Turabi as a liability to Libya's political and economic interests. Sudan's becoming a political burden for Libya also stemmed from the West's perception of the Khartoum regime as a patron of international terrorism. This was indicated in the early 1990s by Sudan's adopting a radical ideology; hosting Illich Ramirez Sanchez, better known as "Carlos the Jackal," one of the world's most notorious terrorists; and providing shelter to former Saudi financier Osama bin Laden, who later became head of al-Qaida. These activities made friendship with Sudan extremely damaging for Libya, especially in light of the US determination to eradicate international terrorism. Tension over the June 1995 assassination attempt on Mubarak in Addis Ababa exacerbated Egypt's conflict with Sudan, which was blamed for the attack. Since Egypt was Libya's sole international ally at this time, Qaddafi could not afford to be seen as friendly toward Khartoum. Egypt, for its part, viewed its backing of Libya as a means of weakening Sudan's position in the nations' triangular relationship.

Still, Qaddafi found it difficult to ignore the Sudanese regime entirely given their common enemy, the United States. The 1993 appearance of Sudan on the US blacklist of terrorist states, which had long included Libya, increased their common interests. Libya hosted first Turabi, a visible symbol of

Islamism, and then Bashir himself: At the twenty-fifth anniversary celebration of Qaddafi's revolution in September 1994, the president was among the few heads of state (mostly from Africa) to participate in the event and was all the more prominent in Mubarak's absence. The visit proved the success of Qaddafi's diplomatic maneuvers in the complicated web of Libyan-Egyptian-Sudanese relationships. Nevertheless, concerned with irritating neither the Mubarak government nor the US administration as well as with the Islamist threat, Libya restricted its ties with Sudan mainly to formal mediation in Sudan's regional disputes with Egypt and Uganda. This was enough to maintain the facade of friendship, as signified by Bashir's attendance at Qaddafi's twenty-sixth anniversary celebrations in Tripoli on 1 September 1995, when the Sudanese "guest of honor" described Libya as no less than the "beating pulse of the Arab nation."[20]

Libya concurrently intensified its efforts to preserve political ties with Egypt, mainly because of its role in stimulating the Libyan economy. Libya's ability to import essential goods through Egyptian territory—notably food and spare parts for the crippled oil industry—as well as to export hydrocarbon products and steel from the Misurata industrial complex, was crucial. No less vital to the survival of Qaddafi's regime was Egypt's efficacy as a buffer against the further expansion of radical Islam across the region.

However, these interests did not entirely preclude political tension between Tripoli and Cairo. Opposition stemmed from their conflicting positions toward the West and the Middle East peace process—and more specifically toward Cairo's role in incorporating Israel into the economic activity of the region, exemplified by the attendance, over Libya's objections, of Prime Minister Yitzhak Rabin and Foreign Minister Shimon Peres at the Middle East and North Africa Economic Conference held in Casablanca from 30 October to 1 November 1994 under US sponsorship. Similar tensions arose with Morocco and Tunisia, when, prior to the Casablanca conference, both announced their decision to establish diplomatic relations with Israel at the level of interest offices. Qaddafi, who rejected Israel's right to exist, certainly objected to the political rapprochement between Israel and Oman as well as to the 1994 peace agreement between Israel and Jordan, known formally as the Treaty of Peace between the State of Israel and the Hashemite Kingdom of Jordan. These Arab overtures toward Israel highlighted what Qaddafi perceived as a paradoxical process, wherein Israel was advancing to the center of the Arab world while Libya was being relegated to its margins.

Not forgetting Tunisia's valuable position as one of Libya's only two gateways to the outside world, Tripoli refrained from endangering its ties with Tunis. Therefore, during the mass expulsion of Arab and African workers in the fall of 1994, the large Tunisian community working in Libya legally and illegally remained untouched. This episode contrasted with the massive expulsion of Tunisians a decade earlier, when Tripoli was not in any need of Tunisian goodwill. Libya was also cautious in its relations with Algeria, sharing with its war-plagued government the priority of combating Islamic extremism, which threatened the rulers of both Algiers and Tripoli. Qaddafi met with Algerian president Liamine Zeroual in Algiers on 19 and 20 April 1995, declaring that "Algeria is the fortress on which we rely in the Arab Maghrib."[21]

Despite his care not to aggravate relations with the major Maghribian countries, Qaddafi withdrew Libya's recognition of Mauritania "as an Arab country" following its establishment of diplomatic ties with Israel in 1995, recalling the Libyan ambassador from Nouakchott, cutting off all economic assistance, and expelling Mauritanian workers. Mauritania, marginal in the region as well as to Libya's interests, thus became a scapegoat for Tripoli's anger over Arab relations with Israel. Tripoli also dismissed the AMU, angry at its "failure" to achieve "real unity" against the "colonialist Western states"—in other words to influence the United States and Britain to lift, or at least mitigate, the UN sanctions.[22]

When, in 1996, Washington accused Libya of building a huge underground chemical-weapons plant, Qaddafi again turned to Egypt, still his sole Arab partner in warding off both US and Islamist perils. Qaddafi's talks with Mubarak first at Sidi Barrani on the Egyptian border on 18 January 1996 and then in Cairo from 24 to 29 May, touched on both threats. Though Qaddafi characterized the international conference to combat terrorism that Egypt hosted at Sharm al-Shaykh in March 1996 and that included Israel as dangerous to the Arab nation, he did not let it eclipse his relations with Mubarak. This policy proved worthwhile as Mubarak came to Libya's defense in the face of the US campaign, maintaining that Washington had no concrete evidence for its accusation and thus implicitly reinforcing Libya's claim that it was the innocent victim of a political witchhunt. Ultimately, Egypt's backing was instrumental in eliminating the chemical-weapons issue from the US-Libyan agenda, and Qaddafi publicly praised Mubarak for "heroically standing up to the unjust US imperialist stance against Libya."[23] Qaddafi visited Egypt from 24 to 29 May 1996 and again the following month for the Arab League summit, daring to defy the UN embargo and travel to Cairo, counting on Mubarak's support and his connections in Washington. Not surprisingly, Qaddafi did not repeat earlier threats to pull Libya out of the League.

In May 1996, with US backing, the UN imposed sanctions on Sudan aimed at forcing it to extradite to Ethiopia the three Egyptian nationals who were allegedly responsible for the attempt on Mubarak's life in Addis Ababa in June 1995. Concurrently, ties between Libya and Egypt continued to be important for both states. On the Egyptian side of the equation, the interest was mainly in mobilizing Libya in the fight against radical Islam in the region and in cementing an anti-Sudanese position. To fortify this bilateral front,

Mubarak visited Tripoli on 2 and 3 December 1996 and Tobruk on 12 and 13 June 1997, thus solidifying Egypt's image as a central pillar of the Arab world and as a credible mediator in regional and international conflicts.

Concerned with deteriorating domestic conditions due to the fourth year of UN sanctions in 1996, Qaddafi also tried to improve the position of his country on the Maghribian scene. He declared his willingness to assume the rotating post of president of the AMU, a post he had been scheduled to fill a year earlier but had refused in protest of the organization's failure to support Libya's struggle against the UN sanctions. He also visited Tunisia, arriving by land on 28 October 1996, having postponed a visit the previous August after the government had refused to allow him to enter by air in defiance of the UN embargo. Although circumstances had not changed, Qaddafi's tactics had, as he reverted to the slogan of Arab unity.

In an effort to mobilize Egypt and Tunisia to counter US hostility toward Tripoli, the Libyan head of state clarified that "unlike the military or political arena, the economy [is] one area where the Arabs could successfully confront the West and persuade the US to lift the sanctions."[24] Qaddafi organized a widely publicized "massive unity march from all over the Great Jamahiriyya headed to sisterly Tunisia" on 1 November 1997, similar to the massive Libyan unity march to Egypt in the early 1970s. Arriving at the border, the Tunisians met the Libyans in "a beautiful scene of unity . . . during which chants for Arab unity overwhelmed the area." Qaddafi emphasized that "total Arab unity is the only means to guarantee Arab power [that] enables [the Arab nation] to enter the next century, where there is no place for pygmy entities."[25] Though aware it lacked any practical significance, Qaddafi continued to wave the flag of Arab unity. Indicative of Qaddafi's efforts to promote Maghribian unity was his move to restore diplomatic relations with Mauritania on 12 March 1997 in the expectation that it would add its voice to those of the other AMU states calling on the United States to lift the sanctions.

At the Arab League meeting in Cairo in the fall of 1998, the countries of the Maghrib and the Mashriq failed to press for the removal of the UN sanctions. Insulted once again by his "Arab brothers" who, unlike the OAU, did not call for noncompliance with the air embargo, Qaddafi appeared more determined than before to leave the Arab League. At that juncture, the cumulative threats were exacerbated by an alleged assassination attempt on Qaddafi by the Islamist opposition on the night of 31 May 1998 near Sidi Khalifa, east of Benghazi, an area known as a stronghold of armed Islamist groups.[26]

As Qaddafi's expectations of the Arab world entirely dissipated, he turned the focus of his foreign policy to Africa, gaining there what his "Arab brothers" had failed to provide him and saying, "I have been raising slogans of Arab unity and brandishing the standard of Arab nationalism for forty years, but it was not realized. That means I was talking in the desert. . . . I have no more time to lose talking with Arabs . . . I now talk about pan-Africanism and African Unity." By way of demonstration, he redefined Libya's mission to the Arab League in Cairo as resident rather than permanent and abolished the pan-Arab affairs ministry, officially called the General People's Committee, from his cabinet.

Furthermore, Qaddafi announced with considerable fanfare his decision to desert *al-'Aruba* (Arabism) in favor of *al-Zanuja* (Negroism, also known as Africanism). "Arabism has turned into a farce, descended into chaos, and brought only humiliation under the Israeli and US occupation," stated Libyan foreign minister Mustafa al-Muntasir.[27] Libya repeatedly pointed to the impotence of the Arab world in the 1990s, which held only two Arab summits throughout the decade—in 1990 and 1996, respectively—and thus failed to effectively tackle what Libya regarded as burning issues on the Arab agenda, such as the Iraqi invasion of Kuwait and the ascent to power of Benjamin Netanyahu's right-wing government in Israel.

Qaddafi visited Cairo between 5 and 13 March 1999, in order to mobilize maximal political support among the Egyptian political elite for the imminent extradition of the Lockerbie suspects. He sought legitimacy from the Egyptian government that would also serve as a safety net should the extradition move prove to be a miscalculation. Qaddafi further hoped to diminish political difficulties with the expatriate community and lessen opposition to his regime. He received a warm welcome from "many resident Libyans" while en route to Cairo in a cavalcade of some 200 vehicles, which was described by an Egyptian weekly as resembling "a British royal trip to America more than it did a typical Arab revolutionary on a state visit, [especially one from] an isolated country." Mubarak, beginning an election campaign for a fourth term, was a cordial host, embracing Qaddafi politically and presenting him with a welcome gift—the containment of Islamist violence, which had cast a shadow over Egypt since 1992, claiming over 1,200 fatalities by 1999.[28] Mubarak showed Qaddafi that the Islamist peril could be contained.

Libya's Arab Policies in the Postsanctions Period

The extradition of the Libyan suspects to the Netherlands in spring 1999 to stand trial for the Lockerbie bombing, achieved through Saudi and South African mediation, represented a breakthrough in Libya's foreign policy as well as its domestic affairs. The subsequent suspension of the UN embargo endowed Libya with growing diplomatic legitimacy and made it attractive to foreign investors. In these circumstances, Qaddafi's Arab neighbors also increased their interest in Libya. This interest was reflected in visits to Tripoli by Sudan's President Bashir in April, September, and December 1999 and

Qaddafi's visit to Khartoum in June 1999, as well as in the meetings among the Libyan, Sudanese, and Egyptian heads of state in Khartoum and Cairo in January and April 2000. Additional high-level contact included visits to Tripoli by Bashir in June 2000 and by Mubarak in July 2000. King 'Abdallah bin Hussein of Jordan visited Tripoli on 1 and 2 September 2000 as the guest of honor at the 1 September celebration of Qaddafi's advent to power. Tunisian president Zayn al-'Abidin bin 'Ali visited Tripoli on 3 and 4 June 2000, reciprocated by Qaddafi's visit to Tunis from 2 to 4 August 2000. He also toured Egypt, Jordan, Syria, Saudi Arabia, and Sudan from 11 to 14 October 2000. The visit of Algerian president 'Abd al-'Aziz Bouteflika to Tripoli on 22 October 2000 can also be viewed in the context of renewed Libyan participation in Arab affairs. This stream of top-level exchanges, not seen in Libya for almost a decade, attested to Qaddafi's interest in rehabilitating his domestic and foreign political prestige in the postsanction era as well as to the desire of Arab states to benefit from Libya's return to the international fold and to presumed economic prosperity.

In this new atmosphere, Qaddafi initiated a process of rapprochement with Sudan, from which he had remained relatively aloof during the 1990s due to his perception of its militant Islamic regime as a security threat and an alliance with such a state as a liability. By 2000, however, the Sudanese leadership had publicly softened its Islamist profile. Bashir removed Turabi, the Islamist hard-liner, from power and restored diplomatic relations with Egypt and Libya, which jointly mediated to find a solution to Sudan's civil strife. The war between the Khartoum government and the rebels in southern Sudan, which had raged for almost two decades since its rekindling in 1983, had devastated Sudan and caused instability in the region. The bilateral negotiation for peace produced no direct results. However, it strengthened relations between the three countries, which in turn buffered Sudan from the threat to its political stability and territorial integrity posed by separatists in the southern rebel movement. Qaddafi was concerned that if the rebels, who had close ties with the United States, achieved an independent state, it would become a launching pad for US policies in the region and might also pose difficulties for Mubarak's regime. Cairo, for its part, feared that an independent Sudanese state might construct dams to reduce the flow of the Nile into Egypt. While it had an agreement with Sudan regarding the allocation of Nile water, the establishment of a new state in the south would require a second agreement—one potentially far less suitable to Egypt's needs.

Qaddafi also embarked on mediation to settle the dispute between Sudan and Eritrea, which first erupted in 1995 as Sudan supported antigovernment Islamic groups in Eritrea and Eritrea supported the opposition in Sudan. These separate peacemaking maneuvers, typical of Qaddafi's overtures toward African governments at the beginning of the 2000s, proved an effective platform for Libya's Arab policy as well.

Following a short period of dynamism on the Arab scene, Qaddafi diverted most of his energies to the West, where Tripoli was being courted economically and diplomatically. He had a lot to gain from this move, especially since the Lockerbie trial was still in process. Besides, his success in suppressing the activities of the Islamist opposition after more than a decade of real threat to his regime had largely reduced the urgency of his need to cooperate with Libya's Arab neighbors and hence the level of his interest therein.

Therefore, Qaddafi did not attend the emergency Arab Summit Conference held on Egypt's initiative in Cairo in October 2000 to deal with the new eruption of violence in the Israeli-Palestinian conflict, known as the al-Aqsa intifada, that had broken out in September. At this point, with the Lockerbie verdict still pending, Qaddafi's foreign-policy priorities involved Libya's international standing. Besides, Qaddafi—a seasoned veteran of Middle East politics—presumably did not expect any significant decisions, either practical or ideological, to come out of the forum. Moreover, with Arab apathy toward Libya's plight during the Lockerbie saga still fresh in his mind, Qaddafi preferred to remain aloof from the League, which, he felt, had betrayed him.

As the intifada gained momentum in the West Bank and Gaza, Qaddafi amplified his anti-Israel rhetoric and gestures of sympathy for the Palestinians. He increasingly demonized Israel, presenting it as a reckless imperialist aggressor and the source of all evil, one that aspired to annihilate the Arab world. He warned that Israel could take over Syria, Lebanon, and even Iraq and might also "extend its borders from the Nile or from the Suez Canal . . . and Judaize North Africa." Qaddafi also alleged that the United States and Israel were jointly plotting to take control over oil supplies in the Gulf, exploiting the weakness of the Arab world. The United States, he claimed, "would help and support [the Israelis] to occupy the Gulf. At the end [the United States] would prefer the oil to be in the hands of the Israelis rather than the Arabs because the latter are moody . . . [and] unpredictable. . . . Therefore, the Israeli borders might extend from Iran to the Atlantic and to the Turkish border." Detailing further his apocalyptic vision, he warned, "the Israelis claim that Mecca was built by Abraham. Therefore, Mecca is theirs and Medina is also theirs. They like to make inane biblical claims such as this." Qaddafi sought to settle political scores both with the United States and with what he repeatedly portrayed as the "treacherous" Arab world. He positioned them together with "malicious" Israel to highlight Libya's place on the side of the Palestinians.[29]

However, under the shadow of the Palestinian uprising, the Arab world was more amenable than before to Tripoli's militant stance. Egypt recalled its ambassador from Israel for consultations; Tunisia, Morocco, and Qatar severed their official ties with Israel; and Jordan announced that its newly appointed ambassador, who had not yet taken up his post, would remain at home indefinitely.

In late March 2001, Qaddafi attended the thirteenth Arab League summit, which convened in Amman, Jordan. He was probably convinced to come by King 'Abdallah of Jordan during his official visit to Tripoli on 11 February 2001. In Amman, Qaddafi "detonated a bombshell," as an Arab publication wrote, stating that the Jewish state should be allowed to join the Arab League as a full member on condition that it meet several prerequisites, above all the establishment of an independent Palestinian state with Jerusalem as its capital, the return of the Palestinian refugees, and nuclear disarmament. This statement, not at all typical of Qaddafi, should primarily be viewed against the backdrop of his disillusionment with Arab solidarity. However, it can also be viewed in light of Qaddafi's renewed efforts to placate the West, particularly the United States, in the aftermath of the Lockerbie trial. He therefore used the media spotlight in Amman to project the image not of a fanatic advocate of Pan-Arabism but rather of a responsible leader prepared to conduct his country's affairs pragmatically. During the summit, he proposed a solution to the Palestinian problem similar to "the one in South Africa," and called on Arafat "to be the Mandela of the Palestinians."[30]

Aware that rhetoric and humanitarian aid alone would not enable the Palestinians to "resist the Israeli occupation," Qaddafi said that what was really needed was "the opening of Arab borders to Arab resistance."[31] However, the discrepancy between Qaddafi's militant ideology and his noninterventionist policy indicated the degree of his adherence to realpolitik. Considering the adverse implications for Libyan interests inherent in any active involvement in the Israeli-Palestinian conflict, Qaddafi prioritized political expediency over ideology.

During the early 2000s, Libya's interest in Arab affairs further diminished. Its successful diplomacy in Africa, with the promotion of Qaddafi's notion of a United States of Africa as its centerpiece, underscored the failure of other Arab states to provide similar dividends even as Egypt's domination over the Arab League diminished Libyan influence. Therefore, Tripoli concentrated its foreign-policy resources on promoting its respectability and economic attractiveness to the international community, particularly the United States. This was of pressing concern because the UN-imposed sanctions were, at least formally, still valid, and because Libya urgently needed to improve its domestic conditions.

Early 2002 witnessed intensive inter-Arab diplomatic activity aimed at smoothing the way to the Arab League's summit in Beirut, scheduled for 27 and 28 March. The Lebanese Shi'ite community opposed Qaddafi's arrival in Beirut on the grounds that he was holding its spiritual leader, Imam Musa al-Sadr, captive. The prominent Iranian-born Lebanese imam had disappeared in

1978 under mysterious circumstances during a visit to Libya and had not been seen since. Shi'ite groups held Qaddafi responsible for Sadr's disappearance but Tripoli repeatedly denied it, claiming that Sadr had left Libya for Italy, disappearing only after his departure, and that the Lebanese organization Shi'i Amal was responsible for his disappearance in any case.[32] The affair adversely affected Libya's relations with both Lebanon and Iran.

In response, meanwhile, Qaddafi threatened to pull Libya out of the "joke that has become the Arab League." Only an intense round of diplomacy headed by Egypt convinced him to remain. However, he did not attend the summit, sending a top-level official to represent the country in his stead. Formally, he explained his absence as a protest against the League's failure to implement the decisions of the 2001 Amman summit, where he had presented his plan to solve the Arab-Israeli conflict and establish one state for the Palestinians and Israelis.[33] Qaddafi argued that "the region [that] lies between the Jordan River and the Mediterranean Sea is too small to accommodate two states. . . . It is like trying to put two bodies into one item of clothing, or two men trying to wear the same pair of trousers. This is impossible." He concluded: "If the Palestinian state is declared, I will not recognize . . . either [of the states] because they are false." On another occasion, he argued that only a Palestinian state that stretched from the Jordan River to the Mediterranean Sea could be recognized by Libya.[34]

On 24 October 2002, Qaddafi officially announced that he was pulling Libya out of the Arab League, citing the organization's inefficiency in dealing with fundamental Arab issues, particularly the Iraqi and the Palestinian crises. This decision prompted Mubarak to visit Qaddafi several days later. Soon afterwards, the Libyans suspended their threat to withdraw and continued to attend the League's forums, though the tension remained.

These tensions came to a head at the Arab League summit at Sharm al-Shaykh in March 2003, which was devoted to a discussion of the Arab position on the imminent US war in Iraq. Mubarak's visit to Tripoli in mid-January 2003 convinced the Libyan leader to attend the summit, during which Qaddafi repeated his call to Arab countries to find their own solutions to regional crises, particularly the crisis in Iraq. He criticized Crown Prince 'Abdallah bin 'Abd al-'Aziz al-Sa'ud for the Saudi kingdom's "pact with the American devil." The Saudi Prince responded by calling Qaddafi a liar who should not speak on subjects he knew nothing about, accused Libya of being an agent of imperialism, and concluded, "The grave is in front of you."[35] This exchange was caught live by the media, aggravating Qaddafi's long-held grudge against the Saudis.

This outburst of animosity toward the ruling royal family in Riyadh had erupted a year earlier during the Arab League Summit in Beirut when Libya rejected recognition of Israel and thus, effectively, the Saudi peace initiative based on the principle of "land for peace." Saudi Arabia was also one of the main supporters of US policy in the Middle East and cooperated closely with Washington on a broad range of issues, while Libya, despite strenuous efforts, had failed to end its conflict with the United States. The Libyan-Saudi hostility was an exception in Libya's inter-Arab affairs in this period, since its policy was generally to maintain conciliatory, albeit low-key, relations with other Arab countries, particularly as the Lockerbie affair had not yet been settled. Likewise, Libya took extreme care not to antagonize the United States, keeping condemnation of the war in Iraq to a minimum.[36]

Libya's foreign-policy priorities—the normalization of relations with the United States foremost among them—were manifested on 19 December 2003 when it made a dramatic renunciation of its weapons of mass destruction. This move triggered criticism from various Arab countries, including Egypt. Saif al-Islam, Qaddafi's son and an influential political figure in his own right, fended off this criticism, stating that Libya's renunciation of WMD was caused by, among other things, the misconduct of the Arabs themselves. "Libya sought modern weapons in order to strengthen the Arab world against the West," he argued, but since the Arabs "are constantly conspiring against each other, Libya no longer wants to bear such costs."[37]

Clearly, however, Libya's renunciation of WMD was not connected to its inter-Arab relationships but rather to its efforts to improve relations with the United States. Bearing in mind both the crushing US defeat of Iraq in 2003 and the Arab world's total lack of response, Libya stepped up its efforts to resolve the conflict with Washington. By mid-2004, Libya had made significant advances toward rehabilitating its image in the United States, without any help from the Arab world.

No longer needing Cairo's immediate diplomatic assistance in Washington, Qaddafi repeated his threat to withdraw from the Arab League. Since the country most vulnerable to the threat was Egypt, intensive diplomatic activity soon ensued between Cairo and Tripoli, with the former endeavoring to convince Qaddafi to stay in what Egypt and other Arab players termed "the House of Arabs."[38] The renewed threat reflected not only Qaddafi's wish to protest what he regarded as the League's incompetence and betrayal but also Libya's rising tension with Egypt. This tension came to a head in January 2004 as a result of Libya's displeasure regarding criticism it had received in the Egyptian press after its renunciation of WMD. Libya imposed travel restrictions on Egyptians, and Egypt retaliated with its own set of restrictions. Meanwhile, the Libyan embassy in Cairo allegedly filed a complaint in the Egyptian courts against fifteen Egyptian journalists from both independent and opposition newspapers over the aforementioned reports. But the matter was soon forgotten as neither Libya nor Egypt had any interest in fueling a bilateral crisis. Libya's foreign ministry released a statement in late January 2004 to the effect that there was no basis for a feud between Libya and Egypt, adding that "some people who want to inject tension in these good relations are behind the current media clamor." Tripoli also emphasized that "Libya has Arab blood, people, and history. We have not changed our Arab identity"; therefore, "Libya's borders are open to all the Arabs."[39]

Mubarak's visit to Libya in February 2004 reflected the shift in power dynamics, as Egypt was now the party more eager to defuse bilateral animosity. Qaddafi rewarded Mubarak's gesture by withdrawing his application to host the African Union's new parliament, an honor Egypt wanted for itself (along with South Africa, now its main competition).[40] There were no further breakthroughs in Libya's relations with Egypt, mainly due to Libya's dwindling interest. Even Qaddafi's visit to Cairo on 11 July 2004 was characterized as a mere gesture of courtesy following Mubarak's recovery from back surgery.

After the opening session of the Arab summit in Tunis on 22 May 2004, Qaddafi held a press conference:

> I regret that Libya has been forced to boycott the [earlier] sessions of the summit. The reason is a lack of agreement on the agenda. There is an agenda that is submitted by the Arab peoples and there is an agenda for the Arab governments. The agenda of the peoples is not here, and what we find in front of us is the official agenda of the governments. Libya is a people and not a government. Libya is a state of the masses. It is not a kingdom or a republic, Libya is a jamahiriyya. So it sides with the peoples, not [with] the governments . . . in these dangerous circumstances. There is a lack of integrity on the part of the secretariat of the Arab League, because we proposed a Libyan draft on establishing an Arab union. I believe that it has been proposed by other Arab countries . . . , but the clause on establishing an Arab union was removed from the agenda of the summit and I believe that the secretariat of the Arab League was responsible for that, unless the secretariat of the League conspired with other parties to remove it.
>
> The second thing that is not on the agenda is the proposal that I put forward at the summit in Amman on the Palestinian issue, which I then put down in the White Book, which I have presented to the world. The summit decided in Amman to form a committee of foreign ministers of seven Arab states under the chairmanship of the secretary of the Arab League to work with the proposal. Yet the proposal remained shelved. The lack of respect for summit resolutions is a travesty and a farce by the secretary of the Arab League.[41]

On the same occasion, Qaddafi went on to protest the Arab League's failure to discuss the fate of "two Arab presidents who were being detained by their enemies," Saddam Hussein and Yasser Arafat. Seemingly recalling the difficult days of the 1990s when the Arab League avoided any public support of his leadership, he elaborated, "It means no member of the summit can rely on his brothers to save him." Qaddafi also referred to Syria's right "to liberate its land by force" if Israel did not unconditionally withdraw from the Golan Heights. In the same breath, he repeated his rejection of the principle of "land for peace" as a means of solving the Arab-Israeli conflict.[42]

The Libyan leader was so preoccupied with his one-state solution for the Israel-Palestinian conflict—which he called Isratin—and with his attempt to shape the summit's agenda that he ignored the fact that for the first time in about a decade and a half, all five members of the AMU, Libya included, were attending an Arab League forum. Qaddafi believed that the Maghribian organization should join the African Union rather than be connected to the Middle East. He was also troubled by a French plan, announced in mid-2004, to strengthen the collaboration of several European countries with Morocco, Tunisia, and Algeria, ignoring Libya altogether. Mauritania's accusation a short while later that Libya had backed a failed coup in Nouakchott, although denied by Tripoli, served to underscore Libya's problematic standing in the Maghrib.[43]

At the end of 2004, the strain on relations between Libya and Saudi Arabia was further aggravated. Saudi Arabia expelled the Libyan ambassador from Riyadh and withdrew its own diplomatic envoy from Tripoli, accusing Qaddafi of a plot to assassinate Crown Prince 'Abdallah bin 'Abd al-'Aziz Sa'ud and other prominent members of the Saudi government. Libya appealed to the Arab League to investigate "this strange matter," so that Saudi Arabia "would disclose the [real] reasons that prompted [it] to recall [its] ambassador."[44] There was a measure of irony in this appeal, given that Libya had repeatedly snubbed and threatened to withdraw from the "impotent" League.

The alleged conspiracy was first exposed in summer 2004. Libya denied any role, emphasizing its "sheer surprise" at the "fabricated accusations," implying they were an attempt by the Saudis to distract attention from the growing political violence within the kingdom by ascribing the security problems to outside agents rather than domestic Saudi groups. The alleged Libyan plot was first described by US investigators in their case against a prominent Muslim American activist, 'Abd al-Rahman al-'Amudi, who was found guilty in July 2004 of business dealings with Libya at a time when the country was still subject to sanctions. 'Amudi allegedly served as an intermediary between Saudi dissidents and the Libyan government, which was suspected of providing the plotters with "hundreds of thousands of dollars." The alleged plot unfolded against a backdrop of tension in Libyan-Saudi relations that stemmed from sharply conflicting ideologies and interests, particularly with respect to Saudi Arabia's political and military cooperation with the United States. Libya made no attempt to conceal its animosity toward the ruling royal family in Riyadh, but any motives it would have had for plotting against 'Abdallah, just when it was making strenuous efforts to rid itself of the label of terrorist sponsor, are unclear. The crisis was particularly embarrassing for Qaddafi, eclipsing his otherwise successful bid to gain worldwide diplomatic respectability and shed his image as a chronic enfant terrible. Libya was once again accused of political terrorism by a state intimately linked to the United States—just as Libya was improving its ties to the superpower in mid-2004, but before it had managed to overcome all obstacles to a normal relationship.

In March 2005, the Arab summit met in Algiers, commemorating the League's sixtieth anniversary. It was attended by only thirteen of twenty-two Arab heads of state, however, including Qaddafi but not Mubarak. The forum did not discuss the Libyan-Saudi dispute that had overshadowed previous summits. The Algerian host attempted to steer away from controversy, particularly regarding normalization in the Arab-Israeli peace process. Qaddafi clarified his position toward the Arab-Israeli conflict by stating that "the so-called state of Israel . . . is definitely an illegal state. [But] that land has two owners. Unilaterally declaring a state [solely for either] of the two owners is illegal. According to international law, that is illegal and cannot be recognized. Personally, and as long as I am alive, I will never recognize either an Israeli state or a Palestinian one." He reiterated his idea for a single state: "The sole possible solution" to the conflict was "to establish one democratic state for both the Palestinians and the Jews . . . a state lying between the [Jordan] river and the [Mediterranean] sea . . . called Isratin."[45]

In summer 2005, Saif al-Islam stated further that Libya's "state of war with Israel is practically over. . . . We participated in the war when Egypt fought [against Israel] and when the Palestinian factions fought [against it]. But if the Palestinians are negotiating today and sitting at the same table as the Israelis, Egypt, Jordan, and all the Arab countries who are having direct ties and negotiations with Israel and they have embassies [there]—the story is over."[46] This message might well be viewed in the context of Israel's implementation of the plan to disengage from the Gaza Strip, which was rewarded by a measure of Arab and Muslim sympathy for Israel, at least in this immediate phase.

On 29 and 30 March 2006, the Arab League held its annual summit in Khartoum. Fewer than ten of the twenty-two Arab heads of state attended. The war-plagued venue probably reinforced the forum's lack of political appeal. Mubarak visited Tripoli on 5 March to persuade Qaddafi to attend; he agreed but did not contribute to the discussions, protesting the dismissal of his proposals at earlier Arab summits. Mubarak himself did not attend. Cut short by a day in the absence of any substantive discussions, the summit extended the term of the League's secretary-general, Egyptian 'Amru Musa, for five more years and dealt mainly with the situation in Iraq, the Palestinian agenda in the aftermath of the Hamas election victory, and the decline of Syrian-Lebanese relations. After the summit, Musa said, "I was anguished by the vast potential that the Arab world possesses and the obstacles and challenges preventing the optimum exploitation of such assets to serve the interests of the Arab world."[47] Comparing the 2006 summit in Khartoum to the famous "three *no*'s" summit held in 1967, an Arab pundit commented that "the so-called common Arab action is in its last throes."[48] This was Qaddafi's conclusion as well.

Conclusion

During his more than three-and-a-half decades in power, Qaddafi moved from one extreme of Arab politics to another: from the self-assumed and ardent guardianship of Nasser's pan-Arabism to a position of aloofness, even antagonism, toward the Arab world. Qaddafi's oft-repeated, if never actually implemented, threat to withdraw from the Arab League—the symbol of Arab solidarity—clearly indicated the wane in Libya's Arab identification, as did the fact that his calls for the annihilation of Israel were gradually replaced by sporadic allusions to its right to exist. Such sharp oscillations were not simply the result of Libya's inter-Arab affairs; they also reflected broader changes in Libya's domestic and foreign relations, most significantly those with the United States.

Since the 1970s, the Arab world repeatedly impaired Libya's prestige, most dramatically in 1973 when Egypt and Syria concealed from Qaddafi their plans for the war against Israel despite his advocacy of the Jewish state's military annihilation and also during the Egyptian-Israeli peace process, which culminated with the 1979 peace agreement. These shocks magnified Qaddafi's already damaged position in the Arab world following the rejection by numerous Arab countries, including Egypt, of his grand vision of Arab unity.

Qaddafi also found it difficult to accept the Arab world's full compliance with the sanctions the UN imposed on Libya from 1992 to 1999. Libya was diplomatically isolated and humiliated as well as damaged socially and economically. In turn, the regime's grasp on power was significantly weakened as it faced a host of internal and external dangers. The unexpected lack of political support from his supposed Arab allies was something Qaddafi neither forgot nor forgave.

Throughout the first decade of the twenty-first century, however, as a result of its newly rehabilitated position in the West—particularly with respect to the United States—as well as its enhanced position in Africa, Libya could afford to vent its rancor against those who had betrayed the pan-Arab legacy and denied it a leadership role in the Arab arena. It no longer identified significantly with the Arab world, which had also proven itself a broken reed in the marsh of world affairs.

In short, Libya no longer considered itself the last stronghold of Pan-Arabism. In the summer of 2006, Qaddafi put it clearly, "There were hopes and aspirations to have a strong Arab nationalist entity of which we would be a part. Unfortunately, this has failed, that era has ended, and a new era has begun."[49]

Notes

1. On the Arab world's place in the New World Order and on its effect on inter-Arab relations in the wake of the Gulf conflict, see, for example, E. Salem, "A New Order"; Hermann, "The Middle East and the New World Order"; Maddy-Weitzman, "A New Arab Order?"; and Podeh, "In the Service of Power."

2. For Syria's inter-Arab arena at this phase, see Zisser, "Syria (Al-Jumhuriyya al-'Arabiyya al-Suriyya)," 1990, pp. 655–656 and 1991, 675–682.

3. Tripoli TV, 17 January 1991 (DR). For more on Maghribian positions toward the Gulf conflict, see Zoubir, "Reactions in the Maghrib."

4. JANA, 27 January 1991 (BBC); Tripoli TV, 14 February 1991 (DR).

5. JANA, 15 and 23 February 1991 (DR). For more details on Arab mediation, see Maddy-Weitzman and Kostiner, "From Jedda to Cairo."

6. Radio Tripoli, 28 March 1991 (DR).

7. Foreign Minister Bishari in a statement to *al-Masa'i,* 28 May 1991.

8. For Islamist pressures in the region, see Ronen, "The Sudanese-Egyptian-Libyan Triangle"; Martinez, "Why the Violence in Algeria?"; and Entelis, "Islamist Politics and the Democratic Imperative."

9. This expression has been used repeatedly by the Libyan media since the early 1990s. For example, see *al-Fajr al-Jadid,* 17 April 1996.

10. For the Lockerbie dispute and the UN sanctions, see Chapter 3.

11. *Al-Jamahiriyya,* 11 and 18 June 1992; *al-Zahf al-Akhdar,* 17 July 1992.

12. *Middle East,* May 1992; *al-Jamahiriyya,* 1 September 1992.

13. *Al-Fajr al-Jadid,* 5 November 1993. The supranational pan-Arab ideology emerged after World War I with the aim of establishing Arab unity. This idea was based on the perception that the Arabs had a common language and civilization, a shared emotional and ideological consciousness, a collective Arab-Islamic identity, and a history of joint struggle against foreign Western colonialism and against Israel, considered integral to the Western postcolonial presence in the region. The demise of pan-Arabism began in 1967 after the Six Day War, "which marked the Waterloo of pan-Arabism." See 'Ajami, "The End of Pan-Arabism."

14. *Al-Suraqiyya* (London), 8 February 1993.

15. *Al-Fajr al-Jadid,* 5 November 1993.

16. *Al-Jumhuriyya* (Cairo), 2 November 1991 and 6 February 1992.

17. *Al-Hayat,* 28 January 1994; Middle East News Agency, 27 January 1994.

18. Tripoli TV, 27 February 1994 (DR).

19. *Al-Hayat,* 28 January 1994.

20. *Al-Shams,* 4 September 1995. For Sudan's hostile relations with the United States, see Ronen, "Sudan and the United States."

21. Tripoli TV, 21 April 1995 (DR).

22. Tripoli TV, 20 November 1995 and 16 February 1995 (DR), respectively. For Mauritania's position on the fringe of the Arab world, see Z. Salem, "Mauritania: A Saharan Frontier-State." In late 1999, Mauritania upgraded its relations with Israel to full diplomacy.

23. Middle East News Agency, 17 April 1996 (DR).

24. Tripoli TV, 29 May 1997 (BBC).

25. *Al-Shams,* 8 November 1997.

26. For more details on the event, see *al-Hayat,* 14 and 19 June 1998; *al-Sharq al-Awsat,* 25 June 1998; and *Libya: News and Views,* 13 and 27 June 1998.

27. Ronen, "Libya's Diplomatic Success in Africa," 2002, p. 68; *al-Suraqiyya,* 6 September 1999; Radio Tripoli, 25 January 1999 (BBC).

28. *Middle East Times,* 14 March 1999. For the containment of Egyptian Islamist violence, see Hatina, "Jumhuriyyat Misr al-'Arabiyya."

29. Ronen, "Libya's Qadhafi and the Palestinian Conflict," 2004, pp. 93–94.

30. Tripoli TV, 28 March 2001 (BBC); *al-Quds al-'Arabi,* 29 March 2001. For more on the summit's decisions, see *al-Wasat,* 2 April 2001.

31. Ronen, "Libya's Qadhafi and the Palestinian Conflict," 2004, pp. 94–95.

32. For Libya's denial of any connection to the affair, see for example, *al-Sharq al-Awsat,* 14 January 2002. For the accusation against Shi'i Amal, see *al-Quds al-'Arabi,* 29 November 2000, quoting Libya's official news agency.

33. *Al-Hayat,* 3 March 2002; Qaddafi, in an interview on al-Jazira satellite TV, quoted in *al-Quds al-'Arabi,* 27 March 2001.

34. See Ronen, "Libya's Qadhafi and the Palestinian Conflict," 2004, p. 85; Qaddafi, from a presentation of his *White Book (al-Kitab al-Abyad)* on the solution to the Israeli-Palestinian conflict, *al-Quds al-'Arabi,* 4 March 2002.

35. Ronen, "The Libyan-Saudi Diplomatic Rupture," 2005.

36. For a broader analysis of Arab politics before and after the US war in Iraq, see Susser, "The Arabs and Iraq," and Podeh, "Between Stagnation and Renovation."

37. From an interview with Saif al-Islam in *Sueddeutsche Zeitung,* 22 December 2003.

38. See Podeh, "Between Stagnation and Renovation."

39. *Al-Bayan,* 24 January 2004; *al-Ahram al-'Arabi,* 17 January 2004, quoting Secretary for Libyan Foreign Affairs Salman al-Shuhumi.

40. "Country Report: Libya," April 2004, p. 18; *al-Ahram al-'Arabi,* 17 January 2004.

41. *Al-Ahram al-'Arabi,* 29 May 2004.

42. Ibid. For a broader survey of the Tunis summit resolutions, see also Podeh, "Between Stagnation and Renovation."

43. *Al-Sharq al-Awsat,* 6 July 2004. For the Mauritanian position, see JANA, 31 August 2004 (DR).

44. Ronen, "The Libyan-Saudi Diplomatic Rupture," 2005.

45. Algiers TV, 23 March 2005 (BBC).

46. Al-'Arabiyya satellite TV, 28 August 2005, quoting Saif al-Islam's interview with LBC TV, 22 August 2005.

47. *Al-Ahram Weekly,* 30 March–5 April 2006.

48. *Al-Quds al-'Arabi,* 29 March 2006. For more on the summit, see *al-Sharq al-Awsat,* 29 and 30 March 2006.

49. *New York Times,* 25 July 2006, quoting the Libyan News Agency, 24 July 2006.

7

Charting a New Course in Africa: Military Involvement in Uganda

On 25 January 1971, Major General Idi Amin Dada launched a military coup, deposed the regime of Apollo Milton Obote, and seized power in Uganda. The coup did not elicit any response from Tripoli since the Qaddafi regime, which had seized power on 1 September 1969, was still preoccupied not only with rallying Libyan society around its leadership but also with inculcating its vision of pan-Arab unity in the Arab arena and especially in Egypt. The Arab world was the sole target of Qaddafi's foreign policy at the time.

Yet in 1971, Qaddafi realized that he and Egyptian president Anwar Sadat diverged ideologically and politically on almost every major issue. Their contradictory views, which soon developed into a militant rivalry, were detrimental to Qaddafi's pan-Arab vision and political prestige. But even as his aspirations to shape the Arab agenda were stymied,[1] a surge in Libya's oil wealth enhanced his self-confidence, and Qaddafi decided to seek foreign outlets for his political ambitions.

Meanwhile, the new Ugandan ruler was rapidly losing credibility at home and abroad, and his country was sliding toward internal turmoil and war on its borders. The Amin regime was threatened by rising socioeconomic distress, financial corruption, administrative malpractice, unrest in the ranks of the military, ethnopolitical hostility, and growing violence among Obote's followers. The deposed Ugandan president, determined to return to power, had taken refuge in neighboring Tanzania, where the government provided him with logistic and military support.[2]

Amin requested urgent financial and military aid from various countries, particularly those that had backed him—including Britain, which had ruled Uganda from 1894 until its independence in 1962, and Israel, which had maintained a strong presence in the country since the early 1960s. He asked Israel to cancel Uganda's debts, mostly so he could pay for military acquisitions such as warships that would take soldiers across Lake Victoria to attack Tanzania.[3] When his appeals to Britain and Israel were flatly rejected, the Ugandan head of state tried a new direction. As a Muslim from the West Nile Kakwa ethnic group,[4] he appealed to the Arab Muslim world—especially to its wealthiest states: Libya and Saudi Arabia. To improve the prospects of Arab Muslim support and perhaps to indicate his own values and perceptions, Amin accompanied these requests with the introduction of pro-Muslim and pro-Arab items onto Uganda's domestic and foreign agendas. Significantly, in late 1971, he also cut off vital military and logistic aid to the non-Muslim, non-Arab southern Sudanese rebels, who were fighting the Arab Muslim regime of Ja'far Muhammad al-Numayri in neighboring Sudan.[5]

Amin's strategic and political activities as well as his Islamic-oriented leadership attracted Qaddafi's attention. He was then ardently waving the banners of Islam, anti-Christianity, and anti–Western imperialism, declaring that "Christianity [is] used as a means of colonialism" and that "Islam is closer to us Africans."[6] The needs of the regime in Kampala converged with the Libyan quest for a new sphere of political and strategic influence as well as for greater ideological impact.

Amin's first official visit to Tripoli took place on 12 and 13 February 1972, followed ten days later by the visit of a Libyan delegation to Kampala. This began a collaboration between the two countries, though geographically remote and different in almost every facet: race, religion, language, culture, historical legacy, population and territorial size, political structure, strategic location, regional and international orientation, economic conditions, national resources, and more.[7] In an attempt to bridge the gaps and establish a base for cooperation, the two heads of state seized the occasion of Amin's visit to Tripoli to vent their animosity toward Israel and declare their support for the "Arab people's rights and just struggle against Zionism and [Western] imperialism . . . and also [for] the Palestinian people's right to return to their land and homes by any means." In addition, the two leaders stated their common commitment to Islam.[8]

Seeking to gain favor from Qaddafi, Amin stepped up his anti-Israeli and anti-Western campaign in Uganda. On 27 March 1972, the Ugandan head of state expelled all Israelis from the country and closed the Israeli embassy in Kampala several days later. He called on other African countries to "extricate themselves from the exploitation of the Israeli economic imperialism" and urged Arabs and Africans to "sit together and crystallize a plan which will eliminate the Zionist entity in the Middle East."[9] Libya and Uganda also opened embassies in each other's capitals in late March 1972.

Amin's anti-Israel, pro-Arab stance earned Tripoli's gratitude in the form of financial grants and military training for the Ugandan army. Libyan military aid was of particular importance, filling the vacuum created by the abrupt expulsion of Israeli military advisers and the consequent cessation of Israeli support.[10] In the wake of Amin's second official visit to Tripoli in June 1972, a trip which enhanced the status of Muslims in his country, bilateral relations gathered further momentum.[11] The Islamic platform was expedient for both leaders, providing them with justification and common ground for strengthening their ties. Amin also began to target "Western imperialism," announcing in the summer of 1972 the expulsion of tens of thousands of Asians from Uganda, many of them British citizens, as well as of Britain's military mission—a move that coincided with Tripoli's denunciation of "British imperialism."[12]

At this stage, Libya's investment of time and resources in Uganda was paying off, as it enhanced Qaddafi's personal and political prestige at home and even, to some degree, in the Arab world. Amin also provided Qaddafi with a springboard into the heart of Africa, which had been a target of influence for Egypt's late president Nasser as well, the only modern Arab leader Qaddafi had ever admired. One may even assume that the Soviet Union watched Qaddafi's deepening encroachment into Africa, marking his potential for advancing Moscow's interests on the continent.

Furthermore, success in Kampala empowered Qaddafi to exert political pressure on Libya's newly pro-Western neighbors Sudan and Egypt and thus, indirectly, on the West. Qaddafi also saw in Uganda a useful instrument for promoting Islam throughout Africa and assisting in the fight against "Western imperialism" and "Zionist expansion"—a central tenet of Qaddafi's ideological and political platform.

The First Active Military Intervention: Setting a Precedent

A dramatic turning point in Tripoli's relations with Kampala—and, in fact, in its foreign policy as a whole—occurred in the fall of 1972, when Qaddafi dispatched five Libyan transport planes carrying 400 technicians and soldiers along with military equipment to Uganda.[13] This move was prompted by the invasion of Uganda on 17 September 1972 by the People's Army, as Obote's opposition forces were called, backed by Tanzanian troops.

The Libyan airlift was brought to international attention by pro-US Sudan, which had intercepted it as it was overflying Sudanese air space without permission. However, the Khartoum government had signed a peace agreement with the rebels in the south only half a year earlier and appeared determined to defuse any foreign threats to the still-fragile settlement of the seventeen-year-long civil war. Fearful of possible political subversion or military retaliation from either Libya or Uganda and cognizant of the crucial support the latter had given the rebels (at least until Amin cut them off), the Khartoum government allowed the Libyan aircraft to fly to Uganda as originally planned.

The September 1972 invasion of Uganda was quickly repelled and Obote's forces, with their Tanzanian allies, withdrew. Both Libya and Uganda avoided releasing details about the military intervention and did not report the departure of Libyan troops from Uganda after the defeat of the anti-Amin forces. It is plausible that they remained in Uganda, serving not only as reinforcements for Amin but also as a deterrent against any new assault by the expelled Ugandan leader and his Tanzanian patron.

Amin thanked Libya by praising Qaddafi and reaffirming Uganda's anti-Western, anticolonialist, and anti-Zionist orientation. In the same spirit, the Libyan leader clarified that his support of Uganda was a gesture for Amin's "commitment to the Arab cause" and "struggle against colonialism and Zionism."[14] Qaddafi sent to Uganda not only Libyans but Palestinians as well to fight for Amin's regime, and Amin's troops trained in Libya itself.[15] The successful military intervention in Uganda—the first sub-Saharan African state to host a Libyan expeditionary force by invitation—accorded Qaddafi a reputation as a reliable political and military ally of any friendly regime in times of crisis and, conversely, as a decisive military opponent to any regime antagonistic to his goals.

Qaddafi's Changing Attitude Toward Amin's Regime

In 1973, Qaddafi seemed to have achieved his desired aims in Uganda, while other affairs both regional and internal now demanded his primary attention. Domestically, his most noteworthy concern was the public dissemination of his self-styled revolutionary ideas, which culminated in the declaration of a popular revolution in spring 1973 and which eventually crystallized into his Third Universal Theory. In foreign affairs, there was Libya's military intervention in the Aouzou Strip along the Libyan border in northern Chad, intended primarily to establish what Libya claimed to be its historic right of sovereignty over the strategically important oil- and uranium-rich region. Other concerns were the renewed attempt to establish a political union with Egypt, tension with Egypt and Syria over their utter disregard for Libya during both the planning stages of the October 1973 war against Israel and the postwar negotiations, and the failure of an attempted union with Tunisia's Habib Bourguiba in January 1974. Finally, and of special importance, were Libya's deteriorating relations with the United States, which were leading to heightened military tension between the two countries.[16]

Libya's demanding circumstances were not Qaddafi's only motivation to distance himself from Amin's regime in 1973. Amin's propensity for fomenting domestic political strife and, indeed, his emerging reputation as a cruel despot who brutally trampled human rights, defied law and order, and shed the blood of many Ugandans diminished his value in Qaddafi's eyes. Having already earned himself the reputation of enfant terrible, Qaddafi felt it politically inexpedient now to be affiliated with Amin, lest the association tarnish his image further and aggravate the strain already characterizing his ties with the West. However, Qaddafi did not desert Amin completely, as a March 1974 tour of Uganda—the first ever by a Libyan head of state—indicated, although it was just a part of a broader African trip following the abrogation of the unity agreement between Libya and Tunisia. In addition, burgeoning ties in the mid-1970s between the Soviet Union and not only Libya but also Uganda—indeed, Moscow was its primary supplier of armaments—further entrenched Qaddafi and Amin on the same side of the Cold War. Yet Tripoli's aloofness toward Kampala continued. Visits by Amin to Libya in June 1973, January and October 1974, and May and August 1975, mainly to request further military support, failed to persuade Libya to restrengthen bilateral ties.

To Amin's distress, mounting internal and external threats to his regime only increased Uganda's need for Libya's help. Therefore, when Palestinians hijacked an Air France plane flying from Israel to France in July 1976 and landed it in Uganda's Entebbe airport, Amin supported them. He hoped thereby to please Qaddafi as well as to air his own political grievances and show support for the Palestinians. Amin even formulated the demands of the hijackers, assuming that his support would gain him further support from Libya, which promoted itself as the most devoted supporter of the Palestinian cause.[17] Indeed, following Israel's rescue operation on 3 and 4 July 1976, Libya—calling it a "terrorist raid"—sent Uganda twenty Mirage jet fighters to replace the MiG aircraft Israel had destroyed.[18] Amin, however, claimed that it was the Soviets who had replaced the aircraft and that Uganda had paid for the replacements, thus wishing to divert the West's growing suspicions about the Libyan-Ugandan strategic and military collaboration. It is noteworthy that the Soviets wished to secure their footing in Uganda not only as a Cold War measure but also as a counterbalance to the rival Chinese influence in Tanzania.[19]

In any case, the Israeli operation in Entebbe served to invigorate the ties between Tripoli and Kampala, as Libya endowed Uganda with a grant of US$50 million to help it pay its debt to Kenya—a term on which Kenya insisted, along with the withdrawal of Ugandan troops from their common border, before it would fully restore its flow of oil to Uganda.[20] Landlocked, Uganda was to a large extent dependent upon the Kenyan port of Mombassa for its trade and oil requirements and therefore for the survival of Amin's regime. Libyan financial aid to Uganda was thus aimed at preventing a war with Kenya that might have placed Libya in a difficult position: either becoming embroiled in combat alongside Amin or risking his removal from power and thus jeopardizing the benefits Libya had gained through its sponsorship of his regime. Libya's fear of an armed conflict was heightened by

Kampala's anger at Nairobi for providing refueling services to the Israelis during the Entebbe operation. From a different direction, the Tanzanian-backed Ugandan opposition continued to threaten Amin's grip on power. Still, the Libyans withheld any substantial military assistance, fearing retaliation by the United States. Qaddafi definitely did not wish to get involved in Uganda's political and diplomatic crises but nor was he prepared to relinquish his stake in the Amin regime.

Renewed Interest in Uganda:
The Reinforcement of Military Support

In 1977, Libya became embroiled in a particularly bitter conflict with its Arab neighbors, mainly Sudan and Egypt, the conflict with the latter even culminating in a four-day war. These two countries, along with Saudi Arabia—all governed by pro-US regimes—accused Qaddafi, together with the Soviet Union, of instigating two attempted coups in the fall of 1975 and the summer of 1976, respectively, against the Sudanese regime in order to change the alliances along the Arab-African seam line in general and in the Red Sea area in particular. Coming at the height of the Cold War, the accusation provoked strong reverberations in the region and detrimentally affected Libya's relations with Egypt as well as Sudan.[21]

The United States, which listed Libya fourth on a list of its potential enemies, put pressure on Qaddafi, halting the delivery of military aircraft that had long since been purchased and reducing its diplomatic representation in Tripoli. At this time, the United States and pro-US Arab countries considered Libya the most dangerous instrument, along with the pro-Soviet regime in Ethiopia, of the Soviet ambition to undermine the political and strategic footing of the West in Arab and African arenas so as to solidify its own interests.[22]

The pressures and threats facing Libya in foreign affairs sharply contrasted with its encouraging domestic scene, marked by an economic boom, increased military power, and remarkable political and ideological success. Qaddafi's security apparatus curtailed the effectiveness of Libyan opposition—most significantly by thwarting 'Umar al-Muhayshi's plot to overthrow him in the summer of 1975 while tightening control over his military and cabinet. His successes continued with the smooth and formal implementation of his professedly revolutionary vision—the People's Power system—in March 1977.[23] Yet the discrepancy between Qaddafi's position at home and his position outside the country caused him to once again seek foreign outlets for his political and ideological goals.

Although Qaddafi did not perceive Amin's Uganda as the best choice, no other alternatives presented themselves at this stage. The dispatch to Uganda (as reported by a foreign source) of 200 Libyan troops on 4 March 1977 should thus be viewed within the context of Qaddafi's ambivalence.[24] Presumably, the timing was dictated by Amin's escape from a coup attempt—one of the most serious of more than a dozen plots to overthrow him. Neither Tripoli nor Kampala revealed details of the scope, mission, or activities of the Libyan military contingent or of the duration of its stay in Uganda. The Libyan troops may have remained there as a deterrent force or may have been called home in the summer of 1977, as the military tension between Libya and Egypt reached a peak.

The End of the Libyan-Ugandan "Romance": Amin's Political Collapse

Amin's visits to Libya in December 1977 and September 1978 indicated his urgent need for political support and military reinforcements. By the fall of 1978, his regime seemed on the verge of collapse as yet another mutiny broke out in one of the army units and swiftly spread through the ranks. Although brutally suppressed, the uprising underlined the fragility of the regime's hold on power. The Ugandan ruler laid the blame for the rebellion, which he portrayed as an invasion, on Tanzanian forces supported by Cuba, Israel, and South Africa. Tanzania maintained an anti-Amin umbrella platform, embracing various exiled Ugandan opponents, including the Uganda Liberation Group and the Uganda National Movement, both based in Zambia. On 1 November 1978, Amin announced that, in reprisal, he was annexing the Kagera Salient region of Tanzania, which, he argued, had historically belonged to Uganda. Some two weeks later, Tanzania retaliated and the fighting between the two countries intensified.[25]

In mid-November 1978, a foreign source reported a new dispatch of Libyan troops to Uganda, although it was not clear precisely when they had arrived.[26] Again, no details were available regarding either their number or their mission, but clearly Qaddafi had decided to act in defense of the Ugandan ruler, in order, among other reasons, to strengthen his own position as a devoted guardian of Islam. The Islamic tide that followed Ayatollah Ruhollah al-Khomeini's revolution in Iran in February 1979 and that indicated Islam's political force, inspired Qaddafi, particularly as it also registered a shift from a primarily domestic agenda to its new anti-Western focus.[27] Moreover, the progress of Egypt's peace process with Israel on the one hand and its anti-Amin policy on the other fueled Tripoli's interest in helping Uganda and thus harming Egypt.

Libya's mediation of the conflict between Uganda and Tanzania in late 1978 and early 1979 reflected its stake in helping them contain their dispute. Qaddafi feared that an escalation of the war would drag his troops into a direct confrontation with the well-armed Tanzanian National Defense Force, reinforced by Ugandan rebels and, ultimately, by Egypt, which supported Tanzania's struggle against Amin politically and militarily. According to a Western source, Tanzania and Egypt were bound by "a secret military agreement," sharing an interest in eliminating the Libyan presence from Uganda.[28] Their success would have hampered Libya's broader ties to the Arab and African regions as well as further aggravated the strain already characterizing its ties with the United States.

Its mediation attempts having failed, early in March 1979 Libya adopted a strategy of deterrence, hoping to prevent the outbreak of war. Tripoli now stated, "We in Libya have already made our decision . . . on whom we would help in the conflict. . . . We know which side is good for Africa. We cannot watch idly if [Tanzanian president Julius] Nyerere insists on destroying Amin. Libya is the real friend of Uganda."[29]

However, Tanzanian troops, together with anti-Amin rebels, soon made inroads into Ugandan territory, attacking a wide range of strategic targets. At the beginning of March 1979, with Amin's position in real danger, Libya reportedly accelerated the airlift of large quantities of arms and military equipment to Uganda, including six Mirage jets, seven MiG-21 jets, and a Tupolev-22 high-altitude bomber. Qaddafi also dispatched an estimated 1,400 troops.[30]

Later in the same month, amid growing fear of not only Amin's downfall but also the resulting loss of his own political and military prestige as well as of troops and equipment, Qaddafi presented Nyerere with an ultimatum: if Tanzania did not withdraw its troops from Uganda within twenty-four hours, he would declare war on Tanzania. Nyerere flatly refused.[31]

Libya dispatched another 2,000 soldiers to Uganda in early April 1979. Logistically, at least, it had no difficulty in sending reinforcements to Uganda, as the compulsory conscription law of May 1978 had significantly increased the size of the Libyan army, which numbered 42,000 soldiers in 1979.[32] This increase took on special importance in light of not only the intervention in Uganda but also Libya's increasing military involvement in Chad as of the spring of 1979, when a reported force of 2,500 launched military operations deep within the country.[33]

Both Libya and Uganda continued to deny any Libyan military involvement in the Ugandan war; such reports came only from foreign sources. According to some of them, Libyan warplanes had bombed the advancing Tanzanian and Ugandan opposition forces within Tanzanian territory, and Tanzania's air force had responded by shutting down the Entebbe airport, thereby preventing other Libyan aircraft from taking off and landing. It would also have prevented any further airlifts of Libyan troops and weapons as well as the evacuation of casualties, while leaving many more Libyan soldiers wounded in the Mulago Hospital in Kampala.[34]

Amin's regime was finally overthrown in early April 1979, leading to an immediate withdrawal of all Libyan troops and embassy staff from Uganda. After Amin and his entourage fled the country on 10 April, his whereabouts remained unknown until, two months later, it was alleged that he was in hiding in Libya.[35] Qaddafi first confirmed that Amin was in the country but later stated that he was "back in northern Uganda gathering his forces."[36] It later became clear that Amin had found temporary refuge in Iraq before moving to Saudi Arabia, where he remained until his death in 2003.

On 11 April 1979, Yusuf Lule—a senior Ugandan politician who was also a Christian, a professor at Makerere University, and a sworn enemy of Amin—seized power in Kampala, gaining recognition throughout Africa and the West. Libya entered a phase of strained relations with the new Ugandan leadership, which was now under the influence of Tanzania, and acted to conceal its defeat from the public eye and contain the damaging domestic and foreign fallout. Even after Lule was removed from power in the summer of 1979 and replaced by Christian jurist Godfrey Binaisa, who ruled the country until May 1980, Libya's ties with Uganda did not improve. When Obote eventually returned to power, no rapprochement occurred, especially since Tanzania's influence was still dominant. Rather, wishing to accelerate a regime change in Uganda, Libya rendered military and financial assistance to Yoweri Museveni's National Resistance Army, which fought unsuccessfully to topple Obote. Obote ruled his country until the summer of 1985, when he was deposed in a coup led by General Tito Okello.[37]

Okello's reign lasted only until early 1986, when Museveni finally succeeded in taking power. However, despite the interest he shared with Qaddafi in the early 1980s, Museveni showed no desire to renew contact. Although in the 1990s, there was a thaw in relations between the two countries, the focus of Qaddafi's foreign affairs had long since shifted from Uganda.

Conclusion

Libya's active military commitment to Idi Amin's regime marked a milestone in Qaddafi's foreign policy in the 1970s, his first decade in power. It was the first time that Libya penetrated Africa militarily and undertook to safeguard a regime in a geographically remote country in the continent's heart. Certainly, Qaddafi expected that this involvement would generate wide-ranging dividends for his country and regime.

However, the military intervention, which was accompanied by great fanfare in 1972, ended in a debacle. This failure exposed not only the chaos of Ugandan domestic affairs but also the gap between Qaddafi's aspirations and Libya's ability to realize them, at least in the 1970s. Significantly, the Libyan failure in Uganda exposed the limits of military power in a geographically remote and politically and ethnically diverse region where other powerful international forces were also deeply involved. Nevertheless, in the first year of its involvement alone, Libya contributed to fending off the Israeli presence in Kampala and, subsequently, in many other African states, while also damaging the position of "Western imperialism" throughout the continent. In retrospect, the next seven years of costly investment in Uganda failed to achieve any further advantages and negatively impacted Qaddafi's foreign and domestic plans.

Libya paid a high price for its commitment to Amin's regime. Libyan troops reportedly endured about 400 casualties and the loss of large quantities of military equipment. In addition, Libya was forced to pay Tanzania and the new regime in Uganda the sum of US$60 million to ensure the safe withdrawal of its forces and secure the release of its captured troops.[38] Libya also suffered a diplomatic backlash across the African continent.

However, the fiasco in Uganda did not benefit the Libyan opposition at home, where Qaddafi emerged unscathed, significantly maintaining the loyalty of the army—a major cornerstone of his power and a key instrument of his foreign policy throughout the 1970s. Drawing his own conclusions from the crushing defeat in Uganda—namely that it was due partly to the disadvantages of deploying armed forces so far from home—Qaddafi decided instead to focus his country's political-military endeavors in neighboring Chad, where Libya had many more interests germane to its security and its economic and political well-being as well as to its historical and religious legacy. Even before this decision, Libya had been meddling militarily in Chad since the early 1970s, although on a relatively low level, with the aim of ousting the incumbent pro-Western regime and promoting its own wide-ranging interests.

Notes

1. For details on Qaddafi's disappointment in the Arab world and in his incompatibility with Sadat, see Chapter 5.

2. On the domestic and foreign threats that Amin faced in the aftermath of his ascent to power, see Legum, *Africa Contemporary Record,* 1972, pp. B226–B252. For more on Tanzania's support of the Ugandan opposition, see Martin, *General Amin,* pp. 65–66, 170–171, 177–197.

3. Bell, "Israel's Setback in Africa," p. 23; Legum, *Africa Contemporary Record,* 1973, p. A135.

4. Some of the southern Sudanese rebels belonged to Amin's ethnic group, who lived on both sides of the Sudanese-Ugandan border. Most were Christian or animist. Amin's father, however, was Muslim, while his mother was a Christian of the Lugbara ethnic group.

5. For details on Sudan's civil war, which erupted in 1955, see for example, Collins, *The Southern Sudan*; Beshir, *The Southern Sudan*; Voll, ed., *Sudan: State and Society in Crisis*; Ronen, *Sudan in a Civil War,* 1995, and "Religions at War, Religions at Peace," 2005.

6. *Arab Report and Record,* 16–31 March 1974.

7. Qaddafi erroneously assumed that Uganda was 70 percent Muslim. See Martin, *General Amin,* pp. 163–164; Muslims in Uganda during the early 1970s reportedly comprised between 5 or 6 percent of the population, of which the majority was Christian. See also Oded, *Uganda and Israel,* p. 134.

8. Libyan News Agency, 14 February 1972 (BBC).

9. For the Israeli presence in Uganda and its subsequent withdrawal, see Martin, *General Amin,* pp. 158–164, and Oded, *Uganda and Israel,* pp. 21–55, 132–133.

10. Legum, *Africa Contemporary Record,* 1973, p. B55; Arnold, *The Maverick State,* p. 70.

11. Kokole, "Idi Amin, 'the Nubi' and Islam in Ugandan Politics," p. 48; Kasozi, "Christian-Muslim Inputs," pp. 241–244.

12. See, for example, Radio Tripoli, 11 August 1972, (DR). For details on the Asian exodus from Uganda, see Legum, *Africa Contemporary Record* 1973, pp. A7–A19, C88. For further details on Uganda's foreign affairs in the early 1970s, see Tandon, "An Analysis of the Foreign Policy of African States." For Britain's interests in Libya in the post–Cold War period, see J. Wright, *Libya: A Modern History,* pp. 44–118, and Kelly, "Britain, Libya and the Start of the Cold War."

13. Legum, *Africa Contemporary Record,* 1973, p. B276.

14. Legum, *Africa Contemporary Record,* 1972, p. B55.

15. Haley, *Qadhafi and the United States Since 1969,* p. 36, quoting Obote.

16. For details on these issues, see Chapters 2, 5, and 8 of this book.

17. Kyemba, *State of Blood,* p. 176. For more on the Entebbe operation, see Netanyahu, *Entebbe.*

18. Radio Tripoli, 7 July 1976 (DR); *Arab Report and Record,* 1–15 July 1976, p. 420.

19. Legum, *Africa Contemporary Record,* 1977, pp. B394–B95.

20. Oded, *Uganda and Israel,* pp. 156–157.

21. Regarding Libya's relations with Egypt, Sudan, and the Maghribian countries during this period, see Chapter 5; see also Dishon and Ben Zvi, "Inter-Arab Relations."

22. For Qaddafi's relations with the United States in the second half of the 1970s, see Chapter 2 and, for example, Gera, "Libya and the United States." On Libya's relations with the USSR, see Chapter 4.

23. For details on Muhayshi's plot, see Chapters 2 and 5. For more on the People's Power system, a major pillar of Qaddafi's Third Universal Theory, see the "Declaration on the Establishment of People's Power," in Gera, "Libya," 1978, pp. 531–533. It concerns changing Libya's name to Jamahiriyya (the state of the masses), declaring the Quran as the code of society, implementing "People's Power," and initiating general military training.

24. Radio Nairobi, 17 March 1977 (BBC).

25. Nyeko, "Exile Politics and Resistance to Dictatorship." For further details on Uganda's affairs and the regime's precarious position in late 1978 and early 1979, as well as on Kampala's allegations of widespread foreign subversion and its battle with Tanzania, see Legum, *Africa Contemporary Record,* 1980, pp. B393–397, B421–434; *Africa Confidential,* 15 December 1978; and *Africa Research Bulletin,* January 1979, p. 5118.

26. *The Observer,* 12 November 1978.

27. Qaddafi, who opposed the pro-US rule of the Shah, provided Khomeini with moral, political, and financial support in late 1978 and early 1979. See the statement by Libya's information and culture secretary Muhammad Abu al-Qasim al-Zuway in *al-Ra'y al-'Amm* (Kuwait), 30 January 1979.

28. *Foreign Report,* 2 May 1979.

29. Legum, *Africa Contemporary Record,* 1979, pp. B428–429, B432.

30. *International Herald Tribune,* 7 March 1979; *Africa Research Bulletin,* March 1979, p. 5185; *New York Times,* 8 March 1979.

31. *The Guardian,* 28 March 1979.

32. International Institute for Strategic Studies, *The Military Balance 1979–80.* In 1977, the number of armed forces was only 29,200 out of a population of 2,630,000. See, ibid., 1977–1978.

33. *Arab Report* (London), 9 May 1979; *The Observer,* 1 July 1979.

34. Legum, *Africa Contemporary Record,* 1980, p. B433; *Jerusalem Post,* 1 April 1979.

35. *Der Spiegel* (Hamburg), 11 June 1979.

36. Reuters, 22 May 1979.

37. Oded, *Uganda and Israel,* p. 192. Obote, like many other toppled African despots, lived the rest of his life in exile, far from his homeland. He died in Johannesburg in October 2005 and was buried in Uganda after much public debate.

38. *Africa Research Bulletin,* April 1979, p. 5221; *International Herald Tribune,* 16 May 1979; *New African,* May 1979.

8

Intervention in Chad:
Warfare and Collapsed Aspirations

Buoyed by unprecedented military strength and immense oil wealth and driven by revolutionary zeal and political and economic aspirations both domestic and extraterritorial, Qaddafi first intervened militarily in Chad at the beginning of the 1970s. He considered Chad an asset of vital strategic importance, one that could serve as a lever for promoting his ideology and interests along the Arab-African seam line and into the heart of the African continent.

Libya's conflict with Chad began before Qaddafi came to power and stemmed from Libya's historic claim of sovereignty over the Aouzou Strip in northern Chad (roughly 144,000 square kilometers), which stretches along the Libyan border. This claim was based on the strong presence and trade activities of the Libyan-based Sanusi Islamic religious order there. From 1899 to 1902, the capital of the Sanusi Order was based in Quru in northern Chad. Founded in Mecca in 1837 and spreading into Libya in the early 1840s, this Sunni order aimed to purge Islam of heterodoxy and return to the original teachings of the Prophet and the Quran. From the early twentieth century, the Sanusi Order developed into a political force as well.

From 1911 until World War II, Italy had colonial control of Libya. According to the Laval-Mussolini Rome Agreement of 1935—negotiated to fulfill promises made to Italy by Britain, France, and Russia with the Treaty of London in 1915—the borders of Eritrea, Somalia, and Libya were changed in return for Italy's readiness to enter the First World War on the side of the Entente. One of these alterations, as Libya repeatedly stressed, accorded the Aouzou Strip to Libya.[1] Furthermore, Libya claimed that its border with Chad had been drawn illegally in 1899 by France and Britain, which had not obtained the consent of the Ottoman Empire when delimiting their respective spheres of influence. After Libya's independence in 1951, Libya also claimed that the Toubou Muslim nomads on both sides of the border in the Aouzou region were part of the Libyan ethnic fabric. In line with this position, Libyan forces under King Idris al-Sanusi—the grandson of the founder of the Sanusi Order—attempted to occupy Aouzou in the mid-1950s, but they were repulsed by colonial French troops.[2]

Chad's civil war, which first erupted in the mid-1960s,[3] stemmed from the refusal of the Toubou Muslims in the north to accept the shift of power dictated by French colonial rule to non-Muslim southerners of Sara ethnic origin. The retention of a strong French politico-military presence in Chad in the postindependence era—from 11 August 1960 onward—sustained the political status quo to the further detriment of the Muslim north. By the end of the 1960s, some 2,000 French troops were still stationed in Chad under a joint defense treaty, occupying a permanent base in the capital, Fort Lamy (known since 1973 as N'Djamena).[4]

In 1966, the rebel Front de Libération Nationale du Tchad (FROLINAT), which consisted of northern-based Muslim Chadian insurgents, was established by Ibrahim Abatcha in Nyala in western Sudan. After his death, Abba Siddiq led FROLINAT, shifting its base from Sudan to neighboring Libya. It was not long before the new Qaddafi regime, which advocated a militant foreign policy in general and in its immediate geopolitical vicinity in particular, backed FROLINAT. After 1969, FROLINAT gradually became a semiregular army, often clad in Libyan uniforms and dispatched along what was known as the Ho-Chi Minh Trail—which stretched from Kufra in western Libya to northern Chad—to transfer arms and reinforcements to the antigovernment Chadian forces.[5] Since FROLINAT was at war with Chad's central government, which was based in the predominantly Christian and animist south and headed by Christian president Françoise (N'Garta as of 1973) Tombalbaye, Libya's support was tantamount to a declaration of war against Tombalbaye.

Influenced by the socialist, anti-Western, and anti-colonialist Nasserist ideology, FROLINAT perceived Tombalbaye's government as a dictatorial regime that did not represent Chad's independent status or its Muslim populace and that, in fact, was merely a sub-Saharan African facade for continued French colonialism. FROLINAT's platform was consistent with Qaddafi's pro-revolutionary principles and political agenda. Tombalbaye's government was the embodiment of everything he opposed,[6] including the political, economic, and military entrenchment of the neocolonialist West, here represented by France, which continued to shape Chad's internal and foreign policies and encouraged Fort Lamy to bolster ties with the "Zionist enemy," thereby indirectly facilitating Israel's penetration into Africa. Libya also feared that the Chadian government would provide Israel with potentially threatening access to Libya's southern security perimeter.[7]

From Military Intervention to Full-Scale War:
Libya's Conquest of N'Djamena

Qaddafi's antagonism toward the Tombalbaye government intensified, cul-minating in Libya's attempt to topple the regime on 27 August 1971 and install a puppet government. Success, Qaddafi believed, would not only end the French influence but also settle the struggle over Aouzou and improve the strategic conditions on Libya's southern border. Economics also moti-vated Libya's claims to the Aouzou Strip, which was rich in iron, uranium, and oil deposits. However, the coup failed and the Tombalbaye government subsequently severed diplomatic relations with Libya and let Libyan politi-cal opposition use Chad's territory as a base of operations against Qaddafi. In response, Libya officially recognized FROLINAT as the only legitimate representative of the people of Chad, training the rebels within its territory and supplying them with arms and funds.

In 1972, the two countries drafted an agreement of friendship and Tom-balbaye, in what seemed to be a tactical move, agreed to cede the Aouzou Strip to Libya. Libya, in return, was supposed to halt its support of FROLINAT and to provide financial aid to Chad.[8] However, Libya failed to fulfill its promises and the agreement soon became irrelevant. To realize his territorial claim to the strip, Qaddafi instead sent his armed forces into Chad and suc-cessfully took control of Aouzou in 1973. He built a complex of religious, educational, and social institutions as well as airfields and prepared to exploit Aouzou's natural resources, primarily its uranium deposits.[9] Soon afterward, Libya included the annexed region on all government maps and publications.[10] The Tombalbaye government, however, rejected the Libyan claims to Aouzou and responded with a counterclaim to the Fezzan region of southern Libya to which, it alleged, Chad had "historical rights."[11] Libya ignored the claim, which seemed mainly for Chadian political consumption.

Following the failed rapprochement, animosity between the two coun-tries reached new heights in mid-1973 and did not abate even after the assas-sination of Tombalbaye in a military coup on 14 April 1975 and subsequent rise to power of his southern, Christian chief of staff, General Felix Mal-loum. Malloum's government adopted the same stance as the previous regime and denounced Libya's occupation of the Aouzou Strip. Qaddafi acted to thwart Malloum's reconciliation efforts with the Chadian Muslim north and even backed a coup, which failed, against Malloum in the spring of 1976. Throughout 1977, Libya continued to attack strategic Chadian targets and Malloum cut off diplomatic ties with Qaddafi on 6 February 1978. This break was of short duration and mainly reflected Chad's fear of Libya.

In the second half of the 1970s, the volatile situation in Chad prompted Sudan and Egypt to provide diplomatic and military aid to the government in N'Djamena, probably with the financial backing of the United States and Saudi Arabia, in order to curb Soviet penetration into the Horn of Africa and the Red Sea. Sudan and Egypt signed a Joint Defense Agreement in mid-1976 in the aftermath of an attempted coup against the Numayri regime in Khartoum allegedly instigated by Libya—which categorically denied any complicity—and backed by the Soviets and their Ethiopian and Cuban allies. The perception that Libya was the spearhead of Soviet expansionism in Africa and along the Arab-African seam line informed Sudanese, Egyptian, and, more discreetly, Saudi Arabian foreign policies in the later 1970s. Growing Soviet-Cuban involvement in Ethiopia during that period heightened fears that Moscow was attempting to establish a base on the Red Sea and control the Nile flow to Sudan and Egypt, thus not only threatening the alignment of global power in the region but also endangering the interests of pro-US Arab countries.

In the late 1970s, Qaddafi grew concerned about the consolidation of a US-backed anti-Libyan regional coalition and anxious to avoid any further provocation of France (paradoxically, an important arms supplier to Libya in the early 1970s). In de facto control of the Aouzou Strip, Qaddafi was now interested in maintaining the status quo in Chad, so he changed tactics and took diplomatic steps early in 1978 to de-escalate the civil war in Chad. Malloum's government immediately responded to Tripoli's initiative, having suffered a series of military defeats at the hands of the combined forces of Libya and FROLINAT, which had conquered most of the northern Chad region of Bourkou-Ennedi-Tibesti (an area vacated by the French garrisons in 1964), including its capital, Faya-Largeau.

The Libyan leader held a series of summits between the warring Chadian factions in the Libyan towns of Sebha and Benghazi in February and March 1978. The talks resulted in the Benghazi Agreement of March 1978, which stipulated formal recognition by the Chadian government of the FROLINAT movement, the withdrawal of all French troops from Chad, and a cease-fire in the thirteen-year Chadian war. Ironically, Libya became a supervisor of the agreement and, alongside Niger and Sudan, its guarantor.[12]

Shortly afterward, however, the agreement broke down and heavy fighting resumed. The combined Libyan-FROLINAT forces, now led by Goukouni Oueddei—the head of the FROLINAT splinter organization, the Inter-Army Council—won some important victories. It was not long until they extended their control further into Chad's heartland; only the bombardment of Libyan convoys by the French air force in the summer of 1978 prevented the rebel forces from entering N'Djamena. Commanded by Libyan officers and equipped with modern weapons, including SAM-9 missiles, Goukouni's forces were positioned in Faya-Largeau, ready for a further thrust southward. On the threshold of further armed confrontation, Tripoli and Paris found it expedient to reach an agreement, partitioning Chad along the sixteenth parallel into de facto Libyan and French spheres of influence. In effect, this agreement turned Chad into a joint Libyan-French domain.

This situation endured until the spring of 1979. Earlier in the year, Libya had shifted its military focus to Uganda, helping Idi Amin's regime oppose a takeover by Tanzanian and Ugandan opposition troops. By spring, however, Amin's regime had collapsed and Libya withdrew its forces from Uganda. Immediately thereafter, Chad again became more attractive to Libya, which needed an alternative foreign arena for rehabilitating the regime's prestige and the army's morale—both damaged due to the debacle in Uganda—and for coping with mounting tensions in its relations with Egypt, Sudan, and, more important, the United States. Determined to achieve these goals, Libya made further military thrusts into the Chadian heartland in the summer of 1979, but French forces defended the government in N'Djamena and helped Chad curb the encroachment.

Libya's motivation to control N'Djamena increased following another coup in Chad in early 1979. Felix Malloum's regime was replaced by a new, coalition government, known as the Gouvernement d'Union Nationale de Transition. Pro-Libyan Goukouni Oueddei—who had earlier challenged Siddiq's leadership of the FROLINAT and was now leader of the northern Muslim Forces Armées Populaires—was named Chad's president; Hissene Habre—leader of another northern Muslim faction, the Forces des Armées du Nord—became defense minister. Habre was a known critic of what he termed "imperialist Libya," portraying it as Chad's "enemy number one" and even suggesting Qaddafi subscribed to "the theory of an Islamic living space," in keeping with Hitler's theory of lebensraum.[13]

By this time, Chad was divided along pro- and anti-Libyan lines, with Muslims fighting on both sides. Deep factional rivalry soon undermined the viability of the new government, which led to conflict between Goukouni's and Habre's forces from early 1980 onward. While Habre enjoyed the military assistance of anti-Libyan Egypt and Sudan, Goukouni relied upon Libya for support. Taking advantage of the opportunity to accelerate Libya's incursion into Chad, two Libyan infantry brigades, backed by tanks, artillery, and helicopters, advanced toward N'Djamena in November 1980. Concurrently, Soviet-made Toupolev-22 bombers attacked areas held by Habre's forces. The Libyan assault had been planned during the summer and fall of 1980, so large numbers of troops and military equipment were already mobilized to enter Chad and take control of bases and airfields that had been vacated by the French troops near the capital. Foreign sources—all of them hostile to Libya—put the number of Libyan troops then in Chad's heartland at 3,000 to 4,000; they also reported that not only had Soviet and East German technicians helped the Libyan military formulate its strategy but that Soviet pilots were flying some of its air force planes.[14] The Soviet Union itself was then preoccupied with the invasion of Afghanistan, which served, in a way, as a legitimizing precedent and model for Libya's involvement in Chad. In late 1980, the breakdown of governmental authority in Chad was a fact, facilitating the rapid advance of the Libyan military machine toward N'Djamena.[15] Libyan troops and tanks entered the capital on 15 December 1980. His forces routed, a wounded Habre fled to Cameroon.

In order to gain maximum political advantage from the military success, Libya cautiously avoided further provocation of the foreign powers invested in Chad and issued no statement acknowledging Libyan military involvement there, quoting instead Goukouni's announcement that it was his own troops that had entered N'Djamena. "No evidence of Libyan forces in Chad," stressed the headline of a Libyan state-controlled periodical shortly thereafter.[16]

The Failure to Translate Military Victory into Political Gain

Soon after the capture of the Chadian capital, at the conclusion of Goukouni's second visit to Tripoli in late 1980, a joint communiqué announced that Chad and Libya had decided "to achieve full unity between the two countries—[Libyan-style] *jamahiri* unity—in which authority, arms, and resources are in the hands of the people[,] their instruments being the People's Congresses and Committees [according to Qaddafi's People's Power model] . . . [and] to support the strategic and inevitable alliance between the two countries and to regard any aggression on one to be aggression on the other." Moreover, they announced their readiness to fight in one another's defense. The communiqué further stipulated that "in accordance with the official request by the Goukouni-led Government of Chad, [Libya] will send a number of military men to assist in preserving security and maintaining the peace, which was achieved by the ending of the civil war, and also assist in the rebuilding of a Chadian national army and security forces."[17] According to Qaddafi, who felt "entirely free to articulate his belief in the value of African and Islamic unity without considering himself guilty of hegemonism," it was appropriate that the allied regime in N'Djamena, as "a fellow progressive" regime, should unify with Libya, adopting the same political structure and ideology Qaddafi had conceived as the perfect system.[18]

The joint announcement caused immediate alarm in the Arab region and in Africa, with the OAU condemning both the military intervention and the unification and calling for the withdrawal of Libyan troops from Chad.[19] Concern was also voiced internationally, mainly by the United States and France.[20] The USSR was itself fending off international pressure related to the intervention in Afghanistan, now in its second year, and had little interest in publicly supporting Libya.

Qaddafi issued a series of explanations designed to downplay the significance of the political union and thus mitigate Western alarm. This union, he argued, was aimed at achieving not a "merger" but "unity"—and even then not "constitutional political unity" but rather "integration and identity between the two countries in their political and social systems." Wishing to dispel the wide perception that the union was forced, Libya specified that it would take place gradually, and only after a general referendum was held in both countries.

Furthermore, Libya implied willingness to leave Chad as soon as the Goukouni government deemed its presence no longer necessary, or, in Qaddafi's words, "as soon as the danger posed by French and other forces ends, as soon as the government of Chad feels reassured."[21] To lend credence to these declarations, Qaddafi withdrew from Chad 200 of the thousands of soldiers stationed there in late March 1981. This token gesture failed, however, to ease the strain that had developed between Qaddafi and Goukouni— who, reportedly, had indeed been compelled to sign the "merger" communiqué, either in fear for his life or in order to lessen political pressure on Libya by African and other states, especially France.[22]

On 21 and 22 May 1981—month after an official visit to Moscow, where the Kremlin had cautiously declared support of Libya's "positive role" in Chad[23]—Qaddafi made a state visit to N'Djamena that failed to either produce an understanding with Goukouni or dispel regional and international concerns. Qaddafi publicly referred to three goals: safeguarding Libya's security, protecting the Chadian Muslims, and perpetuating Libyan control over Aouzou: "We will not allow ourselves to be encircled by hostile regimes. . . . If [anti-Libyan and pro-Western] Habre had succeeded, had France succeeded . . . had the US succeeded . . . had [Egypt's] Sadat [and] the Israelis succeeded . . . had all these captured Chad, the war would have been on the Libyan border; the fighting would have been in Libya. Libya's action was thus taken in self-defense."[24] Regarding his commitment to the Muslims, Qaddafi declared, "We cannot be indifferent to [the] problems [of the large Muslim population in Chad]. We are Muslims and advocate the liberation of and rapprochement between Muslims."[25] He also reiterated what he believed to be Libya's legitimate sovereignty over Aouzou, which "[had] always been . . . Libyan territory."[26]

Facing growing political and military collaboration among the region's pro-US Arab states, Libya formed the Tripartite Friendship and Cooperation Treaty with the Soviet-oriented PDRY and Ethiopia in August 1981, intended to "counter US moves aimed at expanding its military foothold in the Arab region and . . . Africa."[27]

By the fall of 1981, Goukouni, whose attitude toward Libya had become unequivocally hostile, repeatedly and publicly asked Tripoli to withdraw its troops from Chad[28] and rejected a new union scheme proposed by Libya.[29]

Because Goukouni had initiated Qaddafi's intervention, his call for Libya's withdrawal removed any pretext for Libya's continued presence in Chad. France, the United States, Egypt, Sudan, and other Middle Eastern and African states, especially Nigeria and Cameroon, exerted further pressure on Libya to withdraw. At this point, Qaddafi himself had an interest in pulling out some of his forces, or at least in appearing to do so, in order to promote his image as a peaceseeking leader.

This was particularly important as Qaddafi wished to host the 1982 OAU summit in Tripoli and then to become the organization's chairman, enhancing his standing at home and abroad. Moreover, news of the casualties the Libyan forces in Chad had incurred by late 1981 prompted widespread draft dodging and desertion while swelling the opposition's ranks.[30] The hostility that grew between Washington and Tripoli throughout 1981 and 1982 was also becoming a serious threat to Qaddafi's political future. There had been aerial clashes between the United States and Libya over the Gulf of Sirte, and the United States had imposed an embargo on the purchase of Libyan oil as well as a ban on the sale of technology to Libya. France likewise took a tough stand on Libya's interventionist policy in Chad, and the crisis in relations between Tripoli and Paris were further heightened when Qaddafi threatened France with an oil embargo while France, in turn, halted the delivery of missile-launching patrol boats Libya had ordered.[31]

Meanwhile, Qaddafi intensified his efforts to install a pro-Libyan regime in N'Djamena that would serve his interests should he be forced to disengage from Chad. On 29 October 1981, he carried out an abortive attempt to overthrow Goukouni and replace him with longtime ally Ahmad Asil, leader of the pro-Libyan Conseil Démocratique de la Révolution. Goukouni again demanded that Libya withdraw, fixing 31 December 1981 as the deadline.[32] This time, Libya responded promptly, announcing in mid-November that "the last Libyan Arab soldier [had] arrived back from N'Djamena."[33] Nevertheless, Libya's occupation of the Aouzou Strip continued as before.

From Failure to Failure: The Road to a Crushing Defeat

Libya's partial withdrawal from Chad allowed a weakened Habre, with French support, to return to Chad from exile, and, in a coup d'état in the spring of 1982, to topple the Goukouni government and become Chad's president. This was a serious setback to Qaddafi's interests, who had renewed a cordial relationship with Goukouni.

Another bitter disappointment for Qaddafi followed: He had failed to gain the necessary consensus to hold the OAU summit in Tripoli in August 1982 and thus become the organization's chairman for 1983 and 1984. Although Tripoli blamed this failure on a US "plot,"[34] the summit had actually been postponed in the event of a split caused by the admission of the Polisario's provisional government, the aforementioned SADR, as a full member of the OAU.[35] At least fourteen countries had supported Morocco's refusal to accept the SADR's admission, announcing their intention to boycott the summit unless the decision was reversed. Despite strenuous diplomatic efforts, Libya failed to ensure that two-thirds of OAU members would be present to achieve the required quorum. The summit was cancelled and a second attempt to hold it in Tripoli in November of that year was again aborted—this time, due to Qaddafi's insistence that Habre must not occupy Chad's seat at the conference table. Qaddafi thus became the first African leader in the history of the OAU to be denied the chairmanship, which indicates how low his status in African politics was during this period.

The OAU summit was finally held in Addis Ababa on 8 and 9 June 1983. Although Qaddafi attended, he stormed out when Habre was unanimously recognized as Chad's formal representative. Within weeks of the summit, Libya resumed military intervention in Chad alongside Goukouni's forces. Recognizing Goukouni as the legitimate leader of Chad, Tripoli provided his forces with a Libyan-operated radio station broadcasting from Bardai in northern Chad, where he based his headquarters. In addition, Libya provided air-surveillance support to Goukouni's forces and furnished them with arms and military equipment.[36] By June 1983, Goukouni captured Faya-Largeau, the strategically important northern oasis on the road to N'Djamena that had changed hands intermittently throughout the conflict. Shortly thereafter, Goukouni forces captured the important outposts of Oum Chalouba and Abeche closer to the capital.

Libya, backed by its Chadian ally, denied any military intervention in the war in Chad. Moreover, the Libyan media insisted Qaddafi was taking a neutral stance between Habre and Goukouni.[37] Meanwhile, Habre's military position was deteriorating, and he asked France and the United States for reinforcements. Alarmed, Qaddafi warned in early July 1983 that "any foreign intervention will be regarded by us as an act of war against Libya and [will] be treated accordingly." Later that month, he became more specific, citing France, the United States, Egypt, Sudan, Israel, and Zaire as countries that "constitute a direct threat to the security and stability of the Jamahiriyya."[38]

Habre projected himself as the embodiment of Chadian nationalism and the defender of the state's territorial integrity, providing an umbrella for the impressive array of states that backed his pro-Western government in Chad. In addition to his usual supporters, Iraq came to Habre's aid, supplying him with military equipment and serving as a mediator between his government and the Arab Muslim factions in northern Chad. Iraq's involvement in the dispute was, however, merely a means of promoting its war against Iran, with which Libya sided. In the early 1980s, pragmatic considerations overrode Saddam Hussein's earlier political and ideological commitments. Thus

Baghdad's rapprochement with Cairo—an important supporter of pro-Western Habre—was a prominent development, with both countries sharing enmity toward Libya. Supported by Egypt, Sudan, Saudi Arabia, and others, Iraq was clearly in the anti-Libyan camp regarding Chad.

Other African states, including the Côte d'Ivoire, Gabon, Burkina Faso, Senegal, and Benin, also provided support and mediation services to Habre. Zaire's contribution to preserving Habre's regime was particularly conspicuous. Zaire dispatched 2,000 paratroops to help guard strategic points in N'Djamena, freeing Habre's troops to fight against Goukouni and the Libyans in the north.[39] Indeed, by July 1983 Habre had recaptured Abeche, Oum Chalouba, and Faya-Largeau.

In the late summer of 1983, Libya reinforced its military forces in Chad and prepared to fend off any threat to its presence there. According to Western sources, Libyan combatants in Chad then numbered between 3,000 and 5,000, some of them belonging to the Islamic Legion that Qaddafi had formed for foreign interventionist missions—including the one in Uganda in the 1970s, which included Palestinians in its ranks.[40] A French source reported numerous bombing raids by Libyan aircraft on Habre's targets in northern Chad. With Libyan help, Goukouni recaptured Faya-Largeau in mid-August 1983, and Libya's flag was seen flying in the region.[41] Nevertheless, Tripoli continued to deny the presence of Libyan troops in Chad, arguing further that none would arrive "unless Libya acquiesces to Goukouni's request by sending in forces in order to balance French support for Habre."[42]

In January 1984, Goukouni's forces attacked Ziguey, a northern outpost controlled by Habre, where a large French force had been stationed. During the operation, a French Jaguar fighter plane was shot down and its pilot killed by a Soviet-made SAM-7 surface-to-air missile. Qaddafi denied any involvement in the incident and stated that "for a long time we have been trying to convince [Goukouni] not to attack the French forces, but at present we cannot control him."[43] However, foreign sources claimed that Qaddafi had complete control over Goukouni, to the extent that he could restrict the Chadian leader's freedom of movement and deny him and his forces access to arms or ammunition.[44]

In fact, tension was mounting between Qaddafi and Goukouni. The Libyan leader felt that Goukouni had proved unsatisfactory in helping him to achieve his ambitions in Chad and was not an effective counterweight to Habre. He sought another Chadian leader more amenable to Libyan authority, as he implied in an interview by stating that Goukouni "has already said that he does not want power."[45] Yet publicly, Qaddafi insisted that "Libya's stand with Goukouni . . . is firm [and] there will be no betrayal. We fought side by side . . . and we should continue fighting until the end."[46]

In April 1984, Libya announced its readiness to withdraw its forces from Chad—denials of their presence notwithstanding—provided that France, which was "colonizing Chad under the pretext of countering a Libyan presence there," did likewise.[47] The escalating tension with not only Goukouni, France, and the United States but also with Britain (although for reasons unconnected to the war in Chad),[48] combined with increased domestic and expatriate opposition activity,[49] convinced Qaddafi that Libya's resources were overextended and should be devoted to other priorities.

Following a period of secret negotiations, both Libya and France announced their agreement in September 1984 to begin a "total and mutual" withdrawal of troops from Chad, to be completed by mid-November. As the deadline arrived, France declared that it had indeed withdrawn; Qaddafi, however, had according to foreign sources failed to fulfill his part of the agreement. A meeting on 15 November 1984 between Qaddafi and French president François Mitterrand in Crete produced no tangible result and France soon returned its troops to Chad. Even so, Libya insisted that it had evacuated its troops, excluding those stationed in the Aouzou Strip, which Qaddafi regarded as Libyan territory. It even proposed to set up a joint French-Libyan-Greek commission (the Greeks had sponsored the September 1984 withdrawal agreement) to inspect Chad "inch by inch" and establish proof of its claim.[50] A ceasefire was more or less sustained throughout 1985, accompanied by Libya's continuing denials of interventionism.

Meanwhile, the Libyan-Sudanese-Egyptian triangle—a problematic arena for Libya's foreign policy, with important implications for its domestic scene—underwent some dramatic changes. Numayri's sixteen-year-old regime in Sudan was toppled in the spring of 1985. Tripoli embarked on political rapprochement with Khartoum, elbowing Cairo aside to court the new regime headed by General 'Abd al-Rahman Muhammad Siwar al-Dahab. Thus, less than four years after Sadat's assassination in Egypt, Numayri—who, like Sadat was anti-Libyan and pro-US—disappeared from politics as well, an event that somewhat alleviated the strain along Libya's border with Chad, which was also Sudan's neighbor.

In 1985—the twelfth year of Libya's de facto control of the Aouzou Strip—the Libyan flag flew over the two most important oasis towns in northern Chad, Faya-Largeau and Fada. The population was compelled to use Libyan currency. Travel in the area was permitted only to holders of passes issued by the Libyans. Arabic was the only language allowed; French, the language of the former colonial power, was expressly forbidden. Qaddafi explained these measures in a statement to an interviewer: "Chad is an extension of our country and we are an extension of Chad."[51]

In early 1986, the lull in fighting ended. Libyan forces, alongside those of Goukouni, attacked the two strategic towns of Kouba-Olanga, 450 kilometers northeast of N'Djamena, and Oum Chalouba, just south of the "Red Line"—the sixteenth parallel that divided the two warring sides and their respective foreign allies. A Libyan Tupolev-22 bomber attacked the N'Djamena airport in retaliation for an air strike by French bombers on 16 and 17 February 1986 targeting a new military airfield built by Libya at Wadi Doum, a Goukouni outpost in northern Chad.[52] These air raids coincided with ground fighting. It is unclear what actually motivated the resumption of hostilities at this stage; each side blamed the other. Indeed, Libya denied any intervention in the fighting and urged N'Djamena to publicly display the Libyan prisoners it claimed were captured during the fighting in February and March 1986.[53]

In the aftermath of the traumatic aerial bombing of Tripoli and Benghazi by the United States on 15 April 1986, Qaddafi's attention shifted. Fearing further US steps to undermine his regime, including fresh military strikes, Qaddafi lowered his military profile in Chad. Internal threats—especially the economic downturn caused by a decline in oil revenues on the one hand and growing Islamist dissent on the other—required his attention. Libya's economy had been hard hit by the mid-1980s decline in world oil prices; its annual oil income had fallen from a peak of US$22 billion in 1980 to US$10 billion in 1985. The resulting socioeconomic difficulties only encouraged the growth of anti-Qaddafi Islamist opposition.[54]

Perceiving Goukouni to be a negative asset, Libya shifted support to his rival, al-Shaykh Ibn 'Umar, a senior figure in the Gouvernement d'Union Nationale de Transition and a leader of pro-Libyan, breakaway faction the Conseil Démocratique de la Révolution. Anxious to bolster this new alliance, Libya resumed its offensive, attacking Goukouni-controlled areas in northern Chad and rounding up his supporters. Goukouni himself was reported to be seriously wounded while resisting arrest by Libyan forces in mid-October 1986.[55]

In November 1986, al-Shaykh Ibn 'Umar formally replaced Goukouni as head of the Gouvernement d'Union Nationale de Transition. (Goukouni was believed to be in a Tripoli hospital, or, as another source claimed, in a prison in Sebha in southern Libya.)[56] Soon afterward, the new leader paid a visit to Tripoli, where his hosts used the occasion to denounce the "French-American-Zionist colonialist intervention on the side of agent Habre."[57] Within days of the visit, Libyan troops went on the offensive once again, this time attacking a series of outposts in the Tibesti mountain area south of the Aouzou Strip. The Libyan offensive, which involved both ground forces and aircraft, also targeted Goukouni-controlled areas.

A counteroffensive was soon launched by Habre's forces, which had now combined with Goukouni's forces in a typical demonstration of Chad's fluid, opportunistic factionalism. The new Habre-Goukouni forces, supported by France and the United States—which delivered military supplies valued at US$15 million to Habre's government at the close of 1986[58]—was determined to crush the Libyan military presence in Chad. In what was described by an observer as a "brilliant desert blitzkrieg,"[59] the Habre-Goukouni forces stormed Fada—the strategic garrison located 192 kilometers north of the sixteenth parallel and held by Libya since 1983—and thus delivered a severe blow to the Libyan troops in the first days of 1987. Indeed, 800 Libyan soldiers were reportedly killed in the battle, while 81 were taken prisoner and some 1,000 fled.[60] Libya made no reference to the Fada defeat, adhering to its denial of any military intervention in Chad's war. "The Libyans have nothing whatsoever to do with what happened and what is happening" in Chad, Tripoli stated unequivocally, although the claim was contradicted by the public display of over 100 Libyan prisoners, including army officers and a Soviet-made Sukhoi fighter-bomber pilot, in N'Djamena in early January 1987.[61] Attempting to repair his credibility, Qaddafi "revealed" that "a Libyan military unit" of "a few hundred persons" had entered northern Chad in the autumn of 1986 in order "to locate the whereabouts of twenty Libyan technicians" allegedly kidnapped by Goukouni's men, who thought that their leader was imprisoned in Tripoli.[62] The capture of Fada marked a turning point in Libya's involvement in Chad's civil war; the opening of a second military front in northeastern Chad proved detrimental. Notably, however, reports of these battles came almost exclusively from official Chadian or anti-Libyan Western sources, whereas Tripoli maintained total silence.

On 4 January 1987, Libyan MiG-23s bombed Arada 120 kilometers south of the sixteenth parallel.[63] This time, Tripoli acknowledged that Libyan forces had crossed the sixteenth parallel, although it neglected to mention the bombing. Tripoli referred to the action as an "exceptional reprisal" that would not be repeated unless there was "renewed [French or French-backed] aggression";[64] indeed, it seemed to serve as a warning that if France did not curb its intervention, Libya would change the rules of the game and draw the French military into large-scale hostilities. Several days later, French aircraft retaliated by destroying six radar installations on the military airstrip Libyans had built two years earlier at Wadi Doum, northeast of Fada.[65] This blow, which immobilized Libya's main airstrip and logistics center in northern Chad, sent a clear signal to Qaddafi that France was determined to force him to withdraw from Chad.

Libya warned that it "would not accept—whatever the justification—the installation of a hostile regime in Chad, which would be used by imperialism to destabilize the security and stability of the Libyan Arab people inside [its] borders."[66] Tripoli accompanied the warning with the statement that Chad was "geographically and demographically [a] natural extension of Libya" and that therefore the US-French intervention in Chad was "basically [aimed against the] Jamahiriyya."[67] In February 1987, Libya raised the number of troops in Chad from an estimated 8,000 to about 15,000 (French and Chadian sources put the figure closer to 20,000).[68] French troops, too, were steadily reinforced.

To reinforce its troops, Libya relied on the informal military presence it maintained in the ethnically disputed, and economically neglected, indeed famine-stricken, region of Darfur in western Sudan, across the Chadian border. Under the guise of "relief missions," this force steadily increased in size, as did its artillery and logistical capabilities. It was equipped with lorries carrying supplies, oil products, medicines, medical equipment, rocket launchers, anti-aircraft guns, antitank guns, tanks, and hundreds of vehicles. By 1986, it was clear Qaddafi had decided to use the Darfur region as a rear base against Habre's army, hoping not only to improve his troops' strategic and military capabilities but also to avoid French air retaliation in pro-Western Sudan. Enjoying Darfur's proximity to both Chad and Libya as well as its geographical and political distance from Khartoum—which was in political chaos due to the weakness of the new government in any case—Qaddafi ignored repeated requests that he leave the area, denying that he had any forces in the Sudanese territory.[69] The situation revealed the increasing danger of the war's regional and international complications.

Indeed, Libya's new military and strategic advantages did not end Habre's military momentum. In March 1987, the Libyan army suffered further severe setbacks in the Fada area, where almost 1,000 soldiers were killed and over 100 were taken prisoner; fighting at Wadi Doum claimed over 1,200 Libyan casualties and nearly 450 prisoners, according to a Chadian source.[70] Western reports estimated that in the first three months of 1987 alone, Libya lost much of the territory it had held, between US$500 million and US$1 billion in armaments, and a third of its estimated 15,000–20,000 troops.[71] Given the source, however, Libya seldom responded to such reports. Qaddafi's greatest setback was the late March loss of Wadi Doum, Libya's only hardtop air base. This meant that the gateway to southern Chad, Faya-Largeau—which was located on an exposed plain between the Tibesti and Ennedi mountains—was now being deprived of vital air cover as well as food and military supplies and was in danger of being encircled. To prevent such an eventuality, Libya tactically withdrew from Faya-Largeau northward to the Aouzou Strip on 25 March 1987.

The evacuation of Faya-Largeau enabled Habre's forces to advance northward. Not long afterwards, Habre announced that his forces were in "total control" of the Bourkou and Ennedi regions in the north, which were now "free of Libyan troops."[72] N'Djamena's troops approached the Aouzou Strip, threatening Libya's control there for the first time since Qaddafi had annexed the region in 1973. Fearing an attack, Tripoli warned that "Aouzou is an indivisible part of the Libyan Arab land, and . . . was not in the past, is not in the present, and will not be in the future an object of bargaining, international arbitration, or secession."[73] Announcing that he would continue the war until the "liberation of the last inch of Chadian territory is achieved,"[74] Habre in effect pledged to continue the campaign into the Aouzou Strip. Well-publicized visits by Habre to Washington and Paris indicated that his two patrons would assist in this endeavor, prompting Tripoli to warn that it would view "any military action against Aouzou as a declaration of war against Libya."[75]

On 8 August 1987, Habre's forces, backed by their foreign allies, took control of the oasis town of Aouzou, the administrative center of the strip. Habre announced that 650 Libyans were killed and 147 captured in the operation.[76] Retaliating, the Libyans bombed the region, declaring that "we are repelling aggression against our international borders. The Libyans are now in a situation of legitimate self-defense. . . . We have no colonialist ambitions in Chad at all. We would like to put an end to this game . . . [and] to be an ally of the people in Chad."[77]

This message attested to Tripoli's anxiety about what appeared to be a US policy to help Habre eject Libya from Chad. To this end, the United States had transferred US$32 million in aid and armaments to Chad, including Redeye anti-aircraft missiles, and announced a decision to supply Stinger missiles.[78] The Stinger, a sophisticated, shoulder-launched missile, was expected to upgrade Chad's military strength at a time when France appeared reluctant to increase its supply of arms to N'Djamena.

An attack led by Habre in early September 1987 against Ma'tan al-Sarah—a key launching base for Libyan air raids—represented the first penetration of Chad's armed forces into Libyan territory (by about 100 kilometers). N'Djamena reported its troops had destroyed the base, killed 1,713 soldiers, and demolished some two-dozen Libyan aircraft.[79] Habre's victory dealt the final blow to the Libyan army.

Libya promptly accepted an OAU proposal for a ceasefire, formally announcing the end of the war and the "complete closure [of] the border with Chad, thus leaving Chad to the Chadians" on the condition that Chad abstain from incursions into the Aouzou Strip, which, it reemphasized, was sovereign Libyan territory. "Aouzou is indisputably a Libyan Arab region . . . [and we] do not see any justification for subjecting a portion of our national territory and sovereignty to international arbitration."[80] Chad, which otherwise also accepted the OAU proposal, responded by stating that the "war can only end when Libya evacuates occupied Chadian territory," clearly referring to Aouzou.[81]

Libya had reached one of the lowest points in its foreign and domestic affairs. Rising opposition to the regime was exacerbated by a power struggle between Qaddafi and his second in command, 'Abd al-Salam Jallud. According to various sources, Qaddafi held Jallud responsible for the military reversal in Chad. Jallud was thought to be less enthusiastic about the intervention and thus less inclined to prolong it.[82] The growth of expatriate opposition was also causing the regime in Tripoli serious concern; indeed the defection of the commander of the occupying forces, Colonel 'Abd al-Qassim Khalifa Haftar, and several hundred of his soldiers to one of the most important Libyan exile groups—the aforementioned National Front for the Salvation of Libya (NFSL)—indicated the direct connection between the Libyan debacle in Chad and the mounting political agitation in Tripoli.[83]

The Denouement of Libya's Involvement in Chad

Toward the end of the 1980s, Qaddafi concluded that the disadvantages of perpetuating the conflict with Chad outweighed the benefits and might even cost him his position. The war arena in Chad had become the locale for an international anti-Libyan alliance and domestic socioeconomic and political unrest. Libya's low status in the Arab and African arenas and its contentious relations with the West also played a considerable role.

Qaddafi announced Libya's official recognition of Habre's government in May 1988. Presenting the move as a gift to the African continent, Qaddafi stressed that Africa, presumably Chad in particular, "must eliminate Western military bases" from its soil.[84] Qaddafi still refused to compromise over the Aouzou Strip, however, thus precluding any significant reduction of tensions with Chad or its Western and Arab backers. Still, the ceasefire held; an ad hoc committee of the OAU established to discuss the sovereignty of the Aouzou Strip was about to meet, and both sides decided that resuming military operations at that time would be deleterious to their aims.

Tensions mounted in the spring of 1989, when Chad accused Libya of involvement in a failed coup launched by Idriss Déby, former Chadian chief of staff and one of the leaders of an armed faction allegedly supported by Tripoli. Habre also accused Qaddafi of planning a new military attack on Chad.[85] Denying these charges, Libya insisted that its war in Chad was over and that it "[did] not occupy any Chadian territories," deliberately ignoring the Aouzou Strip.[86] Habre kept up the pressure on Libya over the issue, relying on the backing of foreign powers led by the United States. Qaddafi had little choice but to begin negotiations with N'Djamena.

In June and July 1989, two separate attempts sponsored by African countries to bring Libya and Chad to the negotiating table ended in deadlock. The third round of talks, held in August 1989 and hosted by France and Algeria in Paris and Algiers, respectively, with the mediation of Kuwait, eventually culminated in an agreement to submit the dispute over Aouzou to the ICJ in The Hague if it were not settled after a year of bilateral talks. The parties also agreed to cease all hostile media campaigns, release all prisoners of war (there were some 2,000 Libyan captives in Chad), and refrain from interference in each other's domestic affairs.[87] The conciliatory atmosphere was reflected in the presence of an official Chadian delegation at the 1 September 1989 celebrations in Tripoli, the first since Habre's advent to power seven years before.

Nevertheless, Libya and Chad soon engaged in a new series of hostilities. In late March 1990, Chad accused Libya of supporting the National Salvation Front, the rebel force led by Idriss Déby.[88] Déby, who was indeed supported by Libya, intensified his attacks on Habre's troops in eastern Chad, using his base in neighboring Darfur as a launching pad for the attacks. (Under new leadership since 30 June 1989, Sudan was now politically distanced from the United States and Egypt, which is not to say it supported Déby; after all, it was all but impossible to monitor remote parts of Sudan's vast western territory.)

The foreign ministers of Chad and Libya met in Libreville under the auspices of Gabon—which chaired the ad hoc OAU committee—but the talks ended in deadlock, as did successive rounds of talks in Tripoli, N'Djamena, and Rabat in the summer of 1990. Apart from their major disagreement over the Aouzou Strip, the two countries differed over the issue of the Libyan prisoners of war still held by Chad. The latter's reluctance to release them was an obstacle to progress in bilateral ties, as Qaddafi could not politically afford to abandon them and face the consequences from the army.

In November 1990, the Chadian government claimed that "2,000 Libyan-backed attackers" led by Déby had crossed the border from Sudan and inflicted a deathblow on Habre's regime. On 2 December 1990, Déby seized power in N'Djamena; Habre fled to Cameroon and from there to Senegal, where he took refuge at the invitation of President Abdou Diouf.[89] Libya denied Chadian and Western claims that it was involved in the clashes and advised Chad "not to denigrate the name of Libya every time . . . internal problems erupt in N'Djamena."[90] Yet Déby's release of 400 Libyan prisoners only one day after his ascent to power, suggested a close connection between Déby and Qaddafi, as did the visit to Tripoli of an official delegation headed by Déby's brother, also on 3 December. Qaddafi officially recognized the Déby regime and praised him for removing Habre, the "knife which was mercilessly held at the throats of all the Chadians."[91] With the war over and Déby in power, Libya could now take care of its interests both at home and in Chad—just as it faced a new set of global conditions following the USSR's collapse.

Libya and Chad handed over the contentious issue of Aouzou to the ICJ. Its ruling, issued on 3 February 1994, unequivocally established Chad's sovereignty over the region. The ruling was an example of the trend, which began in the 1970s, toward international discouragement against occupation on territorial grounds, as many important multilateral accords were drawn to force states to withdraw from foreign countries[92] (although, the establishment of Eritrea in 1993, following a prolonged war against Ethiopia, certainly deviated from this pattern).

Perhaps because of growing internal dissent[93] as well as increasing external pressures—chief among them the Lockerbie dispute and the resulting UN sanctions imposed due to the incident—Qaddafi abided by the ICJ verdict. He completed the evacuation of his troops from Aouzou in May 1994. Shortly thereafter, the two countries signed the Historic Friendship, Good Neighborliness, and Cooperation Treaty *(Mu'ahadat al-Sadaqa wa-Husn al-Jiwar wa-al-Ta'awun),* and Qaddafi followed the occasion with a display of political support for President Déby: "From now on, [Libya] will not stand alone [in its struggle against the West]. We will stand by you and you should rely on us."[94] Déby's attendance at the anniversary celebration of Qaddafi's ascent to power on 1 September 1994 further symbolized the end of the Chadian quandary, which had plagued Libya for so long.

From the late 1990s and into the new millennium, Libya shifted its continental focus from Chad to broader sub-Saharan Africa, where it found significant leverage for its foreign interests and domestic prestige. In 1998, Tripoli formed a new regional bloc, known as Tajam'u Duwal al-Sahel wal-Sahara, or the Community of the Sahel and the Saharan States (COMESSA, which was renamed in 2001 the Community of Sahel-Saharan States [CEN-SAD]). COMESSA included Libya, Chad, Sudan, Niger, Mali, and Burkina Faso and attested to Qaddafi's continued determination to spread his political and ideological views throughout the Arab African world. He carved out an important niche in the organization for Chad.

Conclusion

Paradoxically, the settlement of the Aouzou dispute and the consequent withdrawal from Chad turned out to be the sole positive development in Libya's foreign affairs in the 1990s, otherwise the most devastating period of Qaddafi's regime. Finally acknowledging Chad's de jure and de facto control over Aouzou, Libya discarded its territorial burden and began to rehabilitate its seriously damaged position both at home and abroad. The end of the Chadian muddle also paved the way to eventual compromise in a more critical foreign dispute, the Lockerbie conflict.

Military intervention in Chad was pivotal to Qaddafi's foreign policy throughout much of his time in power. Ironically, Qaddafi garnered greater benefits from his ultimate defeat in Chad than from his earlier successes. Political rapprochement between Libya and Chad, which gathered momentum with Déby's advent to power in 1990, was further boosted in 1999, at least symbolically, when Déby awarded Qaddafi the highest Chadian medal on a visit to Tripoli that reciprocated Qaddafi's official visit to N'Djamena the year before. After introducing a multiparty constitution and injecting a new measure of political stability, Déby won Chad's first postindependence presidential election in 1996 and was reelected in 2001, with Libya's support.

Qaddafi underscored his continuing interest in Chad and its leadership in a statement made while hosting Déby in Tripoli in 2002:

> In the end, we do not want rewards or thanks [from Chad]. We did our duty toward the African continent and at the forefront of this is fraternal Chad. . . . Conflicts and disturbances in Africa drain its resources and impede the

process of the African Union. Consequently, it is in our supreme interest to put an end to these conflicts . . . so that we save our resources and potentialities in order to build the African Union and face Africa's enemies. . . . In fact, I am much obliged to the sons of the Chadian people, those in the government and those in [the northern Muslim region of] Tibesti, because they put the interest of Chad and that of the Chadian people . . . above internal matters and differences. . . . We have made a pledge of men and achieved the peace of the brave and are now in one rank and one trench in Libya and in Chad. . . . Weapons will be laid down and we will move toward development in Tibesti and the construction of Chad, Libya, and Africa.[95]

Déby's public support for Qaddafi reflected not only his gratitude to the leader for installing him in power and backing his government but also the increasing influence Tripoli had over N'Djamena's politics in 2005.

The two major political-military crossroads in Libya's foreign relations in Africa during Qaddafi's first two decades in power, in Uganda and Chad, differed in initiation, scope, and consequences. They dominated both Libya's foreign agenda and domestic affairs, and gouged deep scars in the collective conscience of Libya's society and leadership.

The three heads of state whose countries were militarily entangled with Qaddafi's Libya during the 1970s and 1980s had all been removed by 1990. Idi Amin, Uganda's president between 1971 and 1979, died in Saudi Arabia in the summer of 2003; Anwar Sadat, Egypt's president from 1970 to 1981, was assassinated in Cairo in the fall of 1981; and Hissen Habre, Chad's president from 1982 to 1990, was living in exile in Senegal while awaiting trial for crimes against humanity as of 2006. By contrast, after more than three-and-a-half decades of leadership, Mu'ammar al-Qaddafi continues to hold the reins.

Notes

1. For a comprehensive work on interstate boundaries and the use of force to alter them, see, for example, Day, *Border and Territorial Disputes,* and Zacher, "The Territorial Norm." For an examination of Libya's arguments regarding Aouzou and their historical accuracy, see Neuberger, *Involvement, Invasion and Withdrawal,* pp. 29–30; Lemarchand, "The Case of Chad," pp. 107–108; and Simons, *Libya and the West,* pp. 60–81.

2. Neuberger, *Involvement, Invasion and Withdrawal,* pp. 22–24; St. John, *Libya and the United States,* pp. 125–126. See also Joffé, "Reflections on the Role of the Sanusi," and J. Wright, "Chad and Libya: Some Historical Connections."

3. For a comprehensive analysis of the issue of war initiation (and termination), see Scott and Stam, "The Duration of Interstate Wars, 1816–1985," and Stedman, "Conflict and Conflict Resolution in Africa."

4. For the extent of the French military presence in Chad, see *Arab Report and Record,* 16–31 August 1971, p. 442. For an analysis of the war-torn Chadian setting

and its ethnic, religious, social, economic, and political diversity, see Neuberger, *Involvement, Invasion and Withdrawal,* pp. 9–21; Foltz, "Reconstructing the State of Chad," pp. 16–20; and Decalo, "Chad: The Roots of Centre-Periphery Strife."

5. Neuberger, *Involvement, Invasion and Withdrawal,* p. 25.

6. Ogunbadejo, "Qaddafi's North African Design," p. 156.

7. On 28 November 1972, Tombalbaye submitted to Libyan pressure and cut off diplomatic ties with Israel. For further details on Israel's connections with Chad, see Lemarchand, "The Case of Chad," p. 110, and Cooley, *Libyan Sandstorm,* p. 98. For Israel's position on the African continent in the early 1970s, see Oded, *Africa and the Middle East Conflict,* pp. 1–7, 161–174.

8. Neuberger, *Involvement, Invasion and Withdrawal,* pp. 27–28.

9. Ibid., p. 29.

10. Per Terrence Mirabelli in a report from Tripoli, *The Middle East,* October 1976, pp. 26–29.

11. Simons, *Libya and the West,* p. 54.

12. For the text of the agreement, see Legum, *Africa Contemporary Record,* 1980, p. C87.

13. Neuberger, *Involvement, Invasion and Withdrawal,* p. 35. *Lebensraum* is the German term for "habitat"; used in both ecological and sociological contexts, it literally means "living room." It refers to the expansionist policies of the Nazi government, which aimed to provide space for the growth of the German population.

14. *Le Monde,* 26 November 1980; *Africa Research Bulletin,* 1–30 November 1980; *New York Times,* 17 December 1980; *Washington Post,* 7, 8, and 15 January 1981.

15. For details, see Foltz, "Reconstructing the State of Chad," p. 15.

16. Radio Tripoli, 16 December 1980 (DR); *Jamahiriyya Review,* December 1980.

17. For the text of the communiqué, see JANA, 6 January 1981 (BBC). The jamahiri unity stems from the term jamahiriyya. With the formal establishment of the People's Power system in March 1977, Libya's official name became *al-Jamahiriyya al-'Arabiyya al-Libiyya al-Sha'biyya al-Ishtirakiyya* (the Arab Libyan People's Socialist State of the Masses).

18. Joffé, "Reflections on the Role of the Sanusi," p. 48.

19. See St. John, *Libya and the United States,* p. 132. For a review of Qaddafi's broader relationship with the OAU, see Pondi, "Qadhafi and the Organization of African Unity."

20. For a comprehensive survey on US and French policies in Chad and the surrounding region, see Selassie, "The American Dilemma on the Horn"; Keller, "United States Foreign Policy on the Horn of Africa"; Lemarchand, "The Crisis in Chad"; and Joure, "France and Crisis Areas in Africa."

21. *Jerusalem Post,* 8 January 1981, quoting a report from the Tripoli government; Radio Tripoli, 15 February 1981 (DR).

22. *Eight Days* (London), 21 March 1981; AFP, 27 March 1981 (DR); *Africa Research Bulletin,* 1–31 January 1981.

23. TASS, 29 April 1981 (BBC).

24. *Now* (London), 5 December 1980; *Jamahiriyya Review,* March 1981.

25. *Le Monde,* 22 January 1981.

26. JANA, 19 March 1979 (DR).

27. *Jamahiriyya Review,* November 1981.

28. Radio Paris, 18 September 1981 (DR); *Le Monde,* 21 October 1981.

29. *Le Monde,* 15 September 1981.

30. *The Economist,* 10 October 1981; *al-Watan al-'Arabi,* 30 October–5 November 1981.

31. JANA, 14 January 1981 (DR); *Le Monde,* 3 March 1981.

32. AFP, 30 October 1981 (DR).

33. Radio Tripoli, 15 November 1981 (DR).

34. *Foreign Report,* 12 August 1982.

35. *Africa Economic Digest,* 13 August 1982.

36. For the recognition of Goukouni's government, see JANA, 31 October 1982 (DR). For more on Libya's arms supplies, see *Foreign Report,* 27 January 1983.

37. See, for example, Radio Tripoli, 25 June 1983 (BBC), and Radio Bardai (a clandestine, Libyan-operated radio station broadcasting from Bardai in northern Chad), 4 July 1983 (BBC).

38. *The Jamahiriyya Mail* (Tripoli), 2 July and 11 July 1983 (DR).

39. For further details on the international repercussions of Qaddafi's occupation of Chad and the African states' motives for backing Habre, see Ogunbadejo, "Qaddafi and Africa's International Relations." See also Foltz, "Reconstructing the State of Chad," pp. 26–27, and Huliaras, "Qadhafi's Comeback."

40. *The Guardian,* 11 August 1983; AFP, 1, 2, 8, and 18 August 1983 (DR).

41. *Daily Telegraph,* 19 August 1983.

42. From Qaddafi's interview with Radio Paris, 30 January 1984 (DR); *al-Zahf al-Akhdar,* 4 February 1984.

43. AFP, 25 January 1984 (DR); Radio Paris, 30 January 1984 (DR), quoting Qaddafi.

44. *Africa Confidential,* 20 June 1984.

45. Radio Paris, 30 January 1984 (DR).

46. *Al-Zahf al-Akhdar,* 25 February 1984.

47. Qaddafi, quoted at a press conference on 2 May 1984 by Radio Tripoli, 3 May 1984 (BBC).

48. Britain severed its diplomatic ties with Libya in the spring of 1984 in response to the killing of a British policewoman and the injury of eleven others in an anti-Libyan demonstration in front of the Libyan embassy in London. Britain blamed Libya for the violence. See Ronen, "Libya's Conflict with Britain," p. 274.

49. The growing activity of the Libyan opposition was reflected in, among other things, an armed attack on Qaddafi's office and residence in the Bab al-'Aziziyya barracks in Tripoli on 8 May 1984. The scale of the assault took Qaddafi by surprise and evoked concern.

50. See, for example, the interview with 'Abd al-Salam al-Turayki, Libya's foreign minister, *al-Watan,* 18 December 1984; JANA, 27 January 1985 (BBC).

51. *Le Monde,* 24 April 1984. For more on Libya's rule in Aouzou, see *The Guardian,* 17 March 1984; *Africa Confidential,* 20 June 1984; and *Christian Science Monitor,* 18–24 January 1986.

52. Radio N'Djamena, 12 February 1986 (BBC); *Le Monde,* 18 February 1986; AFP, 18 March 1986 (DR). Intentionally, this research work does not provide systematic coverage of the fighting.

53. JANA, 14 and 18 February 1986 (DR); AFP, 20 March 1986 (DR).

54. "Country Report: Libya," 1986, p. 10. For further details on Libya's economy in the 1980s, see Vandewalle, "Qadhafi's 'Perestroika'." For the Islamist threat, see Ronen, "Qadhafi and Militant Islamism." For background on the broader opposition to Qaddafi, see L. Anderson, "Qadhafi and His Opposition."

55. AFP, 30 October, 1 November 1986 (DR).

56. *The Economist,* 22 November 1986; *al-Dustur* (London), 17 November 1986.

57. *Al-Fajr al-Jadid,* 7 December 1986.

58. "Country Report: Libya," 1987, no. 1, p. 9.

59. Lemarchand, "The Case of Chad," p. 121.

60. Radio N'Djamena, 2, 3, and 4 January 1987 (DR).

61. For Libya's denials, see, for example, JANA, 2 and 3 January 1987 (BBC). For Chad's claims, see, for example, AFP, 14 January 1987, and Radio N'Djamena, 20 January 1987 (BBC).

62. Qaddafi, in an interview with *Libération,* 5 January 1987.

63. Radio N'Djamena, 5 January 1987 (DR).

64. AFP, 6 January 1987 (DR), quoting a communiqué issued by the Libyan Embassy in Paris.

65. *International Herald Tribune,* 8 January 1987, quoting French defense minister André Giraud.

66. From Qaddafi's interview with *Politique Internationale,* quoted by Tripoli TV, 14 February 1987 (BBC).

67. *Al-Zahf al-Akhdar,* 5–19 January 1987.

68. *Jerusalem Post,* 10 February 1987, quoting data issued by the French defense ministry; Habre's interview with *Jeune Afrique,* 18 February 1987.

69. *Al-Siyasa* (Khartoum), 24 March 1987; JANA, 24 and 27 March 1987 (DR). See also Burr and Collins, *Africa's Thirty Years' War.*

70. Radio N'Djamena, 20, 25 March 1987 (DR).

71. *International Herald Tribune,* 3 April 1987; *Wall Street Journal,* 15 April 1987; *The Times,* 13 May 1987.

72. Radio N'Djamena, 3 April 1987 (DR).

73. JANA, 12 April 1987 (DR).

74. *Africa Research Bulletin,* 15 July 1987.

75. JANA, 12 July 1987 (DR).

76. AFP, 12 August 1987 (DR), quoting the Chadian ambassador in Paris.

77. Tripoli TV, 1 September 1987 (BBC).

78. *The Guardian,* 11 September 1987; *New York Times,* 6 November 1987. For further details on US aid to Habre, see Ogunbadejo, "Qaddafi and Africa's International Relations," p. 45.

79. Radio N'Djamena, 8 September 1987 (DR).

80. *Al-Majalla,* 16–22 September 1987, from an interview with a senior Libyan diplomat.

81. JANA, 17 September 1987 (DR); *Financial Times,* 19 September 1987.

82. *Foreign Report,* 5 February 1987; *Mideast Markets,* 16 February 1987; and "Country Report: Libya," 1987, no. 2, pp. 5–7.

83. AFP, 25 March 1988 (DR).

84. Tripoli TV, 29 March 1989 (DR).

85. *Al-Hayat,* 6 April 1989; AFP, 5 May and 4 June 1989 (DR).

86. JANA, 4 June 1989 (DR).

87. Radio Algiers, 31 August 1989 (DR).

88. AFP, 27 March 1990 (DR).

89. In 2000, a Senegalese judge, responding to Chad's demand, indicted Habre on charges of torture and crimes against humanity. A short while later, the Senegalese Supreme Court overturned the ruling, stating that he could not be tried there. Habre's victims then filed complaints in Belgium under its "universal jurisdiction" law. As the Belgian probe continues toward an indictment and extradition request, the case has also opened a new possibility for bringing Habre's accomplices to justice in Chad itself. See *Human Rights Watch,* http://hrw.org/justice/habre/ and http://www.fidh.org/article.php3?id_article=997 (accessed 28 April 2008).

90. JANA, 11 and 20 November 1990 (DR).

91. JANA, 5 December 1990 (DR).

92. Zacher, "The Territorial Norm," pp. 244–246. On the end of armed interstate conflicts, see Scott and Stam, "The Duration of Interstate Wars," and Wittman, "How a War Ends."

93. Consider, for instance, the broad-based military uprising that reportedly took place in mid-October 1993 in the Bani Walid region southeast of Tripoli, home of the Warfallah tribe. The rebellion, which was promptly crushed, was planned by Colonel al-Rif'i 'Ali al-Sharif, who had commanded a Libyan military force in Chad during the 1980s. See *al-Hayat,* 20 and 31 October 1993, and *al-Wasat,* 1–7 November 1993.

94. As quoted in *al-Shams,* 16 July 1994.

95. JANA, 22 January 2002 (BBC).

9

A New Quest for Unity and Leadership in Africa

In the late 1980s, Libya began to gear its African policy toward mending diplomatic relations on the continent, where it once wrought so much havoc—while also making strenuous efforts to create a new vehicle for Qaddafi's leadership.

At that time, Libya's standing in the international community had reached its nadir. The country's conflict with the West and especially the United States was escalating alarmingly; the Soviet Union's disappearance from the international stage only further exposed Qaddafi to unremitting international pressure. Moreover, Libya's poor relations with the Arab world—along with its diminished standing in Africa—made clear that its foreign policy needed to be revitalized, especially in light of developments at home, where social and political restiveness engendered by economic recession and Islamist opposition also threatened Qaddafi's rule.

All this led Qaddafi to conclude that Africa was the one arena that could offer Libya substantial political and diplomatic benefits. Thus he sought to highlight Libya's inseparability from and major contributions to the continent. On 25 March 1988, he declared that "Libya is an active state in the African family. It constitutes the northern gate of Africa . . . [and] is also the Mecca of African revolutionaries."[1] This claim starkly contrasted with Qaddafi's belligerence toward Africa during the 1970s and most of the 1980s, when he fought in Uganda and Chad and supported various insurgencies, coups, and radical organizations—which he called "liberation movements"—all over sub-Saharan Africa. Conspicuous among these were uprisings in Angola, Guinea-Bissau, Namibia, Zimbabwe, and Mozambique.[2]

Qaddafi seized highly publicized occasions on the continental calendar to project the image of a responsible and peaceseeking leader. On Africa Day in May 1988, he offered to reconcile with eight African countries, all aligned with the West: Kenya, Liberia, Democratic Republic of Congo (then

Zaire), Mauritius, Gabon, Senegal, Gambia, and the Côte d'Ivoire. Diplomatic relations were soon resumed with many of them, including Senegal—which had broken off relations with Libya in 1980 on the grounds that it was involved in subversive activities against the Senegalese government—as well as Democratic Republic of Congo and Liberia, with which Qaddafi had cut ties in 1984 in protest of their relations with Israel. At the same time, he further improved diplomatic relations with Nigeria, Niger, Burkina Faso, Ghana, and Somalia. The decision to reopen relations with countries that had maintained their connections with Israel reflected the newly pragmatic thrust of Qaddafi's foreign policy.

Qaddafi continued his campaign to render Libya a pivotal component of the African continent at the OAU Defense Committee meeting on 28 March 1989. This occasion followed a prolonged boycott of the Libyan capital as a venue for official OAU gatherings, which ended only after Libya had withdrawn its troops from Chad. Qaddafi used the meeting to stress the mutual concerns of Libya and sub-Saharan Africa. His list included fighting "Western imperialism," which "is determined to violate Africa's independence and sanctity as well as drain its resources and which thinks that every individual who lives on the African continent is a slave to the white Europeans"; the rejection of South Africa's apartheid government; and the elimination of any "foreign [Western] military presence" from the continent.[3] Just as the USSR was collapsing and the United States was achieving global dominance in international politics, Qaddafi was waving his twenty-year-old banner against Western imperialism in Africa. The politically inexpedient move indicated that, for all his newfound pragmatism, Qaddafi's adherence to ideology was still strong.

Qaddafi's African policy at this time was highly selective; he chose causes he wanted to promote, mainly through rhetoric, proclaiming that "Libya is the guard of Africa. . . . It will remain the gate which will not be crossed by the enemy except over the dead bodies of Libya's sons." Repeatedly referring to his country as "the gate to Africa" indicated the historic centrality of Africa to the Qaddafi regime's identity. The regions comprising the modern Libyan state tended to be demarcated by the trade routes across the Sahara from central Africa and the Sahel rather than by East-West routes. This fact helped integrate Fezzan urban centers such as Ghadames, Ghat, Kufra, and Sabha into the fabric of the Mediterranean coast as well as into the great commercial centers of the Sahel.[4]

In the summer of 1989, Qaddafi embarked on a tour to Mali and Niger, providing further evidence of his new spirit of reconciliation toward Africa. On 1 September of that year, the participation of approximately fifteen African heads of state in Qaddafi's twentieth-anniversary celebrations indicated that his efforts had paid off—Libya had indeed improved its status on the continent.

A number of exceptions to the rule of reconciliation, however, reflected the increasing dialectic between ideology and pragmatism. A telling example was the diplomatic crisis with Burundi, arising in mid-1989 due to Libya's alleged involvement in an abortive plot on the life of Burundian president Pierre Buyoya during a military parade on 11 March 1989 and culminating in the expulsion of all Libyan nationals and diplomats.[5] Libya denied the accusation. Another example of Qaddafi's deviation from the declared policy of mediation was Libya's sending of a high-ranking military delegation to Guinea-Bissau to mediate in the dispute. This act of "mediation" was taken in Qaddafi's capacity as president of the COMESSA (also known as CEN-SAD), but a Senegalese source claimed that the so-called mediators took part in training and arming the combatants.[6] The case was reminiscent of other alleged instances of Libyan subversion in Niger, Mali, Nigeria, Cameroon, Gabon, Gambia, and Ghana, dating back to the early 1980s.

Africa's Role in the Lockerbie Resolution

At the end of the 1980s and early 1990s, Qaddafi believed that the United States was determined to eradicate him politically. He was also concerned about the crisis in the Gulf, which culminated in the US-led Operation Desert Storm in early 1991. In late 1991, the United States and Britain accused Libya of responsibility for the 1988 bombing of a Pan Am airliner over Lockerbie, Scotland and the French blamed it for the 1989 explosion of a DC-10 over Niger. The West now perceived Libya to be a state sponsor of world terrorism; refusing at this stage to be held accountable, Libya lost any international legitimacy it may have had.

By the spring of 1992, the UN Security Council, at the behest of the United States and Britain, imposed economic and diplomatic sanctions on Libya for its refusal to extradite the two Libyan nationals suspected of the Lockerbie bombing. The sanctions, periodically extended during the 1990s, had a debilitating effect on all facets of Libyan life, resulting in diplomatic isolation, economic stagnation, social and political restiveness, and, most perilous to the regime, growing threats of violence by the militant Islamist opposition. The broad-based military uprising in the army camps at Misurata and Bani Walid near Tripoli in October 1993, aimed at overthrowing the regime, signaled that even Qaddafi's traditionally loyal army was turning against him.

In the post–Cold War era, Africa's significance in global affairs was largely diminished and the continent was in dire need of international support. Qaddafi identified this need, which perfectly meshed with Libya's own objectives. Many African nations were likewise eager to foster bilateral ties, hoping that their political support of Libya would convince Washington to reevaluate its policies toward the continent and increase economic support. Furthermore, other positive policy developments during the first half of the 1990s enhanced Libya's prestige on the continent, thus smoothing the way for African states to promote rapprochement with Tripoli. Most noteworthy among these were the final withdrawal of Libyan forces from Chad and the restoration of Libya's diplomatic ties with South Africa following the collapse of the apartheid regime.

Libya's diplomatic overtures included providing financial aid to various African countries. Gambia restored diplomatic relations after Qaddafi granted it some US$6 million in November 1994;[7] two years later, a grant to Niger of US$2 million helped avert a budgetary crisis, and a donation of US$200,000 to Mali went toward development and defense.[8] Though not huge, these grants were important as symbols of Libya's support and as a potential pledge for the future.

From 24 through 27 February 1997, the annual OAU meeting of foreign ministers convened in Tripoli. The forum unanimously declared "Africa's support for and solidarity with Libya" and set up a five-member committee of foreign ministers (from Niger, Chad, Burkina Faso, and Mali as well as Libya) "to liaise between Libya and the West for the resolution of the Lockerbie dispute." Encouraged after nearly five years of diplomatic isolation, Qaddafi addressed the delegates with the slogan "Africa for the Africans" and blamed the United States for strife on the African continent.[9] The following May, addressing a mass prayer assembly marking the Muslim New Year in Niger's capital, Niamey, he admonished African Muslims to obey the word of God rather than that of the UN Security Council, which he claimed was under the sway of "anti-Islamic Christian colonialism."[10] In Kano, the Muslim center of northern Nigeria, Qaddafi addressed a massive Muslim audience, calling on "millions of Muslims" to battle "America and Europe." Attacking Western capitalism, he urged "millions of Muslims [in Africa] to demonstrate . . . the power of Islam and its ability to defy and counter these campaigns of humiliation."[11] During a successful public-relations tour in May 1997, Qaddafi received Nigeria's medal of honor from General Sani Abacha at a state banquet in Kano. Qaddafi also gained political revenue by defying the UN air embargo, as he traveled around Africa aboard a Libyan aircraft without penalization.

The thirty-third annual OAU summit in Harare, Zimbabwe, in June 1997 saw a diplomatic achievement of even greater significance for Libya, as African leaders pledged to take action to solve the Lockerbie dispute. "These obnoxious sanctions," the plenum noted, "affect not only the Libyan people but also the rest of Africa and, therefore, merit full African mobilization alongside Libya."[12] Following up on this resolution, the presidents of Burkina Faso, Chad, Mali, and Niger met in Tripoli from 15 through 17 August 1997 to work out a solution to the dispute.

South African president Nelson Mandela, a longtime supporter of Qaddafi, paid two visits to Tripoli in late October and early November 1997, respectively. During his second trip, he condemned the United States and other Western states for playing the "policemen of the world"—Qaddafi's perception precisely—and awarded Qaddafi South Africa's "highest decoration to a citizen of a foreign country" for having helped fight apartheid.[13] This further improved the Libyan leader's reputation in Africa.

Girding Its Loins:
The Formation of the COMESSA Bloc

To further mobilize effective political support, Libya invested heavily in the sub-Saharan region. On 3 February 1998, Qaddafi convened a two-day meeting of the Sahel and the Sahara states in Tripoli, which culminated in the formation of a new regional bloc, the aforementioned COMESSA, comprising Libya, Sudan, Niger, Mali, Burkina Faso, and Chad. The density of the area's Muslim population evidently inspired the cooperation plan.[14] Led by Qaddafi and based in and financed by Tripoli, the new body aimed to establish "efficient and fruitful cooperation to face up to the challenges of the next century, when there will be no place for small entities."[15]

The establishment of the bloc demonstrated Qaddafi's growing diplomatic influence and relatedly Libya's emerging prominence in Africa, especially the sub-Saharan region. Libya's state-controlled media widely covered the summit, glorifying Qaddafi's "victory for the unity of the African continent" as evidence of his ability as "a backer of Africa's causes and a defender of its rights and freedoms."[16]

The dynamics of the Lockerbie dispute changed in late February 1998 when the International Court at the Hague ruled in favor of Libya, stipulating that the trial be held in a third country before a Scottish judge in accordance with Scottish law. This ruling, which implied that the Lockerbie proceedings could not be exclusively controlled by Washington or London, paved the way for Libya's new African friends to convince the UN Security Council to hold a debate on the sanctions. Behind the scenes was a deal between Gambia—which then held the rotating presidency of the Security Council—and Libya, which agreed to pay off Gambia's debt to the UN. Gambian ambassador Abdoulie Momodou Salah was instrumental in steering the debate, held on 20 March 1998, along lines favorable to Tripoli.[17]

Qaddafi continued to cultivate relations across the continent. This was exemplified by, among other things, Eritrean president Isaias Afeworki's visit to Tripoli between 31 January and 3 February 1998, which led to the reestablishment of diplomatic ties. Afeworki—whose government was known for its pro-US orientation—pledged solidarity with Libya against the US-led sanctions, a stand that Tripoli perceived as a political rebuke to the United States.[18] Soon there was a stream of visits to Tripoli by African heads of state, including Malawi's President Muluzi Bakili in February 1998 and Gambia's President Yahya Jammeh the following March, both of whom declared their support for the lifting of the sanctions.

Qaddafi's visit to Chad from 30 April to 4 May 1998, when he was given a lavish reception, should be viewed as a similar attempt to bolster his position at home, on the continent, and in the diplomatic battle against the United States. N'Djamena's political embrace of Qaddafi signaled the rehabilitation of bilateral ties and an end to an embarrassing chapter in Libya's history. In return, Qaddafi announced that Libya would supply Chad with electricity and oil and finance a new parliamentary building in N'Djamena. The Chadian head of state, Idriss Déby—who had ascended to power with Qaddafi's help—publicly sided with Libya in its demand to lift the sanctions. The alignment appeared somewhat ironic to Washington, which had supported Chad in its conflict against Libya throughout the 1980s, contributing substantially to the latter's defeat.

Promising economic aid to other African states as well as Chad, Tripoli revealed its determination to harness all its resources in using the continent as a lever against the West despite its economic difficulties. In the 1990s, the Libyan economy endured a cumulative loss of between US$24 billion and US$33 billion as a result of the UN sanctions, which lasted from 1992 to 1999. The steep decline in the world's oil prices had led to a considerable loss of revenues as well. The slump resulted in growing unemployment, a halt to the implementation of infrastructures, the near-cessation of foreign investment, an increase of 200 percent in the price of foodstuffs, and transport problems, mainly for the national airline, due to a shortage of spare parts.[19] Nevertheless, Libya kept its financial promises in return for support against the Lockerbie sanctions.

To help fund the annual OAU summit to be held in Burkina Faso in June 1998, Libya reportedly gave Blaise Campaore—president of both Burkina Faso and, at the time, the OAU—a grant of US$2 million.[20] At the summit, all the states in attendance announced they would immediately cease to comply with the UN air embargo against Libya, at least in the case of religious, humanitarian, and OAU-related flights. Moreover, the organization called on its members to ignore the sanctions after September 1998 unless the United States and Britain agreed to hold the Lockerbie trial in a neutral third country.[21]

Hailing the OAU resolution as "another victory in the just confrontation with Western imperialist American arrogance,"[22] Libya hastened to implement the OAU decision by sending a plane from Tripoli to N'Djamena and back on 23 June 1998. A month later, Blaise Campaore also violated the sanctions and flew to Libya. Encouraged by the absence of any UN penalties, Libya invited a large group of African heads of state to fly to Libya to attend the celebrations of the birth of the Prophet. The invitation was accepted by the presidents of Chad, Niger, Gambia, Eritrea, Mali, Sierra Leone, Zimbabwe, the Central African Republic, and Sudan, thus further demonstrating Libya's growing prominence in African politics.

Qaddafi cultivated his role as mediator in Africa's disputes. He convened COMESSA on 5 and 6 September 1998 in Tripoli to discuss the conflict between Uganda and Democratic Republic of Congo. Known as the World War of Africa, this intrastate conflict became an interstate conflict, engulfing central Africa and undermining the region's political stability. Rwanda, Uganda, and Burundi supported the Congolese rebels against President Laurent-Désiré Kabila, who had the support of Angola, Namibia, Zimbabwe, the Central African Republic, Chad, Sudan, and, according to the rebels, Libya. The COMESSA meeting resulted in a proposal to replace Ugandan and Rwandan troops with peacekeeping forces from other African countries. According to foreign sources, between 1,000 and 1,500 Chadian troops, financed by Libya, were dispatched to aid Kabila's government.[23] Qaddafi followed this peacemaking move with mediation in the dispute between Ethiopia and Eritrea that erupted in 1998. However, Addis Ababa unofficially accused Tripoli of supporting Asmara in the war, donating money, weapons, fuel, and fighter-pilot training.[24] Tripoli insisted Libya was only a mediator.

In August 1998, Qaddafi flew in a Libyan aircraft under the aegis of the OAU, ostensibly on a humanitarian mission to evacuate Arab families from the war zone in the Democratic Republic of Congo.[25] The United States and Britain, faced with violations of the air embargo on what had become an almost routine basis, responded by formulating a compromise proposal in the summer of 1998, agreeing to hold the trial in the Netherlands under Scottish law.

Grateful for their contribution to this outcome, Qaddafi praised his African colleagues for "[trampling] with their feet on the American-inspired resolutions." He expressed his gratitude by declaring a shift in ideological and political focus from the Arab world to Africa: "I had been raising slogans of Arab unity and brandishing the standard of Arab nationalism for forty years but it has not been realized. That means that I was talking in the desert. . . . [Instead,] I now talk about pan-Africanism and African unity."[26] In October 1998, he symbolically changed the name of Tripoli's national radio station from Voice of the Greater Arab Homeland to Voice of Africa, while Libya's daily television-news program replaced its background map of the Arab world with a map of Africa.

Qaddafi's Pursuit of African Unity

Meanwhile, South Africa (along with Saudi Arabia) promoted mediation efforts to resolve the Lockerbie dispute, which resulted in the extradition of the Libyan suspects to the Netherlands to stand trial and the suspension of the sanctions in the spring of 1999. Qaddafi continued to foster his position on the continent, promoting "unity, Islam, and anti-Western colonialism" as the common goals of its states. Africa must enter the twenty-first century "united and renewed" and must "rid itself of the colonizer's religion . . . and bring about the triumph of Islam," he declared, pledging to guard African rights and "extinguish the fire" of its disputes. Making his "Africa first" policy the focus of his foreign agenda, Qaddafi went on to announce that "we Libyans are Africans. Africa is our continent [and] we are proud of belonging to it."[27]

Accordingly, his activism on the African continent continued. On 13 and 14 April 1999, Libya again hosted a summit of the heads of state of the COMESSA. Three days after the adjournment of the summit, Tripoli hosted another summit on the war in the Democratic Republic of Congo, its second that year. The meeting was attended by Qaddafi and the heads of state of Congo, Chad, Eritrea, and Uganda, who drew up an agreement between President Kabila and Uganda's President Yoweri Museveni. The agreement stipulated, among other things, a ceasefire and the deployment of an African peacekeeping force composed of Libyan and Eritrean troops. While the peace initiative lacked the approval of other central actors in the war—including the Congolese rebels and Rwanda—it afforded Tripoli the opportunity to announce a diplomatic breakthrough. Qaddafi hosted two more summits on the conflict in May; though they produced no tangible results, they served his interests by maintaining his image in Africa as a leading peacebroker.

Libya's high-profile peacemaking activities in Africa were further enhanced by Qaddafi's mediation between the warring factions in Sierra Leone's prolonged civil war. Although in the past, Qaddafi had supported the rebel Revolutionary United Front under the leadership of Foday Sankoh, in the late 1990s he embarked on a conciliatory course with Freetown. Thus, on 7 June 1999, following a visit from the president of Sierra Leone, Ahmed Tajan Kabbah, the Libyan leader pledged to appoint a Libyan ambassador to Freetown as well as to pay for the accommodation of Sierra Leone's diplomatic mission to Tripoli.[28]

At the annual OAU summit held in Algiers from 12 to 16 July 1999 Qaddafi—who had been absent from recent summits abroad—proposed a special summit to be held in Libya, the goal of which would be to amend the OAU charter to reflect the realities of globalization. The invitation was accepted and on 8 and 9 September 1999, Libya hosted an extraordinary convention of the OAU in Sirte, attended by 45 African leaders at a cost of US$50 million.[29] The event, timed to coincide with the commemoration of the thirtieth anniversary of his rule, showcased African support for Libya. Libya responded by contributing US$4.5 million to cover the dues of seven OAU member-states that were in arrears, namely Comoros, Guinea-Bissau, Equatorial Guinea, Liberia, Niger, São Tomé and Principé, and Seychelles.[30]

At the conference, Qaddafi promoted his grand design for what he termed the United States of Africa in order "to meet the challenges of globalization in the new millennium." The Sirte Declaration, released at the end of the summit, refused to endorse Qaddafi's United States of Africa framework but agreed to the creation of certain umbrella institutions: a central continental bank, a monetary fund, an investment bank, a pan-African parliament, and a supreme court.[31] The framework for the African Unity agreement had been provided by the 1991 Abuja Treaty, which came into force in 1994 as the first in a series of steps that were to culminate in an Africa Economic Community by 2025.[32] The inspiration for Qaddafi's dream of an African union was the European Union, an organization that grew out of a world war and took more than thirty years to develop. Qaddafi ignored the Arab Maghrib Union established in 1998 but now virtually defunct, although Libya was still a member.

Two ceremonial tours by Qaddafi in the summer of 1999, one to Chad and Zambia and the other to South Africa, further attested to Libya's ongoing diplomatic endeavors and rising status on the African continent. While in South Africa—a potential opponent of his unification endeavor—he marked the retirement of Nelson Mandela and the inauguration of his successor, Thabo Mbeki. His host portrayed Qaddafi as "one of the revolutionary icons of our time."[33]

Tripoli continued to use COMESSA as an effective platform for cultivating Libyan interests on the continent, especially as the regions of the Sahel and the Sahara gained diplomatic prominence. At a summit held in Chad from 2 through 5 February 2000, Gambia, Senegal, and Djibouti joined Libya, Niger, Burkina Faso, Mali, Chad, the Central African Republic, Eritrea, and Sudan to raise COMESSA membership to eleven. In his role as leader of the organization, Qaddafi urged more African countries to join the bloc and thereby "form the cornerstone of an African union."[34]

Focused on his aspiration for unity and cognizant of the pending Lockerbie verdict, Qaddafi continued to promote his vision of a United States of Africa, hosting and visiting various African heads of state. At the time, Africa was in fact the only region friendly to Qaddafi. Despite the suspension of the sanctions, he was still isolated from the West and he disdained the Arab world for its "betrayal" in adhering to the sanctions. The highlight of his new campaign was the OAU summit held in Lomé, Togo, from 10 to 13 July 2000, which was financed largely by Libya.[35] Qaddafi arrived in Togo after making an overland journey from Libya across West Africa via Niger, Burkina Faso, and Ghana that symbolized the goodwill he enjoyed across the continent.

The Lomé summit dealt primarily with the notion of an African union, which Qaddafi had most recently raised at the EU-Africa summit in Cairo in April 2000. Twenty-seven of the fifty-three OAU member-states—two-thirds of those present in Lomé—signed a document that stipulated the formation of a union within one year. The summit also decided to hold an extraordinary conference on the implementation of a union charter in Sirte in March 2001. Following the summit, Qaddafi set off on a tour of West Africa, visiting Benin from 12 to 14 July 2000. There he reiterated his message that the continent must be transformed into a single entity, "thereby erasing the borders demarcated by Western imperialism." In addition, he stressed that "Africa must rid itself of Christianity, the religion of colonization," and replace it with Islam.[36]

In some ways, the union created at the Lomé summit was the old OAU with new labels. The principal organs were renamed but retained their roles: the summit became the Conference of the Union, the Council of Ministers became the Executive Council, the Secretariat became the Executive Commission, and the Ambassadors Committee became the Committee of Permanent Representatives. A new organ, the Pan-African Parliament—a concept borrowed from the 1991 Abuja Treaty—was conceived to design a framework for the development, mobilization, and use of African resources, both human and material, as means toward continental self-sufficiency.

The parliament's formation—like that of the Court of Justice, the Economic, Social, and Cultural Commission, and the financial institutions (the African Monetary Fund, African Central Bank, and African Investment Bank)—was put on hold. However, the reluctance of leading African states, namely South Africa and Nigeria, to relinquish their hard-won position on the union is evident from the sixteen principles set forth in article 4 of the document signed in Lomé. These included "the right of the Union to intervene in a member-state pursuant to a decision of the Conference of the Union in respect to grave circumstances, namely war crimes, genocide and crimes against humanity" (4h), the "non-interference by any member-state in the internal affairs of another" under all other circumstances, and the pledge that "governments [that] come to power by unconstitutional means [will not be] allowed to participate in the work of the Union" (4g).[37]

Threats to Unity:
Violence Between Sub-Saharan Migrants and Libyans

Ironically, while Qaddafi was championing the vision of a borderless United States of Africa for the benefit of the African people, Libya was the site of unprecedented violence against African migrant workers. In the fall of 2000, Libyan citizens began rioting in protest of the economic and security burden posed by the presence of migrants—many of them illegal—whose differing cultural values they also resented. Migrants had been arriving in Libya in ever-increasing numbers since the 1990s, many of them intent on reaching the European "promised land" in search of political asylum and a better life.

They came mainly from impoverished sub-Saharan Africa but also from countries just beyond the Arab-African seam line—countries with membership in COMESSA. Instead of continuing on to Mediterranean Europe however, large numbers of migrants settled illegally in Libya, generating economic, social, cultural, health, and security problems.

Many of these migrants were unskilled agricultural and manual workers who indeed clashed at times with Libyan society. In late September 2000, an unprecedented outburst of violence in the town of Zawiyya west of Tripoli and in the capital itself, resulted in casualties estimated at between 150 and 500 or more. The Libyan authorities claimed that the clashes were the result of a drug war between Libyan dealers and their African competitors ("brothers from beyond the Sahara").[38] Tensions between Libyan citizens and the million-strong migrant community heightened over competition for employment and the perception that the migrants were responsible for a nationwide upsurge of crime, including drug trafficking, robbery, rape, prostitution, and alcohol consumption. Many citizens also believed that the migrants were largely responsible for the increased incidence of HIV/AIDS in the country, although the government itself never explicitly made such accusations.[39] After Libyan rioters indiscriminately killed and injured migrants from Sudan, Niger, Nigeria, Chad, Gambia, Burkina Faso, and Ghana, Qaddafi's vision of an African union was somewhat tarnished, particularly in the eyes of the heads of these African states. Acting primarily to appease them as well as to diminish resentment in local circles, Qaddafi sacked Minister of Public Security and Justice Abu al-Qasim al-Zawi, thereby signaling his serious concern for Libya's relations with its African friends as well as for preventing or deterring the recurrence of further riots—while implicitly shifting the blame for the riots to the ministry.[40]

Many of the African migrant workers were subsequently deported or repatriated by their governments. The airlifting of migrants to their home countries was made possible by the suspension of the UN air embargo a year and a half earlier; by contrast, in 1995, the UN had rejected Libya's request to deport 2,200 illegal African migrants to their countries of origin by plane.[41] The relatively quick and smooth deportation in 2000 was also facilitated by Qaddafi's cautious handling of the crisis, designed to avoid any further diplomatic escalation that might impede the creation of the African Union. The operation was somewhat reminiscent of deportations carried out by the Libyan government in two major waves in the mid-1980s and mid 1990s, when thousands of foreign workers, both Africans and Arabs, were expelled.[42]

Qaddafi downplayed the impact of the riots at the OAU summit held in Tripoli from 7 to 9 November 2000. He reiterated his well-publicized motto that "Africa is one people and one family" and claimed that "foreign hostile hands" were behind the violence in an attempt to "block our [African] unity." Libya's deputy secretary of information in charge of the African Union, Bukhari Huda, denied that racism and xenophobia were motives for the disturbances and noted that "out of 5 million Libyan citizens, 1.4 million are blacks," including "many Libyan civil servants" such as the senior General Yunis Jaber, commander of the Libyan armed forces and secretary of the Provisional Defense Committees.[43] Libyan nationals did indeed include a substantial minority of sub-Saharan Africans, especially in the Fezzan region to the south on the Chadian border, a legacy of the slave trade in precolonial Libya and of French colonial rule over Chad.[44]

Qaddafi's effort to minimize the damage to Libya's regional stature coincided with a similar effort on the part of the economically weak sub-Saharan countries with which he was concerned; they were anxious that the flow of Libyan aid, actual and potential, go unimpeded. This anxiety was highlighted in a statement by Ali Sidi Adam, a presidential adviser in Niger, who accused the international press of "abusively exaggerating" the confrontation between African immigrants and "young Libyans," alluding to the latter's supposed hot-blooded nature rather than any xenophobic or racial motivation. He echoed Qaddafi's argument that, through this confrontation, foreign "invisible hands" were trying "to sabotage the African Union project." Adam also emphasized Libya's helpful attitude to Africans continentwide. "The between 4,000 [and] 5,000 Niger nationals" staying in Libya "are faring very well . . . and are not undergoing any form of harassment by the local population," he stated to the Pan-African News Agency in early December 2000. Niger's position was shaped not only by economic considerations but also by the memory of a 1976 conflict whereby Qaddafi had annexed Nigerien territory while backing a coup attempt against the government in Niamey. Fear of renewed subversion was compounded by the knowledge that the Armées Révolutionairies du Sahara—the only rebel group that had refused a peace agreement with the Nigerien government in the fall of 2000, after all the other groups had ceased fighting—had access to Tripoli.[45]

African states not in need of Qaddafi's support, such as Nigeria, were less deferential, as were the deportees themselves. The Lagos National Human Rights Commission submitted a complaint against the Libyan government for its expropriation of the property of about 2,000 Nigerian deportees. Similar complaints were made by a group of approximately 400 Cameroonian nationals, who alleged following their expulsion that they had been attacked by Libyan citizens while taking refuge in a Libyan camp soon after the riots, despite security measures taken by the authorities.[46] Such hostilities didn't dissuade sub-Saharan migrants from coming to Libya in the early 2000s, however; indeed, their numbers steadily grew, and the government became ever more resolute to stem the tide.

The African Union: Gaps Between Vision and Reality

The obstacles to the full realization of African unity were formidable, especially in light of the reservations of several African states, most noteworthy
among them Nigeria and South Africa.[47] These two leading states were sus-
picious not only of Qaddafi's motives but also of his allegiance to the
African cause, which they imagined was based less on his commitment to
Africa's development and political stability than on Libya's own national
interests. Given their influential standing on the continent, they also feared
Qaddafi's rival bid for leadership and political impact. Mistrust and even
outright rejection of Qaddafi's commitment to Africa also arose from domestic circles disinclined to share their country's economic resources with poor
African countries. The convening of the first session of the Parliament of the
Economic Community of West African States (ECOWAS) from 21 to 26 January 2001 in Abuja, Nigeria, with representatives from fifteen countries,
clearly attested to Africa's political regionalism.

Naturally, the most impoverished countries became the staunchest backers of Qaddafi's unionist policy, hoping their diplomatic support would
ensure the continuation of Libya's economic aid. In keeping with its perspective that money could solve, or at least mitigate, its problems in Africa,
Libya offered Guinea a "gift" of US$500,000, which the latter rejected.[48]
The offer may have been designed to influence Guinea's leaders to align
themselves with Liberia's Charles Taylor, who backed the rebels in Sierra
Leone. Like Taylor, rebel leader Foday Sankoh had allegedly received military training in Libya and was presumed to be politically close to Qaddafi.
Though Libya never confirmed such interventionist activities, they seemed
in line with its efforts to secure political influence in more distant parts of
the continent, even at the risk of open competition with other pillars of the
African community.

In short, the obstacles to African union did not extinguish Qaddafi's
activist ardor; he appeared determined to fight the "battle of African unification." Swept along by his own rhetoric, he stated that "Africa, at the moment,
does not own any intercontinental missiles or nuclear bombs, but now it is
stronger than those who own cruise missiles. Iron will rust, wither, and come
to an end, but Africa's determination will never rust."[49]

On 11 July 2000, twenty-seven heads of state (just over half of the OAU
membership) signed the Constitutive Act of the African Union. While taking
Qaddafi's plan one step further, the Act did not provide for the immediate
creation of a political union. Rather, it laid the foundations for the establishment of key organs that would hasten the process of economic integration.[50]
Libya was then expecting the Lockerbie verdict; it came in January 2001,
sentencing one of the two accused Libyan nationals to life imprisonment

while implicitly holding their government responsible for the explosion of the Pan Am aircraft. Qaddafi was now anxious to have the suspended sanctions formally lifted and relations with the West promptly normalized. Soon, on 1 and 2 March 2001, the final signing of the Constitutive Act took place at the OAU summit in Sirte. It demonstrated the public support of the signatories for Libya's struggle against UN sanctions. On 26 May 2001, the African continent marked a new chapter in its history as the African Union entered into being and the Organization of African Unity (OAU), which had led Africa since 1963, ceased to exist.

The African Union was formally inaugurated in Durban, South Africa, on 9 July 2002. Qaddafi "deserved all the praise heaped on him by the adoring crowd for having led the charge for the Union," one foreign commentator stated; he had emerged as one of the continent's most outstanding political guardians and ideological pillars, commanding significant attention at home and abroad. It was nevertheless ironic that the old Nkrumahist dream of a United Africa had been revived and driven by a North African Arab rather than by a sub-Saharan African.[51]

Qaddafi now assumed the role of peacebroker and political stabilizer as "the Caesar of New Africa," in one Arab commentator's words.[52] Libya's intervention in the Central African Republic in late May 2001 reflected this new position. Though strategically located in the heart of Africa and rich in natural resources, the Central African Republic had became a center of money laundering and arms dealing, as well as an occasional stopover for members of Osama bin Laden's al-Qaida. Libya's declared aims were to minimize its political and military instability, which had the potential of spreading to Libya directly or through neighboring Chad. Tripoli backed the regime of Ange-Felix Patasse in the wake of an abortive coup launched by soldiers loyal to former president Andre Kolingba. In November 2001, Tripoli sent more troops to protect Patasse and even bombed dissident positions. The dissidents again attempted to overthrow Patasse's regime but, aided by Libyan troops, Patasse foiled the scheme. The Libyan soldiers withdrew on 28 December 2002 and were replaced by a new peacekeeping force. It was only in March 2003 that the forces of former army chief of staff François Bozize eventually succeeded in toppling Patasse and seizing power in Bangui.

In 2002 and 2003, Qaddafi was also active in intraconflict negotiations in Chad, where he mediated between the rebel Movement for Democracy and Justice and the Chadian government. Oddly, while the latter accused Libya of trying to manipulate the talks, the former accused it of supplying arms to the government.[53] Granted, Qaddafi had clear stakes in Déby's regime, which was suffering from growing political threats, some indirectly connected to the war that had erupted in Darfur in the early spring of 2003 along the Sudanese-Chadian border.

In the early 2000s, Libya also supplied Zimbabwe with weapons to replenish its arsenal, which had been depleted by the war in the Democratic Republic of the Congo; in addition, it donated a gift of US$1 million to Zimbabwe's President Robert Mugabe for his 2002 presidential election campaign. Qaddafi's "checkbook diplomacy" entailed a promise to supply most of Zimbabwe's fuel requirements in a deal with the Libyan-owned oil-marketing company Tamoil that totaled US$360 million. In return, Libya expected to receive shares in various businesses in Zimbabwe as well as bartered goods. However, the Libyan oil deal soon collapsed, as Zimbabwe failed to keep up payments to Tamoil.[54]

Aware of the importance of COMESSA in African politics, Qaddafi convened its representatives in Sirte in early March 2002. COMESSA now had eighteen member states: Libya, Burkina Faso, the Central African Republic, Chad, Egypt, Sudan, Djibouti, Eritrea, Gambia, Mali, Morocco, Niger, Nigeria, Senegal, Somalia, and Tunisia as well as two new members, Togo and Benin.[55] However, Qaddafi failed to achieve his vision of a United States of Africa that would incorporate all the states on the continent under a single leader—preferably Qaddafi himself. This idea was rejected by the African foreign ministers' summit that convened in South Africa in January 2003. A month earlier, Qaddafi had been excluded from an African peer-review system established under the New Partnership for African Development that was aimed at encouraging Western investment on the continent. The main partners in the program, South Africa and Nigeria, were concerned that Libya's involvement would deter Western support.

However, these failures were eclipsed on 20 January 2003, when African states including South Africa voted for Libya's chairmanship of the UN Human Rights Commission, in the face of US objections. The vote of confidence once again showed the value of the "African asset" to Libya's foreign policy. This was further underscored in early 2003 when Libya's Ministry of African Unity was subsumed into the Ministry of Foreign Affairs and International Cooperation—one of the most powerful executive organs of the government in Tripoli.

Qaddafi's aspirations for a leadership position in a united Africa were demonstrated once again during the African Union summit that convened in Maputo, Mozambique, in July 2003. There he declared that "Africans need not fear the tsetse fly and mosquito, for they are God's armies, which will protect us against colonialists," who would "get malaria and sleeping sickness" should they try to occupy Africa.[56] This somewhat odd message raised certain questions. To which colonizers was Qaddafi referring now, in 2003, when Libya's relations with the formerly colonialist West had substantially improved? It is possible that the Libyan head of state still found it difficult to adjust his old rhetoric to fit changing circumstances. Whatever his intentions were, Qaddafi registered a symbolic achievement at the Mozambique summit by changing the date of Africa Day from 25 May to 9 September, the day of the Sirte declaration on the establishment of the African Union—which also happened to be close to Libya's 1 September Revolution Day.

Africa received less attention from Libya from 2004 onward, especially after the UN sanctions and the EU-related embargo were finally lifted. Tripoli was entering a new era of diplomatic normalization with the West and diverted all its energies to that end. However, African leaders' visits to Libya continued. On 27 January 2005, Olusogun Obasanjo, the president of both Nigeria and the African Union, visited Libya. That same day, the chairman of the Community of the Sahel and the Saharan States (COMESSA), Mali's President Amadou Toumani Touré, also arrived, as did Chad's President Idriss Déby. Somalia's Abduallah Yusuf Ahmad visited Tripoli on 8 April 2005, and Ugandan president Yoweri Museveni came four days later. Côte d'Ivoire's President Laurent Gbago came on 24 April. On 13 May 2005, Qaddafi hosted the presidents of Sénégal and Benin—Abdoulaye Wade and Mathieu Kerekou, respectively—and, two days later, the presidents of Gambia, Nigeria, and Chad. This stream of visitors, of whom the above are merely the highlights, indicates Qaddafi's success in turning Libya into a central diplomatic destination for leading African politicians.

In late May 2005, enjoying his rehabilitation and renewed respectability in the international community, Qaddafi toured Africa again. His visit was reciprocated two months later by the visit to Tripoli of the president of Burkina Faso. On that occasion, Qaddafi reiterated his well-known message of "Africa's need to present a unified front to the world and to speak with one voice" in dealing with both internal and external challenges. "We need a strong African Union to serve Africa and defend the continent's dignity, security, and development." At the opening session of the summit, he proposed that ministerial institutions be established on the level of the African Union and that Africa become a borderless state with a single currency, passport, and pancontinental peacekeeping force.[57] The implication was that he himself should be the leader of this state. Yet it seemed that Qaddafi still had considerable work to do before his vision of African unity could ever be completely realized.

Conclusion

Libya's foreign policy in Africa has undergone dramatic vicissitudes throughout Qaddafi's reign. Nevertheless, its central tenets remained basically unchanged, including the defense of Libya's borders against real or perceived threats; the enhancement of Qaddafi's political position at home and abroad;

the eradication of Western "imperialist" and "Zionist" influences; the glorification of the status of Islam; the propagation of Libya's prorevolutionary theory beyond its borders; the development of potential economic and natural resources; and the fulfillment of long-desired territorial ambitions or "historical claims" in Tripoli's parlance.

While the ends have not varied, the means have undergone far-reaching change, as Tripoli has adjusted its decisionmaking strategies to reflect the altered states of its domestic, regional, and above all international affairs. The collapse of the Soviet Union, for instance, definitely affected Libya's relations with other African states. The strategic, political, economic, and military changes resulting from the end of the Cold War were detrimental for Tripoli, at least in the short- and medium-term. The subsequent emergence of a US-dominated New World Order further destabilized Qaddafi's essential interests and political position, causing him to reevaluate the potential diplomatic assets of Libya's African environs.

Qaddafi's foreign policy in Africa can be schematically divided into two main periods. The first, lasting from Qaddafi's advent to power until the end of the 1980s, was characterized by belligerence as well as frequent reversals on matters of diplomacy and culminated in the failed military interventions in Uganda and Chad. In that period, Qaddafi was seen by many in Africa and beyond as a bellicose and unpredictable leader. The second period, from the beginning of the 1990s onward into the twenty-first century, has been marked by increased diplomatic efforts and peacebrokering since Qaddafi began making Africa the focus of his foreign-policy agenda. Over time, Qaddafi has worked to present himself as a pragmatic and responsible leader—a senior statesman rather than a mere head of state.

Following two unsuccessful attempts at military occupation in the 1970s and 1980s, Libya did not repeat its mistakes in Africa or any other foreign arena. Conceivably, the intervention in Uganda and particularly the one in Chad—which ended in total disaster for Tripoli—convinced Qaddafi that political, economic, and military involvement in its neighbors' affairs would neither automatically secure Libya a leading position on the continent nor promote its interests in Africa or beyond. In fact, these two disastrous interventions damaged almost every facet of Libya's international standing and had social and political repercussions on the home front as well.

The disappearance of the Soviet Union, Libya's sole foreign patron, from the international arena left Qaddafi alone, exposed to Washington's hostile foreign policies. It was not long before the dangerous implications of the New World Order manifested themselves in the US-instigated, UN-imposed Lockerbie sanctions. The sanctions accelerated the deterioration of Libya's internal and external affairs, forcing Qaddafi to expend all his efforts to reverse it. The full compliance of Arab countries, including those of the Maghrib, with the UN sanctions highlighted Libya's low status in the international community.

At that juncture, Qaddafi began to view Africa as a lever uniquely designed to pull Libya out of its foreign-policy swamp. In order to obtain the required leverage, however, he had to employ tactics entirely opposed to those he had used in the first phase of his leadership. Therefore, he began resorting mainly to diplomatic rather than subversive activities, often backing them with economic incentives. Concurrently, Qaddafi became a prominent mediator in regional disputes. These new methods soon proved fruitful for Libya, although they hardly served to lessen conflict in Africa. The Libyan leader gradually rose to the forefront of African diplomacy, successfully spearheading his grand vision of a United States of Africa. Indeed, the speed with which Libya has burst forth into the sphere of African diplomacy since the early 1990s is nothing less than astounding. The substantial role African diplomacy played, however indirectly, in rehabilitating Libya's reputation amid the international community is likewise remarkable. Nevertheless, Qaddafi's personal and political skills and efforts—reinforced by those of his son, Saif al-Islam—are primarily responsible for Libya's return to respectability and legitimacy on the African continent and beyond.

Notes

1. Tripoli TV, 25 May 1988 (DR).
2. For more details, see Huliaras, "Qadhafi's Comeback."
3. Tripoli TV, 29 March 1989 (DR).
4. Tripoli TV, 29 March 1989 (DR). For the historical roots of Libya's African identity and its role as a link between Africa and the Mediterranean coast, see Joffé, "Libya's Saharan Destiny." See also J. Wright, "Enforced Migration."
5. AFP, 5 April 1989 (DR); "Country Report: Libya," 1989, no. 3, p. 8.
6. Huliaras, "Qadhafi's Comeback," p. 20.
7. Legum, *Africa Contemporary Record,* 1996, p. B502; "Country Report: Libya," 1996, no. 2, p. 12; Wiseman, "Military Rule in The Gambia," p. 932.
8. Ronen, "Libya's Diplomatic Success in Africa," p. 62.
9. *Al-Shams,* 24 and 26 February 1997; *al-'Arabi,* 28 February 1997. For a detailed survey of Libya's diplomatic relations with the OAU, see Pondi, "Qadhafi and the Organization of African Unity."
10. Tripoli TV, 8 May 1997 (BBC).
11. *Al-Shams,* 10 May 1997.
12. *Middle East Times,* 13 June 1997; Lewis Machipisa, "Overwhelming Support for Libya from African Leaders," InterPress Service, 4 June 1997.
13. *Al-Fajr al-Jadid,* 14 November 1997.
14. Chad's Muslim population was estimated at 50 percent, Niger's at 85 percent, Mali's at 60 percent, and Sudan's at over 60 percent.
15. JANA, 5 February 1989 (BBC).
16. Tripoli TV, 4 February 1989 (BBC).
17. Huliaras, "Qadhafi's Comeback," p. 15.
18. Radio Tripoli, 3 February 1998 (DR).
19. *The Economist,* 7 February 1998; *al-Quds al-'Arabi,* 4 June 1998; *Middle East,* July 2000; Doyle, "Libya: After (UN) Sanctions."

20. *Africa Research Bulletin,* 1–31 March 1998.

21. JANA, 10 June 1998 (DR).

22. *Al-Shams,* 10 June 1998.

23. *New Vision,* 18 January 1999; AFP, 20 April 1999 (DR). For Libya's denial, see JANA, 7 January 1999 (DR); *International Herald Tribune,* 1 October 1998; *Le Soir,* 28 December 1998; and "Country Report: Libya," 1998, no. 4, p. 15.

24. For details on the war, see Ofcansky, "Ethiopia and Eritrea."

25. JANA, 30 August 1998 (DR).

26. JANA, 6 September 1998 (DR); *Middle East Times,* 26 September 1998.

27. See, for example, *Africa Research Bulletin,* 1–31 March 1999; Tripoli TV, 2 February 1999 (DR); and Tripoli TV, 13 March 1999 (BBC).

28. AFP, 18 June 1999 (DR).

29. *New African,* November 1999, citing a report from Sirte by Gamal Nkrumah.

30. Huliaras, "Qadhafi's Comeback," p. 18; *al-Quds al-'Arabi,* 10 and 11 September 1999.

31. *Al-Hayat,* 10 September 1999.

32. Zartman, "The Future of Continental Regionalism," p. A57.

33. South African Press Association, 13 June 1999 (BBC).

34. AFP, 5 February 2000 (DR).

35. *Africa Research Bulletin,* 1–31 July 2000.

36. Ronen, "Libya's Diplomatic Success," 2002, p. 70.

37. Zartman, "The Future of Continental Regionalism," p. A58. For details on the Abuja Treaty, see Packer and Rukare, "The New African Union and its Constitutive Act."

38. Ronen, "A Libyan-Italian Encounter: The Changing Mosaic of Mediterranean Migration."

39. *Middle East International,* 13 October 2000. For further details on the riots, see Pargeter, "Violence in Libya."

40. *Al-Sharq al-Awsat,* 26 November 2000. Zawi's ousting was part of a more general shake-up of the General People's Committee (that is, Libya's government). Replaced by 'Abd al-Rahman al-'Abbar—a hard-liner with close links to the powerful Revolutionary Committees—Zawi was appointed in late 2001 to the position of Libyan ambassador to Britain, which had restored diplomatic ties with Tripoli after a fifteen-year hiatus.

41. *The Middle East Economic Digest,* 20 October 1995.

42. For more on the earlier mass deportations, see Ronen, "Libya," 1987, pp. 560–561 and 1997, pp. 485–487.

43. Radio Tripoli, 9 October 2000 (BBC); *New African,* November 2000.

44. See Dunton, "Black Africans in Libya."

45. *Africa Research Bulletin,* 1–30 September 2001; Solomon and Swart, "Libya's Foreign Policy in Flux." Libya's close ties with various circles in Niger were further evidenced in 2005, when it granted citizenship to 500 Nigerien rebel refugees from the Touareg. See *al-Quds al-'Arabi,* 16 August 2005.

46. *Africa Research Bulletin,* 1–31 December 2000; *The Vanguard* (Lagos), 9 December 2000.

47. For South Africa's stance toward Qaddafi's unification campaign, see Kornegay, "Beyond the OAU." South African president Thabo Mbeki's visit to Libya in mid-June 2002, on the verge of the African Union's formation in Durban, was apparently connected with these unification activities.

48. *Africa Research Bulletin,* 1–31 March 2001, quoting Minister for African Unity 'Abd al-Salam Turayki.

49. Ronen, "Libya's Diplomatic Success," p. 71.

50. For further details on the Union's Constitutive Act, see *New African,* July–August 2002, p. 30.

51. *New African,* September 2002, citing a report from Durban by Pusch Commey. "The old Nkrumahist dream" refers to the vision of Kwame Nkruma (1909–1972), the founder and first president of Ghana, who was one of the most prominent pan-Africanist statesmen of the twentieth century, known in particular for his anti-colonialist position.

52. *Al-Suraqiyya,* 13 August 2001.

53. "Country Report: Libya," July 2002, p. 16, January 2003, p. 17, and October 2005, p. 17.

54. *Africa Research Bulletin,* 1–30 November 2001, 1–31 December 2001, and 1–28 February 2002. See also Solomon and Swart, "Libya's Foreign Policy in Flux," pp. 7, 12.

55. In 2005, the number of COMESSA's member-states reached twenty-three. See Joffé, "Libya's Saharan Destiny," p. 613.

56. Solomon and Swart, "Libya's Foreign Policy in Flux," p. 16.

57. *Al-Mustaqbal,* 17 June 2005; Xinhua, 5 July 2005 (DR).

10

Conclusion: Qaddafi's Changing Strategies for Survival

Qaddafi "is our spiritual leader, our godfather," stated a well-known Libyan artist when asked to explain his dedication to painting portraits of the Libyan head of state. "I do it out of love," he added, echoing the sentiments of many in Libya toward their leader of almost four decades.[1] Such adoration, which in certain circles borders on a cult of personality, is the result of a combination of factors, pivotal among them the close identification of the man with the state.

The popular equation "Qaddafi is Libya and Libya is Qaddafi" has become seared into the Libyan collective consciousness. This is not surprising given that most of the country's population, estimated at 5.74 million in 2004, is fairly young. Indeed, a 2003 estimate found that Libyans over the age of sixty-five made up only 2.9 percent of the general population; in 2006, statistics showed that more than half the population was under the age of twenty.[2] In other words, most Libyans were born after Qaddafi came to power and have grown up under the revolution, exposed to the pervasive influence of its political and ideological dictates as well as to the constant presence of their author, "Brother Leader" Qaddafi. Thus, having known only "the Colonel" as their leader and being unfamiliar with any alternatives, many Libyans have found it irrelevant to distinguish between Qaddafi's hegemonic leadership and their country's political life.

But it is not only Qaddafi's vigorous charisma, prolonged leadership, or ideological impact, or even a combination of the three, that have secured for him a place in the Libyan pantheon. Indeed, one can enumerate a long list of explanations for his status. One involves the country's abundant petroleum reserves and the economic and political leverage they provided the regime. Another points to a well-marshaled state machinery dedicated to portraying Qaddafi as a supreme leader and ideologue devoted to the welfare of his people and the advancement of "his" state and its society—a devotion that garnered Libya a place of prominence on the global map for the first time in its history, much to the pride of its citizens.

Adopting patterns characteristic of authoritarian regimes—most conspicuously those in the USSR and Eastern Europe, with which he was closely associated and strategically allied during the Cold War—Qaddafi has imposed suppressive measures to block any deviation from his self-styled revolutionary principles and political norms. He has employed a wide variety of means to achieve the objective of popular identification with his leadership and unique ideology. His colorful, larger-than-life portrait gazes down from billboards and tall buildings all over Libya, radiating fatherly love, determination, and self-assurance and projecting an image of Qaddafi and Libya as two sides of the same coin. Qaddafi exudes confidence in the system he has created and the benefits it can bestow on the Libyan state and its people.

Furthermore, during the 1990s, when UN sanctions were causing economic stagnation, social unrest, and diplomatic difficulties, that—along with the growing militancy of domestic Islamist opposition—threatened his control of the state, Qaddafi and his inner circle broadened his leadership to include a more prominent Islamic dimension. This was of particular importance in refuting the Libyan Islamists who claimed that Qaddafi's regime was "infidel" and therefore illegitimate. Interestingly, it was then, in the third decade of his rule, that the government issued a stamp to commemorate the twenty-third anniversary of the revolution that depicted Qaddafi on a white horse leaping into the sky—presumably with a certain resemblance to al-Buraq, the winged white steed that carried the Prophet Muhammad on *al-Isra'*, as his midnight journey from Mecca to Jerusalem is called. This was one of a series of moves undertaken by state-controlled bodies to glorify Qaddafi's religious position and, thus, reinforce his political status. "We value and are proud of your religious leadership of millions of Muslims from East to West, which enables the banner of Islam to be raised high in fulfillment of the will of Allah," stressed a message released by one of the state-affiliated organs in that politically sensitive period.[3]

At the other end of the political spectrum from Qaddafi's stalwart supporters were his opponents, united in their wish to see his regime toppled yet largely fragmented by political, ideological, and personal rivalries. Prominent within this camp were dissidents who were active mostly outside of Libya beyond the reach of Qaddafi's "iron fist." Nevertheless, they succeeded neither in affecting domestic policy nor in changing the political circumstances to the detriment of the regime. The activities of these expatriate opponents—"stray dogs" in the official parlance of the jamahiriyya—remained mainly a nuisance rather than a threat. By contrast, the domestic Islamist opposition, which declared a jihad against Qaddafi's "infidel" regime, did achieve a degree of influence that endangered Qaddafi's control of the country and consequently compelled him to change his approach to affairs of state. Ironically, this camp followed the ways of the regime by resorting to forceful Islamic discourse and violence in order to promote its religious-political agenda. Mindful of its highest priority—retaining its hold on power—the Qaddafi regime fought back, resorting to suppressive methods to combat the Islamist menace which it indeed managed to contain by the end of the 1990s.

At the beginning of the twenty-first century, however, it was difficult to gauge the real extent of popular support for Qaddafi's rule, particularly as the security apparatus and the Revolutionary Committees—made up of the regime's watchdogs—continued to prevent any deviation from the "right path," even though the hard-line model of revolution had become obsolete.[4] Whatever this suggests about the actual strength of Qaddafi's political position, the termination of Libya's dispute with the West and particularly with the United States has largely neutralized the once-dangerous sting of Libyan opposition. Libya's reentry into the global community and its consequent focus on drafting economic reforms, attracting direct foreign investment, channeling oil revenues into infrastructure and development projects, and "Libyanizing" the labor market in order to reduce the staggering 30 percent unemployment rate of the early 2000s have given the Libyan state and society new, constructive momentum.

When the United States removed Libya from its list of state sponsors of international terrorism and restored diplomatic ties in mid-2006, it ended a cycle of enmity between Tripoli and Washington that had lasted about three decades. This cycle encompassed a variety of conflicts fueled, in large measure, by the Cold War, in which Libya sided with the Soviet Union, as well as by a religious-cultural conflict that Qaddafi termed "the war between Christianity and Islam." Thus, the breakup of the Soviet Union at the turn of the 1990s dramatically changed Libya's agenda and the basis for bilateral relations with the United States, for which the terrorist attacks on the World Trade Center on 11 September 2001 provided a similar impetus.

With the disappearance of the USSR from the global stage, Libya lost its international backing. Disappointed by the Arab world's failure to promote Nasser's pan-Arab vision, to establish an effective front against the "Zionist entity" and against the West, and, most painfully, to support Libya during the UN-imposed sanctions crisis, Qaddafi's regime, increasingly isolated and weakened, became "easy prey" for the West. Qaddafi's subsequent abandonment of the Arab world was clear-cut, although sentiments from the old pan-Arab Qaddafi resurfaced when he scathingly criticized Saddam Hussein's execution at the close of 2006 and declared a national period of mourning, thus breaking the Arab world's consensual silence.

During the 1990s, Qaddafi shifted his emphasis from the Arab to the African arena, using his newly established diplomatic position in the sub-Saharan region to become a prominent player on the pan-African stage. This policy was crowned with success; indeed, Libya's newfound allies, generally on the margins of global affairs, accelerated a breakthrough in the Lockerbie stalemate and even played an indirect role in bringing Libya and the West closer. Even if he did not admit it in public, Qaddafi was fully aware of the importance of reconciled relations with the United States and the West to the survival of his regime. The renunciation of weapons of mass destruction at the close of 2003 ended the confrontation with Washington. Qaddafi, who for years had called the home of the US president the "Black House," repainted that house white.

This sharp about-face reflected the interdependency of Libya's domestic and foreign affairs. More than anything else, the Libyan regime's intent to maintain power molded its foreign policies. According to Anoushiravan Ehteshami and Raymond Hinnebusch, "The foreign policy of any individual Middle Eastern state at a given time can only be adequately understood as the outcome of an interaction between the state, sub-/trans-state, and state-systems levels." This observation is certainly apt in Libya's case. "The state system in the Middle East," they further argue, is "shaped by two forces: (1) a series of periodically erupting, systemwide transstate forces—imperialism, nationalism, war, oil, Islam, and globalization; and (2) the behavior of the individual states that collectively 'construct' the system."[5] This, too, is applicable in the Libyan context.

* * *

"A person in need is a slave indeed," writes Qaddafi in his *Green Book,* deeming socialism the solution to the economic problem.[6] As of 2007, Libya, although no longer dogged by foreign hostilities or bound by regional and international constraints, remained dependent on the West to usher it into a better era. Assuming that Libya is still a country in need, it nevertheless finds itself equipped with much more freedom to maneuver in foreign affairs, with considerably broader horizons, and with much improved prospects for its people than it had in 1969, when Qaddafi's revolution began.

Notes

1. Michael Slackman, "Social Issues Clown Their Way to Center Stage in Libya," *New York Times,* 12 March 2007, quoting portraitist Jamal Dawob.
2. "Country Profile: Libya," 2006, pp. 17–18, quoting the Human Development Report of the UN Development Programme (UNDP); Michael Slackman, "Libya Gingerly Begins Seeking Economic but Not Political Reform," *New York Times,* 2 March 2007.
3. Eljahmi, "Libya and the US," p. 17, quoting the Revolutionary Committees Movement sources.

4. See, for instance, Georges Rassi, "Libya's Fractured Opposition," *al-Mustaqbal,* cited in *Mideast Mirror,* 29 July 2005; Hisham Matar, "Seeing What We Want to See in Qaddafi," *New York Times,* 5 February 2007.

5. Ehteshami and Hinnebusch, "Conclusion: Patterns of Policy," p. 335.

6. Al-Qadhafi, *The Green Book: The Solution of the Economic Problem,* Part 2, p. 15.

Acronyms and Abbreviations

AFP	Agence France Presse
AMU	Arab Maghrib Union
ARNA	Arab Revolution News Agency
AWACS	Airborne Warning and Control System
BBC	British Broadcasting Corporation
BWC	Biological Weapons Convention
CEN-SAD	Community of Sahel-Saharan States
COMESSA	Community of the Sahel and the Saharan States
CPA	Comprehensive Peace Agreement
CTBT	Comprehensive Test Ban Treaty
DR	Daily Report
EEC	European Economic Community
ECOWAS	Parliament of the Economic Community of West African States
EU	European Union
FROLINAT	Front de Libération Nationale du Tchad
IAEA	International Atomic Energy Agency
ICJ	International Court of Justice
ILSA	Iran-Libya Sanctions Act
JANA	Jamahiriyya Arab News Agency
LBC	Lebanese Broadcasting Television
MEMRI	Middle East Media Research TV Monitor Project
NFSL	National Front for the Salvation of Libya
NPT	Nuclear Non-Proliferation Treaty
OAPEC	Organization of Arab Petroleum Exporting Countries
OAU	Organization of African Unity
PDRY	People's Democratic Republic of Yemen
PLO	Palestine Liberation Organization

Polisario	People's Organization for the Liberation of Saquia al-Hamra and Rio del Oro
SADR	Saharan Arab Democratic Republic
SPLA	Sudanese People's Liberation Army
TASS	Telegraph Agency of the Soviet Union
UK	United Kingdom
UPI	United Press International
USIS	United States Information Service
USSR	Union of Soviet Socialist Republics
WMD	weapons of mass destruction

Bibliography

Abi-Aad, Naji E. "Libya: Effects of Sanctions on Petroleum Industry." *Middle East Executive Reports* 20, no. 11 (November 1997): 8–9.

'Ajami, Fouad. "The End of Pan-Arabism." *Foreign Affairs* 57, no. 2 (Winter 1978–1979): 343–354.

Allan, John A. *Libya: The Experience of Oil.* Boulder, CO: Westview Press, 1981.

———. "Libya Accommodates to Lower Oil Revenues: Economic and Political Adjustments." *International Journal of Middle East Studies* 15, no. 3 (1983): 377–385.

Alterman, John B. "The Unique Libyan Case." *Middle East Quarterly* 13, no. 1 (Winter 2006): 21–29.

Altman, Israel. "The Arab Republic of Egypt." In *Middle East Contemporary Survey, 1978–79.* Edited by Colin Legum and Haim Shaked. New York: Holmes & Meier, 1980, 390–432.

al-'Anan, Ibrahim, et al. *Qadiyyat Lokerbie wa-Mustaqbal al-Nizam al-Dawli.* Valleta, Malta: Islamic World Studies Centre, 1992.

Anderson, Frank. "Qadhafi's Libya: The Limits of Optimism." *Middle East Policy* 6, no. 4 (June 1999): 68–79.

Anderson, Lisa. "Religion and Politics in Libya." *Journal of Arab Affairs* (1 October 1981): 53–77.

———. "Qadhafi's Islam." In *Voices of Resurgent Islam.* Edited by John L. Esposito. New York: Oxford University Press, 1983, 134–149.

———. "Qadhafi and the Kremlin." *Problems of Communism* 34, no. 5 (September 1985): 29–44.

———. "Qadhafi and His Opposition." *The Middle East Journal* 40, no. 2 (Spring 1986): 225–237.

———. *The State and Social Transformation in Tunisia and Libya, 1830–1980.* Princeton, NJ: Princeton University Press, 1986.

———. "Rogue Libya's Long Road." *Middle East Report,* no. 241 (Winter 2006): 42–47.

Arnold, Guy. *The Maverick State: Gaddafi and the New World Order.* London: Cassell, 1996.

Ayoub, Mahmoud. *Islam and the Third Universal Theory: The Religious Thought of Mu'ammar al-Qadhafi.* London: Kegan Paul International, 1991.

Bearman, Jonathan. *Qadhafi's Libya.* London: Zed Books, 1986.

Becker, Abraham S., and Francis Fukuyama. "The USSR and the Middle East." In *Middle East Contemporary Survey, 1978–79.* Edited by Colin Legum and Haim Shaked. New York: Holmes & Meier, 1980, 59–69.

Behrens, Henning. "The Soviet Occupation of Afghanistan." In *The Soviet Union and the Middle East in the 1980s.* Edited by Mark V. Kauppi and R. Craig Nation. Lexington, MA: Lexington Books, 1983, 247–265.

Bell, J. Bover. "Israel's Setback in Africa." *Middle East International* 9, no. 21 (March 1973): 22–24.

Bengio, Ofra. "Iraq." In *Middle East Contemporary Survey, 1990.* Edited by Ami Ayalon. Boulder, CO: Westview Press, 1992, 379–423.

Beshir, Omer Mohamed. *The Southern Sudan: Background and Conflict.* Khartoum: Khartoum University Press, 1970.

Bienen, Henry. "Perspectives on Soviet Intervention in Africa." *Political Science Quarterly* 95, no. 1 (Spring 1980): 29–42.

Blackwell, Stephen. "Saving the King: Anglo-American Strategy and British Counter-Subversion Operations in Libya, 1953–59." *Middle Eastern Studies* 39, no. 1 (January 2003): 1–18.

Blake, Cecil B., and Saleh Abu-Osba, eds. *Libya: Terrorist or Terrorized? An Inquiry into Politics, Ideology, and Communication.* Canada: Jerusalem International House, 1982.

Blanchard, Christopher M. "Libya: Background and U.S. Relations." Congressional Research Service Report for Congress RL33142, pp. 24–29. http://www.fas.org/sgp/crs/mideast/RL33142.pdf (accessed 12 May 2008).

Blank, Stephen J. *Operational and Strategic Lessons of the War in Afghanistan, 1979–1990.* Carlisle Barracks, PA: Strategic Studies Institute, 1991.

Bolger, Daniel P. *Americans at War, 1975–1986: An Era of Violent Peace.* Novato, CA: Presidio, 1988.

Bowen, Wyn Q. *Libya and Nuclear Proliferation: Stepping Back from the Brink.* Adelphia Paper 30. London: Routledge, 2006.

Brown, L. Carl. *International Politics and the Middle East: Old Rule, Dangerous Game.* Princeton, NJ: Princeton University Press, 1984.

Burgat, François. "Qadhafi's Ideological Framework." In *Qadhafi's Libya: 1969 to 1994.* Edited by Dirk Vandewalle. New York: St. Martin's Press, 1995, 47–63.

Burr, J. Millard, and Robert O. Collins. *Africa's Thirty Years' War: Chad, Libya and the Sudan, 1963–1993.* Boulder, CO: Westview Press, 1999.

Campbell, John C. "Communist Strategies in the Mediterranean." *Problems of Communism* 28 (May–June 1979): 1–17.

Collins, Robert. *The Southern Sudan, 1883–1898.* New Haven, CT: Yale University Press, 1962.

Cooley, John K. *Libyan Sandstorm.* New York: Holt, Rinehart and Winston, 1982.

"Country Report: Libya." London: Economist Intelligence Unit, 1986, no. 2; 1987, nos. 1–2; 1989, no. 3; 1996, no. 2; 1998, no. 4; July 2002; January 2003; April 2004; October 2005.

Davis, Brian L. *Qaddafi, Terrorism, and the Origins of the U.S. Attack on Libya.* New York: Praeger, 1990.

Davis, Christopher. "Country Survey 16, The Defence Sector in the Economy of a Declining Superpower: Soviet Union and Russia, 1965–2001." *Defence and Peace Economics* 13, no. 3 (2002): 145–177.

Day, Alan J., ed. *Border and Territorial Disputes.* Cambridge: Cambridge University Press, 1987.

Decalo, Samuel. "Chad: The Roots of Centre-Periphery Strife." *African Affairs* 79, no. 317 (1980): 490–509.

Deeb, Marius K. "Islam and Arab Nationalism in Al-Qaddafi's Ideology." *Journal of South Asian and Middle Eastern Studies* 2, no. 2 (Winter 1978): 12–26.

Deeb, Mary-Jane. "Inter-Maghribi Relations since 1969: A Study of the Modalities of Unions and Mergers." *Middle East Journal* 43, no. 1 (Winter 1989): 20–33.

———. "Qadhafi's Changed Policy: Causes and Consequences." *Middle East Policy* 7, no. 2 (February 2000): 146–153.

Dhooge, Lucien J. "Meddling with the Mullahs: An Analysis of the Iran and Libya Sanctions Act of 1996." *Denver Journal of International Law and Policy* 27 (1998): 1–60.

Dishon, Daniel. "The Middle East in Perspective: A Review of the Crucial Changes in 1977." In *Middle East Contemporary Survey, 1976–77.* Edited by Colin Legum and Haim Shaked. New York: Holmes & Meier, 1978, 3–17.

———, ed. *Middle East Record 1969–70.* Jerusalem: Israel Universities Press, 1977.

Dishon, Daniel, and Varda Ben Zvi. "Inter-Arab Relations." In *Middle East Contemporary Survey, 1976–77.* Edited by Colin Legum and Haim Shaked. New York: Holmes & Meier, 1978, 163–175.

———. "Inter-Arab Relations." In *Middle East Contemporary Survey, 1977–78.* Edited by Colin Legum and Haim Shaked. New York: Holmes & Meier, 1979, 213–249.

Dishon, Daniel, and Bruce Maddy-Weitzman. "Inter-Arab Affairs." In *Middle East Contemporary Survey, 1979–80.* Edited by Colin Legum and Haim Shaked. New York: Holmes & Meier, 1981, 169–230.

Doyle, Chris. "Libya: After (UN) Sanctions." *Middle East International,* no. 597 (23 April 1999): 8–9.

Dunton, Chris. "Black Africans in Libya and Libyan Images of Black Africa." In *The Green and the Black: Qadhafi's Policies in Africa.* Edited by René Lemarchand. Bloomington: Indiana University Press, 1988, 150–166.

Ehteshami, Anoushiravan, and Raymond Hinnebusch. "Conclusion: Patterns of Policy." In *The Foreign Policies of Middle East States.* Edited by Raymond Hinnebusch and Anoushiravan Ehteshami. Boulder, CO: Lynne Rienner Publishers, 2002, 335–350.

El-Fathaly, Omar, and Monte Palmer. "Institutional Development in Qadhafi's Libya." In *Qadhafi's Libya: 1969 to 1994.* Edited by Dirk Vandewalle. New York: St. Martin's Press, 1995, 164–170.

Eljahmi, Mohamed. "Libya and the US: Qadhafi Unrepentant." *Middle East Quarterly* 13, no. 1 (Winter 2006): 11–20.

ElWarfally, Mahmoud G. *Imagery and Ideology in US Policy Toward Libya: 1969–1982.* Pittsburgh: University of Pittsburgh Press, 1988.

Entelis, John. "Islamist Politics and the Democratic Imperative: Comparative Lessons from the Algerian Experience." *The Journal of North African Studies* 9, no. 2 (Summer 2004): 202–215.

Erlich, Haggai. *The Struggle over Eritrea, 1962–1978: War and Revolution in the Horn of Africa.* Stanford: Hoover International Press, Stanford University, 1983.

———. *Ethiopia and the Middle East.* Boulder, CO: Lynne Rienner Publishers, 1994.

———. *The Cross and the River: Ethiopia, Egypt and the Nile.* Boulder, CO: Lynne Rienner Publishers, 2002.

Esposito, John. *The Islamic Threat: Myth or Reality?* New York: Oxford University Press, 1999.

Faath, Sigrid. "The Problematic Topic of Anti-Americanism." In *Anti-Americanism in the Islamic World.* Edited by Sigrid Faath. London: Hurst, 2006, 1–11.

Falke, Andreas. "The EU-US Conflict over Sanctions Policy: Confronting the Hegemon." *European Foreign Affairs Review* 5 (2000): 139–163.

Feldman, Shai. "The United States and the Middle East in 1986." In *Middle East Contemporary Survey, 1986.* Edited by Itamar Rabinovich and Haim Shaked. Boulder, CO: Westview Press, 1988, 15–32.

Foltz, William J. "Reconstructing the State of Chad." In *Collapsed States: The Disintegration and Restoration of Legitimate Authority.* Edited by I. William Zartman. Boulder, CO: Lynne Rienner Publishers, 1995, 15–31.

Freedman, Robert O. "The Soviet Union and the Middle East." In *Middle East Contemporary Survey, 1981–82.* Edited by Colin Legum, Haim Shaked, and Daniel Dishon. New York: Holmes & Meier, 1983, 36–54.

———. "Moscow and the Middle East in 1985." In *Middle East Contemporary Survey, 1984–85.* Edited by Itamar Rabinovich and Haim Shaked. New York: Holmes & Meier, 1987.

Gera, Gideon. "Libya." In *Middle East Contemporary Survey, 1976–77.* Edited by Colin Legum. New York: Holmes & Meier, 1978, 531–538.

———. "Libya." In *Middle East Contemporary Survey, 1977–78.* Edited by Colin Legum and Haim Shaked. New York: Holmes & Meier, 1979, 628–654.

———. "Libya and the United States: A Relationship of Self-Fulfilling Expectations?" In *The Middle East and the United States: Perceptions and Poli-*

cies. Edited by Haim Shaked and Itamar Rabinovich. New Brunswick, NJ: Transaction Books, 1980, 197–206.

Gershoni, Israel. *The Emergence of Pan-Arabism in Egypt.* Tel Aviv: Shiloah Center for Middle Eastern and African Studies, Tel-Aviv University, 1981.

Gilboa, Eytan. "US Strategy in the Middle East: Effects of the 2006 Congressional Elections and the Baker-Hamilton Report," The Begin-Sadat Center for Strategic Studies, Bar-Ilan University. *Perspectives* 23 (19 December 2006).

Ginat, Rami. "The Soviet Union and the Syrian Ba'th Regime: From Hesitation to Rapprochement." *Middle Eastern Studies* 36, no. 2 (2000): 150–171.

Ginor, Isabella. "'Under the Yellow Arab Helmet Gleamed Russian Eyes': Operation Kavkaz and the War of Attrition." *Cold War History* 3, no. 1 (October 2002): 127–156.

Golan, Galia. "Soviet Policy in the Middle East." In *Middle East Contemporary Survey, 1990.* Edited by Ami Ayalon. Boulder, CO: Westview Press, 1992, 33–55.

Goldberg, David H., and Paul Marantz, eds. *The Decline of the Soviet Union and the Transformation of the Middle East.* Boulder, CO: Westview Press, 1994.

Goldberg, Jacob. "Saudi Arabia." In *Middle East Contemporary Survey, 1979–80.* Edited by Colin Legum and Haim Shaked. New York: Holmes & Meier, 1981, 682–688.

Grey, Robert D. "The Soviet Presence in Africa: An Analysis of Goals." *Journal of Modern African Studies* 22, no. 3 (1984): 511–527.

Grinevsky, Oleg. *Stsenarii dlya tret'ey mirovoy voyny* [The Script for World War III]. Moscow: Olma Press, 2002.

Gunter, Michael M. "Qaddafi Reconsidered." *Journal of Conflict Studies* 21, no. 1 (2001): 122–130.

Habiby, Raymond. "Qadhafi's Thoughts on True Democracy." *Middle East Review* (Summer 1979): 33–39.

Haley, Edward P. *Qadhafi and the United States Since 1969.* New York: Praeger, 1984.

Halliday, Fred. *Nation and Religion in the Middle East.* Boulder: Lynne Rienner Publishers, 2000.

———. "The Iranian Revolution: Uneven Development and Religious Populism." In *State and Ideology in the Middle East and Pakistan.* Edited by Fred Halliday and Hamza Alavi. London: Macmillan, 1988.

Hannah, John P. "The Soviet Union and the Middle East." In *Middle East Contemporary Survey, 1989.* Edited by Ami Ayalon. Boulder, CO: Westview Press, 1991, 34–61.

Harris, D. R. "Tunisia." In *The Middle East and North Africa 1974–75.* London: Europa, 1974, 679–710.

Harris, Lillian Craig. "America's Libya Policy Has Failed." *Middle East International* (10 October 1986): 14–15.

———. *Libya: Qadhafi's Revolution and the Modern State.* Boulder: Westview Press, 1986, 76–82.

Hatina, Meir. "Jumhuriyyat Misr al-'Arabiyya" [Egypt]. In *Middle East Contemporary Survey, 1999.* Edited by Bruce Maddy-Weitzman. Tel Aviv: Moshe

Dayan Center for Middle Eastern and African Studies, Tel Aviv University, 2001, 201–230.

Heikal, Muhammad. *The Road to Ramadan.* London: Collins, 1975.

Henderson, George. "Libya and Morocco: Marriage of Necessity." *Middle East International* (11 October 1985): 17–18.

Hermann, Richard K. "The Middle East and the New World Order: Rethinking U.S. Political Strategy after the Gulf War." *International Security* 16, no. 2 (Fall 1991): 42–75.

Hinnebusch, Raymond. "Introduction: The Analytical Framework." In *The Foreign Policies of Middle East States.* Edited by Raymond Hinnebusch and Anoushiravan Ehteshami. Boulder, CO: Lynne Rienner Publishers, 2002, 1–27.

Hochman, Dafna. "Rehabilitating a Rogue: Libya's WMD Reversal and Lessons for US Policy." *Parameters* 36, no. 1 (Spring 2006): 63–78.

Huliaras, Asteris. "Qadhafi's Comeback: Libya and Sub-Saharan Africa in the 1990s." *African Affairs* 100, no. 398 (2001): 5–25.

International Institute for Strategic Studies. *The Military Balance 1979–80.* London: ISS, 1979.

Jensen, Erik. *Western Sahara: Anatomy of a Stalemate.* Boulder, CO: Lynne Rienner Publishers, 2004.

Jentleson, Bruce W. "The Reagan Administration and Coercive Diplomacy: Restraining More Than Remaking Governments." *Political Science Quarterly* 106, no. 1 (Spring 1991): 57–82.

Joffé, George. "Qadhafi's Islam in Local Historical Perspective." In *Qadhafi's Libya: 1969 to 1994.* Edited by Dirk Vandewalle. New York: St. Martin's Press, 1995, 139–154.

———. "Reflections on the Role of the Sanusi in the Central Sahara." *Journal of North African Studies* 1, no. 1 (Summer 1996): 25–41.

———. "Why Gaddafi Gave Up WMD." BBC. 21 December 2003.

———. "Libya: Who Blinked, and Why." *Current History* (May 2004): 221–225.

———. "Libya's Saharan Destiny." *Journal of North African Studies* 10, nos. 3–4 (September–December 2005): 605–617.

———. "The Status of the Euro-Mediterranean Partnership." http://www .medobs.net/documents/BCN10Joffe.pdf (accessed 1 January 2008).

Joure, Edmond. "France and Crisis Areas in Africa." In *African Crisis Areas and US Foreign Policy.* Edited by Gerald J. Bender, James S. Coleman, and Richard L. Sklar. Berkeley: University of California Press, 1985, 308–320.

Kaldor, Mary, and Paul Anderson, eds. *Mad Dogs: The US Raids on Libya.* London: Pluto Press, 1986.

Kash, Douglas. "Libyan Involvement and Legal Obligations in Connection with the Bombing of Pan Am Flight 103." *Studies in Conflict and Terrorism* 17 (1994): 23–38.

Kasozi, Abdu B. K. "Christian-Muslim Inputs into Public Policy Formation in Kenya, Tanzania and Uganda." In *Religion and Politics in East Africa: The Period since Independence.* Edited by Holger Bernt Hansen and Michael Twaddle. London: James Currey, 1995, 223–246.

Kedourie, Elie. "The Transition from a British to an American Era in the Middle East." In *The Middle East and the United States: Perceptions and Policies.* Edited by Haim Shaked and Itamar Rabinovich. New Brunswick, NJ: Transaction Books, 1980, 3–9.

Keller, Edmond J. "United States Foreign Policy on the Horn of Africa: Policy-making with Blinders On." In *African Crisis Areas and US Foreign Policy.* Edited by Gerald J. Bender, James S. Coleman, and Richard L. Sklar. Berkeley: University of California Press, 1985, 178–193.

Kelly, Saul. "Britain, Libya and the Start of the Cold War." *The Maghreb Review* 31, nos. 1–2 (2006): 42–61.

el-Kikhia, Mansour O. *Libya's Qadhafi: The Politics of Contradiction.* Gainesville: University Press of Florida, 1997.

Kokole, Omari H. "Idi Amin, 'the Nubi' and Islam in Ugandan Politics, 1971–1979." In *Religion and Politics in East Africa: The Period since Independence.* Edited by Holger Bernt Hansen and Michael Twaddle. London: James Currey, 1995, 45–55.

Korn, David A. *Assassination in Khartoum.* Bloomington: Indiana University Press, 1993.

Kornegay, Francis. "Beyond the OAU: African Union or Afro-Jamahiriya?" *Global Dialogue* 5, no. 2 (2000).

Kyemba, Henry. *State of Blood: The Inside Story of Idi Amin.* London: Corgi Books, 1977.

Lannoy, François de. *Afrikakorps, 1941–1943: The Libya Egypt Campaign.* Bayeux: Éditions Heimdal, 2002.

Laskier, Michael M. *Israel and the Maghrib: From Statehood to Oslo.* Gainesville: University Press of Florida, 2004.

Legum, Colin, ed. *Africa Contemporary Record: Annual Survey and Documents, 1971–72.* Vol. 4. New York and London: Holmes & Meier, 1972.

———. *Africa Contemporary Record: Annual Survey and Documents, 1972–73.* Vol. 5. London: Rex Collings, 1973.

———. *Africa Contemporary Record: Annual Survey and Documents, 1976–77.* Vol. 9. New York: Africana, 1977.

———. *Africa Contemporary Record: Annual Survey and Documents, 1978–79.* Vol. 11. New York: Holmes & Meier, 1980.

———. *Africa Contemporary Record: Annual Survey and Documents, 1994–96.* Vol. 25. New York: Africana.

Lemarchand, René. "The Crisis in Chad." In *African Crisis Areas and US Foreign Policy.* Edited by Gerald J. Bender, James S. Coleman, and Richard L. Sklar. Berkeley: University of California Press, 1985, 239–256.

———. "The Case of Chad." In *The Green and the Black: Qadhafi's Policies in Africa.* Edited by René Lemarchand. Bloomington: Indiana University Press, 1988, 106–124.

Leppard, David. *On the Trail of Terror.* London: Jonathan Cape, 1991.

Maddy-Weitzman, Bruce. "Inter-Arab Relations." In *Middle East Contemporary Survey, 1983–84.* Edited by Haim Shaked and Daniel Dishon. Boulder, CO: Westview Press, 1986, 123–157.

———. "Inter-Arab Relations." In *Middle East Contemporary Survey, 1984–85.*

Edited by Itamar Rabinovich and Haim Shaked. New York: Holmes & Meier, 1987, 109–145.

————. "Inter-Arab Relations." In *Middle East Contemporary Survey, 1986.* Edited by Itamar Rabinovich and Haim Shaked. Boulder, CO: Westview Press, 1988, 93–126.

————. "Conflict and Conflict Management in the Western Sahara: Is the Endgame Near?" *The Middle East Journal* 45, no. 4 (Autumn 1991): 594–607.

————. "A New Arab Order? Regional Security after the Gulf War." *Orient* 34, no. 2 (June 1993): 221–230.

Maddy-Weitzman, Bruce, and Joseph Kostiner. "From Jedda to Cairo: The Failure of Arab Mediation in the Gulf Crisis." *Diplomacy and Statecraft* 7, no. 2 (July 1996): 466–490.

Mandelbaum, Michael. "President Bush and the Middle East: One Year On." *PolicyWatch,* no. 598 (2 April 2002). Washington Institute for Near East Policy, http://www.washingtoninstitute.org/templateC05.php?CID=1476 (accessed 18 May 2008).

Martin, David. *General Amin.* London: Faber and Faber, 1974.

Martin, David C., and John Walcott. *Best Laid Plans: The Inside Story of America's War Against Terrorism.* New York: Simon & Schuster, 1989.

Martinez, Luis. "Why the Violence in Algeria?" *Journal of North African Studies* 9, no. 2 (Summer 2004): 14–27.

Mattes, Hanspeter. "The Rise and Fall of the Revolutionary Committees." In *Qadhafi's Libya: 1969 to 1994.* Edited by Dirk Vandewalle. New York: St. Martin's Press, 1995, 89–112.

————. "The Maghreb States: Libya, Tunisia, Algeria, Morocco." In *Anti-Americanism in the Islamic World.* Edited by Sigrid Faath. London: Hurst, 2006.

Mayer, Ann E. "Islamic Resurgence or New Prophethood: The Role of Islam in Qadhafi's Ideology." In *Islamic Resurgence in the Arab World.* Edited by 'Ali E. Hillali Dessouki. New York: Praeger, 1982.

Mefarlane, Robert C. "The Global Oil Rush." *The National Interest* 84 (Summer 2006): 34–36.

Menashri, David. "Iran." In *Middle East Contemporary Survey, 1979–80.* Edited by Colin Legum and Haim Shaked. New York: Holmes & Meier, 1981, 438–500.

————. *The Iranian Revolution and the Muslim World.* Boulder, CO: Westview Press, 1990.

Miller, Clement. "North Africa's Oil Exporters." *Middle East Executive Reports* (2 February 1987): 4.

Morison, David. "The Soviet Bloc and the Middle East." In *Middle East Contemporary Survey, 1977–78.* Edited by Colin Legum and Haim Shaked. New York: Holmes & Meier, 1979, 34–39.

Netanyahu, Iddo. *Entebbe: A Defining Moment in the War on Terrorism—the Jonathan Netanyahu Story.* Green Forest, AR: Balfour Books, 2003.

Neuberger, Benjamin. *Involvement, Invasion and Withdrawal: Qadhafi's Libya and Chad, 1969–1981.* Tel Aviv: Shiloah Center for Middle Eastern and African Studies, 1982.

Neuman, Ronald E. "Libya: A U.S. Policy Perspective." *Middle East Policy* 7, no. 2 (February 2000): 142–145.

Newsom, David. "U.S.-Libyan Relations Since 1969." *Middle East* (October 1980): 60–64.

Niblock, Tim. *"Pariah States" and Sanctions in the Middle East: Iraq, Libya, Sudan.* Boulder, CO: Lynne Rienner Publishers, 2001.

———. "The Regional and Domestic Consequences of Sanctions Imposed on Iraq, Libya and Sudan." *Arab Studies Quarterly* 23, no. 4 (2001): 59–67.

———. "The Foreign Policy of Libya." In *The Foreign Policies of Middle East States.* Edited by Raymond Hinnebusch and Anoushiravan Ehteshami. Boulder, CO: Lynne Rienner Publishers, 2002, 213–233.

Nyeko, Balam. "Exile Politics and Resistance to Dictatorship: The Ugandan Anti-Amin Organizations in Zambia, 1972–79." *African Affairs* 96, no. 382 (1996): 95–108.

Nyrop, Richard F., et al., eds. *Area Handbook for Libya.* Washington, DC: US Government Printing Office, 1973.

Oded, Arye. *Africa and the Middle East Conflict.* Boulder, CO: Lynne Rienner Publishers, 1987.

———. *Uganda ve-Israel: Toldot Yachasim Meputalim* [Uganda and Israel: The History of a Complex Relationship]. Jerusalem: Keter, 2002 (in Hebrew).

Ofcansky, Thomas P. "Ethiopia and Eritrea: Cry Havoc! Background to War." In *Africa Contemporary Record, 1998–2000.* Edited by Colin Legum. New York: Holmes & Meier, 2004, A3–A15.

Ogunbadejo, Oye. "Soviet Policy in Africa." *African Affairs* 79, no. 316 (July 1980): 297–325.

———. "Qaddafi's North African Design." *International Security* 8, no. 1 (Summer 1983): 154–178.

———. "Qaddafi and Africa's International Relations." *Journal of Modern African Studies* 24, no. 1 (March 1986): 33–68.

Ohaegbulam, F. Ugboaja. "US Measures against Libya Since the Explosion of Pan Am Flight 103." *Mediterranean Quarterly* 11, no. 1 (2000): 120–125.

Packer, Corinne A. A., and Donald Rukare. "The New African Union and Its Constitutive Act." *The American Journal of International Law* 96, no. 2 (April 2002): 365–379.

Pajak, Roger F. "Arms and Oil: The Soviet-Libyan Arms Supply Relationship." *Middle East Review,* no. 13 (Winter 1980–1981): 51–56.

Pargeter, Alison. "Violence in Libya." *Mediterranean Politics* 6, no. 1 (2001): 89–93.

Pedaliu, Effie G. H. "Truman, Eisenhower and the Mediterranean Cold War, 1947–57." *The Maghreb Review* 31, nos. 1–2 (2006): 2–20.

Petterson, Donald. "Ethiopia Abandoned? An American Perspective." *International Affairs* 62, no. 4 (Autumn 1986): 627–645.

Podeh, Eli. "In the Service of Power: The Ideological Struggle in the Arab World During the Gulf Crisis." *Conflict Quarterly* 4, no. 4 (Fall 1994): 7–25.

———. "Between Stagnation and Renovation: The Arab System in the Aftermath of the Iraq War." *Middle East Review of International Affairs* 9, no. 3 (September 2005): 52–74.

Podeh, Eli, and Onn Winckler, eds. *Rethinking Nasserism: Revolution and Historical Memory in Modern Egypt.* Gainesville: University Press of Florida, 2004.

Pondi, Jean-Emmanuel. "Qadhafi and the Organization of African Unity." In *The Green and the Black: Qadhafi's Policies in Africa.* Edited by René Lemarchand. Bloomington: Indiana University Press, 1988, 139–149.

Al-Qadhafi, Muammar. *The Green Book: The Solution of the Problem of Democracy.* Part 1. London: Martin Brian & O'Keeffe, 1976.

———. *The Green Book: The Solution of the Economic Problem.* Part 2. Tripoli: Public Establishment for Publishing, 1978.

———. *The Green Book: The Social Basis of the Third Universal Theory.* Part 3. Tripoli: Public Establishment for Publishing, 1979.

Al-Qadhafi, Saif Aleslam. "Libyan-American Relations." *Middle East Policy* 10, no. 1 (Spring 2003): 35–44.

Rabinovich, Itamar. "The War in Lebanon: An Overview." In *Middle East Contemporary Survey, 1981–82.* Edited by Colin Legum, Haim Shaked, and Daniel Dishon. New York: Holmes & Meier, 1983, 109–127.

Reinich, Jacques. "Arab Republic of Egypt." In *Middle East Contemporary Survey, 1977–78.* Edited by Colin Legum and Haim Shaked. New York: Holmes & Meier, 1979, 368–410.

Rivlin, Paul. "Economic Developments in the Middle East." In *Middle East Contemporary Survey, 1999.* Edited by Bruce Maddy-Weitzman. Tel Aviv: Moshe Dayan Center for Middle Eastern and African Studies, Tel Aviv University, 141–160.

———. *The Russian Economy and Arms Exports to the Middle East.* Tel-Aviv: Jaffee Center for Strategic Studies, Tel Aviv University, 2005.

Roberson, B. A. "The Impact of the International System on the Middle East." In *The Foreign Policies of Middle East States.* Edited by Raymond Hinnebusch and Anoushiravan Ehteshami. Boulder, CO: Lynne Rienner Publishers, 2002, 55–69.

Rodman, Kenneth A. "Sanctions at Bay: Hegemonic Decline, Multinational Corporations, and U.S. Economic Sanctions since the Pipeline Case." *International Organization* 49, no. 1 (1995): 105–137.

Ronen, Yehudit. "Libya." In *Middle East Contemporary Survey, 1977–78.* Edited by Colin Legum and Haim Shaked. New York: Holmes & Meier, 1979, 628–654.

———. "Libya." In *Middle East Contemporary Survey, 1981–82.* Edited by Colin Legum, Haim Shaked, and Daniel Dishon. New York: Holmes & Meier, 1983, 734–758.

———. "Libya." In *Middle East Contemporary Survey, 1982–83.* Edited by Colin Legum, Haim Shaked, and Daniel Dishon. New York: Holmes & Meier, 1984, 703–728.

———. "Sudan." In *Middle East Contemporary Survey, 1983–84.* Edited by Haim Shaked and Daniel Dishon. Boulder, CO: Westview Press, 1986, 638–670.

———. "Libya." In *Middle East Contemporary Survey, 1983–84.* Edited by Haim Shaked and Daniel Dishon. Boulder: Westview Press, 1986, 589–590.

————. "Libya." In *Middle East Contemporary Survey, 1984–85.* Edited by Itamar Rabinovich and Haim Shaked. New York: Holmes & Meier, 1987, 560–561.

————. "The Republic of Sudan." In *Middle East Contemporary Survey, 1986.* Edited by Itamar Rabinovich and Haim Shaked. Boulder, CO: Westview Press, 1988, 590–597.

————. "Libya's Intervention in Amin's Uganda: A Broken Spearhead." *Asian and African Studies* 26, no. 2 (July 1992): 173–183.

————. *Sudan be-Milchemet Ezrachim: beyn Afrikaniut, Araviut ve-Islam* [Sudan in a Civil War: Between Africanism, Arabism, and Islam]. Tel Aviv: Hakibutz Hameuhad, 1995 (in Hebrew).

————. "Libya." In *Middle East Contemporary Survey, 1995.* Edited by Bruce Maddy-Weitzman. Boulder, CO: Westview Press, 1997, 471–491.

————. "Personalities and Politics: Qadhafi, Nasser, Sadat and Mubarak." *Journal of North African Studies* 6, no. 3 (2001): 1–10.

————. "Sudan and the United States." *Middle East Policy* 9, no. 1 (March 2002): 9–108.

————. "Qadhafi and Militant Islamism: Unprecedented Conflict." *Middle Eastern Studies* 38, no. 4 (October 2002): 1–16.

————. "Libya's Diplomatic Success in Africa: The Reemergence of Qadhafi on the International Stage." *Diplomacy and Statecraft* 13, no. 4 (December 2002): 60–74.

————. "Qadhafi's Christmas Gift: What's Behind Libya's Decision to Renounce WMD?" *Tel Aviv Notes,* no. 93 (December 2003).

————. "Libya's Qadhafi and the Israeli-Palestinian Conflict, 1969–2002." *Middle Eastern Studies* 40, no. 1 (January 2004): 85–98.

————. "The Libyan-Saudi Diplomatic Rupture." *Tel Aviv Notes,* no. 120 (January 2005).

————. "Religions at War, Religions at Peace: The Case of Sudan." *Zeitschrift fur Politik* 52, no. 1 (March 2005): 80–96.

————. "Libya's Rising Star: Saif Al-Islam." *Middle East Policy* 12, no. 3 (Fall 2005): 136–144.

————. "Libya's Conflict with Britain: Analysis of a Diplomatic Rupture." *Middle Eastern Studies* 42, no. 2 (March 2006): 271–283.

————. "The HIV/AIDS Tragedy: A Window on State and Society in Libya." *Middle Eastern Studies* 43, no. 3 (May 2007): 341–352.

————. "A Libyan-Italian Encounter: The Changing Mosaic of Mediterranean Migration." *The Maghreb Review* 33, no. 1 (2008): 69–81.

————. *"Meshulash haYahasim haSudani-haMitzri-haLuvi betzel haIslam haRadiqali"* [The Sudanese-Egyptian-Libyan Triangle of Relations Under the Shadow of Radical Islam]. *Hamizrah Hehadash.* Jerusalem: The Middle East and Islamic Studies Association of Israel, MEISAI, 2008, vol. 47, pp. 216–236 (in Hebrew).

Ross, Dennis. "Considering Soviet Threats to the Persian Gulf." *International Security* 6, no. 2 (Autumn 1981): 159–180.

Rubin, Alfred P. "Libya, Lockerbie, and the Law." *Diplomacy and Statecraft* 4, no. 1 (March 1993): 1–19.

Rubin, Barry. "The United States and the Middle East: From Camp David to the Reagan Plan." In *Middle East Contemporary Survey, 1981–82*. Edited by Colin Legum, Haim Shaked, and Daniel Dishon. New York: Holmes & Meier, 1983, 26–35.

———. "The Gulf Crisis: Origins and Course of Events." In *Middle East Contemporary Survey, 1990*. Edited by Ami Ayalon. Boulder, CO: Westview Press, 1992, 73–97.

———. "The United States in the Middle East." In *Middle East Contemporary Survey, 1991*. Edited by Ami Ayalon. Boulder, CO: Westview Press, 1993, 21–34.

Rubinstein, Alvin Z., and Donald B. Smith, eds. *Anti-Americanism in the Third World: Implications for U.S. Foreign Policy*. New York: Praeger, 1985.

Sabagh, Nida. *Muhakamat Sh'ab: Lockerbie*. Beirut: Dar al-Sadaqa Lil-Tiba'a wal-Nashr, 1992.

Sabki, Hisham M. "International Authority and the Emergence of Modern Libya." PhD diss., Indiana University, 1967.

Salem, Elie. "A New Order: Settlement Scenarios in the Arab East." *The Beirut Review*, no. 1 (Spring 1991): 3–18.

Salem, Zekeria Ould Ahmed. "Mauritania: A Saharan Frontier-State." *The Journal of North African Studies* 10, nos. 3–4 (September–December 2005): 491–506.

Sandbakken, Camilla. "The Limits to Democracy Posed by Oil Rentier States: The Cases of Algeria, Nigeria and Libya." *Democratization* 13, no. 1 (February 2006): 135–152.

Saunders, Elizabeth N. "Setting Boundaries: Can International Society Exclude 'Rogue States'?" *International Studies Review* 8, no. 1 (2006): 23–54.

Schumacher, Edward. "The United States and Libya." *Foreign Affairs* 65, no. 2 (Winter 1986–1987): 329–348.

Schweitzer, Yoram. "Neutralizing Terrorism-Sponsoring States: The Libyan 'Model'." Jaffee Center for Strategic Studies, Tel Aviv University. *Strategic Assessment* 7, no. 1 (May 2004).

Scott, Bennett D., and Allan C. Stam. "The Duration of Interstate Wars, 1816–1985." *American Political Science Review* 90, no. 2 (June 1996): 239–258.

Sela, Avraham, ed. *The Continuum Political Encyclopedia of the Middle East*. New York: Continuum International, 2002.

Selassie, Bereket H. "The American Dilemma on the Horn." In *African Crisis Areas and US Foreign Policy*. Edited by Gerald J. Bender, James S. Coleman, and Richard L. Sklar. Berkeley: University of California Press, 1985, 163–177.

Shaked, Haim, and Yehudit Ronen. "Simmering Tension: Libyan-Egyptian Relations, 1954–86." In *Conflict Management in the Middle East*. Edited by Gabriel Ben-Dor and David B. Dewitt. Lexington, MA: Lexington Books, 1987, 113–128.

Shaked, Haim, and Esther Webman-Souery. "Libya [Al-Jumhuriyya al-'Arabiyya Al-Libiyya]." In *Middle East Record 1969–70*. Edited by Daniel Dishon. Jerusalem: Israel Universities Press, 1977, 951–952.

Shamir, Shimon, ed. *The Decline of Nasserism, 1965–1970: The Waning of a Messianic Movement.* Tel Aviv: Shiloah Center for Middle Eastern and African Studies, Tel Aviv University, 1978.

———. *Egypt from Monarchy to Republic: A Reassessment of Revolution and Change.* Boulder, CO: Westview Press, 1995.

Shamir, Shimon, and Bruce Maddy-Weitzman. *The Camp David Summit—What Went Wrong? Americans, Israelis, and Palestinians Analyze the Future of the Boldest Attempt to Resolve the Palestinian-Israeli Conflict.* Eastbourne: Sussex Academic Press, 2005.

Shamir, Shimon, and Ran Segev. "Arab Republic of Egypt." In *Middle East Contemporary Survey, 1976–77.* Edited by Colin Legum and Haim Shaked. New York: Holmes & Meier, 1978, 314–316.

Shapir, Yiftah. "Libyan Weapons of Mass Destruction: Qadhafi Redux?" *Tel Aviv Notes,* no. 49 (September 2002).

———. "Syria and Libya: Beyond the Axis of Evil." *Tel Aviv Notes,* no. 37 (May 2003).

Shinn, David H. "Al-Qaeda in East Africa and the Horn," *Journal of Conflict Studies* 27, no. 1 (Summer 2007).

Sicker, Martin. *The Making of a Pariah State: The Adventurist Politics of Muammar al-Qadhafi.* New York: Praeger, 1987.

Siddiqi, Moin A. "Economic Report: Libya." *The Middle East Journal* (July–August 2000): 25–27.

Simons, Geoff. *Libya and the West.* Oxford: Centre for Libyan Studies, 2003.

Smis, Stefaan, and Kim van der Borght. "The EU-US Compromise on the Helmes-Burton and D'Amato Acts." *The American Journal of International Law* 93, no. 1 (January 1999): 227–236.

Solomon, Hussein, and Gerrie Swart. "Libya's Foreign Policy in Flux." *African Affairs* 104, no. 416 (July 2005): 469–492.

Spiegel, Steven L., and David J. Pervin. "The United States and the Middle East." In *Middle East Contemporary Survey, 1989.* Edited by Ami Ayalon. Boulder, CO: Westview Press, 1991. 13–33.

Squassoni, Sharon A., and Andrew Feickert. "Disarming Libya: Weapons of Mass Destruction." Congressional Research Service Report for Congress, 22 April 2004, RS21823. http://www.fpc.state.gov/documents/organization/32007.pdf (accessed 12 May 2008).

St. John, Ronald Bruce. "The Ideology of Mu'ammar al-Qadhafi: Theory and Practice." *International Journal of Middle East Studies* 15 (1983): 471–490.

———. "The United States, the Cold War and Libyan Independence." *Journal of Libyan Studies* 2, no. 2 (Winter 2001): 26–45.

———. *Libya and the United States: Two Centuries of Strife.* Philadelphia: University of Pennsylvania Press, 2002.

Stanik, Joseph T. *El Dorado Canyon: Reagan's Undeclared War with Qaddafi.* Annapolis: Naval Institute Press, 2002.

Stedman, Stephen John. "Conflict and Conflict Resolution in Africa: A Conceptual Framework." In *Conflict Resolution in Africa.* Edited by Francis M. Deng and I. William Zartman. Washington, DC: Brookings Institute, 1991, 367–399.

Susser, Asher. "The Palestinian Liberation Organization." In *Middle East Contemporary Survey, 1982–83*. Edited by Colin Legum, Haim Shaked, and Daniel Dishon. New York: Holmes & Meier, 1984, 285–290.

———. "The Arabs and Iraq." *Tel Aviv Notes*, no. 52 (30 October 2002).

Taheri, Amin. *The Spirit of Allah: Khomeini and the Islamic Revolution*. Castle Rock, CO: Alder & Alder Publishers, 1986.

Takeyh, Ray. "Qadhafi, Lockerbie, and Prospects for Libya." Washington Institute for Near East Policy. Special Policy Forum Report. *PolicyWatch*, no. 342 (1 October 1998). http://www.washingtoninstitute.org/templateC05.php?CID=1220 (accessed 18 May 2008).

———. "Libya's Confident Defiance and ILSA." Washington Institute for Near East Policy, *PolicyWatch*, no. 553 (27 August 2001).

———. "The Rogue Who Came in from the Cold." *Foreign Affairs* 80, no. 3 (May–June 2001): 65–66.

———. "Post-Lockerbie Judgment: What Next for US-Libya Relations?" Washington Institute for Near East Policy, *PolicyWatch*, no. 612 (17 March 2002) http://www.washingtoninstitute.org/templateC05.php?CID=1490 (accessed 18 May 2008).

Tandon, Yashpal. "An Analysis of the Foreign Policy of African States: A Case Study of Uganda." In *Foreign Relations of African States*. Edited by Kenneth Ingham. London: Butterworths, 1974, 191–209.

Tanter, Raymond. *Rogue Regimes: Terrorism and Proliferation*. New York: St. Martin's Press, 1998.

Telhami, Shibley, and Michael Barnett, eds. *Identity and Foreign Policy in the Middle East*. Ithaca, NY: Cornell University Press, 2001.

Tessler, Mark A. "Moroccan-Israeli Relations and the Reasons for Morocco's Receptivity to Contact with Israel." *Jerusalem Journal of International Relations* 10, no. 3 (Spring 1988): 76–108.

Vandewalle, Dirk. "Qadhafi's 'Perestroika': Economic and Political Liberalization in Libya." *The Middle East Journal* 45, no. 2 (Spring 1991): 216–231.

———. "The Libyan Jamahiriyya since 1969." In *Qadhafi's Libya: 1969 to 1994*. Edited by Dirk Vandewalle. New York: St. Martin's Press, 1995, 17–26.

———. *Libya Since Independence: Oil and State-Building*. London: I. B. Tauris, 1998.

———. *A History of Modern Libya*. Cambridge: Cambridge University Press, 2006.

Vicker, Ray. *The Kingdom of Oil*. New York: Charles Scribner's Sons, 1974.

Viorst, Milton. "The Colonel in His Labyrinth." *Foreign Affairs* 78, no. 2 (March–April 1999): 60–75.

Voll, John O., ed. *Sudan: State and Society in Crisis*. Bloomington: Indiana University Press, 1991.

Waddams, Frank C. *The Libyan Oil Industry*. London: Croom Helm, 1980.

Waller, Robert. "The Lockerbie Endgame." *The Journal of North African Studies* 1, no. 1 (1996): 73–94.

Weigele, Thomas C. *The Clandestine Building of Libya's Chemical Weapons Factory: A Study in International Collusion.* Carbondale: Southern Illinois University Press, 1992.

Wharton, Barrie. "'Between Arab Brothers and Islamist Foes': The Evolution of the Contemporary Islamist Movement in Libya." *Journal of Libyan Studies* 4, no. 1 (Summer 2003): 33–48.

Wiseman, John A. "Military Rule in The Gambia: An Interim Assessment." *Third World Quarterly* 17, no. 5 (1996): 917–940.

Wittman, Donald. "How a War Ends: A Rational Model Approach." *The Journal of Conflict Resolution* 23, no. 4 (December 1979): 743–763.

Woodward, Bob. *Veil: The Secret Wars of the CIA, 1981–1987.* New York: Simon and Schuster, 1987.

Wright, Claudia. "Libya and the West: Headlong into Confrontation?" *International Affairs* 58, no. 1 (Winter 1981–1982): 13–41.

Wright, John. *Libya: A Modern History.* Baltimore, MD: Johns Hopkins University Press, 1982.

———. "Chad and Libya: Some Historical Connections." *The Maghreb Review* 8, nos. 3–4 (1983): 91–95.

———. *Libya, Chad, and the Central Sahara.* London: Hurst, 1989.

———. "Enforced Migration: The Black Slave Trade across the Mediterranean." *Maghreb Review* 31, nos. 1–2 (2006): 62–70.

Zacher, Mark W. "The Territorial Norm: International Boundaries and the Use of Force." *International Organization* 55, no. 2 (Spring 2001): 215–250.

Zartman, I. William. "The Future of Continental Regionalism: Birth of the African Union." In *Africa Contemporary Record, 1998–2000.* Edited by Colin Legum. New York: Holmes & Meier, 2004, A56–A60.

Zilian, Fredrick, Jr. "The US Raid on Libya—and NATO." *Orbis* 30, no. 3 (1986): 499–524.

Zisser, Eyal. "Syria (Al-Jumhuriyya al-'Arabiyya al-Suriyya)." *Middle East Contemporary Survey,* 1990, 655–656; and 1991, 675–682.

Zoubir, Yahia H. "The Western Sahara Conflict: Regional and International Dimensions." *Journal of Modern African Studies* 28, no. 2 (1990): 225–243.

———. "Reactions in the Maghrib to the Gulf Crisis and War." *Arab Studies Quarterly* 15, no. 1 (Winter 1993): 83–103.

———. "The United Nations' Failure in Resolving the Western Sahara Conflict." *Middle East Journal* 49, no. 4 (Autumn 1995): 614–628.

———. "Libya in US Foreign Policy: From Rogue State to Good Fellow?" *Third World Quarterly* 23, no. 1 (2002): 31–53.

Zunes, Stephen. "The Function of Rogue States in US Middle East Policy." *Middle East Policy* 5, no. 2 (May 1997): 150–167.

Index

Abatcha, Ibrahim, 158
al-'Abbar, 'Abd al-Rahman, 199(n40)
Abu Nidal, 28–29, 55
Abu Sayyaf, 60
Abuja Treaty of 1991, 189, 190
Achille Lauro highjacking, 28, 98
Adam, Ali Sidi, 192
Aerial incidents: air attack on Omdurman, Sudan (1984), 25, 95; airstrike on Libyan targets (1986), 32–34, 98, 116–117; incident of 19 August 1981, 21–22, 93; incident of 21 March 1973, 12; incident of 24 March 1986, 31, 98; incident of 4 January 1989, 35; intensification of disputes over airspace (1980), 20. *See also* Terrorism
Afeworki, Isaias, 185–186
Afghanistan, 18, 21, 90–93; Qaddafi's reaction to Soviet invasion, 90–92; Soviet preoccupation with, 19, 22, 29, 92–93, 111; Soviet pullout, 118; and the US, 18, 65
Africa: Abuja Treaty of 1991, 189, 190; and collapse of the Soviet Union, 197; COMESSA bloc, 185–189; conflicts between African migrant workers and Libyans, 190–192; Constitutive

Act of the African Union, 193–194; economic aid to African states, 184–186, 193, 195; Economic Community of West African States (ECOWAS), 193; Islam in, 184 (*see also specific countries*); Libyan subversion in, 183; Libyan treaty with Ethiopia and Yemen, 22, 93–94, 163; and Libya's normalization of relations with the West, 196; and Libya's UN Human Rights Commission chairmanship, 61, 195; and Lockerbie dispute, 183–188; Lomé summit of 2000, 189–190; Qaddafi's belligerence in the 1970s and 80s, 181, 197 (*see also* Chad; Uganda); Qaddafi's goals in, 195–197; Qaddafi's quest for African unity, 132, 135, 181–200; Qaddafi's reconciliation and mediation efforts, 181–188, 193–195, 198; Qaddafi's rhetoric on, 181, 182, 184, 187, 190, 193, 195; Sirte Declaration, 189; threats to unity campaign, 190–196; United States of Africa proposal, 189; visits to Libya by African heads of state, 185–186, 196. *See also* Organization of African Unity; *specific countries*

225

About the Book

Libya's enigmatic Muammar Qaddafi has demonstrated a perhaps unprecedented capacity for reinvention and survival, particularly in the realm of foreign policy. Yehudit Ronen traces Libya's sometimes tortuous trajectory in international affairs across the four decades of Qaddafi's leadership.

Ronen addresses a range of critical issues: oil politics, foreign military adventurism, WMDs, international terrorism, the confrontation between Islam and the West, and the constraints of US policy in the Middle East. She also sheds abundant light on the many ways that domestic politics have affected Libya's international role. From internal leadership rivalries to international strategic quandaries, she navigates the major course corrections that have reoriented the country's focus from the Arab Middle East and the Soviet Union to the African continent and the West.

Yehudit Ronen is a senior research scholar at the Moshe Dayan Center for Middle Eastern and African Studies at Tel Aviv University and lecturer in political science at Bar-Ilan University. Her numerous publications include *Sudan in a Civil War: Between Africanism, Arabism and Islam* and *The Maghrib: Politics, Society, and Economy.* She is also author of a novel, *Carob Whiskey.*